JAMES WATT

JAMES WATT

Making the World Anew

BEN RUSSELL

REAKTION BOOKS

Published in association with the Science Museum, London

For Lisa and Eli

Published by Reaktion Books Ltd
33 Great Sutton Street
London EC1V 0DX, UK
www.reaktionbooks.co.uk

In association with
Science Museum
Exhibition Road
London SW7 2DD, UK
www.sciencemuseum.org.uk

First published 2014

Printed and bound in Great Britain
by TJ International, Padstow, Cornwall

A catalogue record for this book is
available from the British Library

ISBN 978 1 78023 375 8

Contents

James Watt's workshop at his Birmingham home, 1924, just before it was dismantled and moved to the Science Museum, London.

INTRODUCTION

Do We Want the Dust?

ON THE AFTERNOON OF 29 December 1924, Edward Collins stood alone, in a large, empty room at the top of a house on the edge of Birmingham. Outside the window, slates on the roofs of an adjoining wash house and dairy were beginning to slip, chimney pots leaned at odd angles, the trees were without leaves and a line of old lamp standards leaned against a wall from which the paint was flaking. The house had been uninhabited for four years and was about to be demolished.[1] Edward Collins was middle-aged, an architect by training, a 'most careful & painstaking man', fastidious about detail, just like his father, who had been his predecessor in the same post.[2] He also described himself as a 'one-man job', with no colleagues, and he had not had a holiday since 1914, ten years earlier.[3] But despite this, he sat down on 29 December and wrote to Sir Henry Lyons, Director of the Science Museum in London. The letter asked: 'The whole of the dust on the floor of the Room was swept up and put in a box for me to sort over at my leisure . . . Am I to understand that there is *no possible chance* of you requiring the dust?'[4]

Answering the question of why Collins felt obliged to collect the dust from the room and send it to the Science Museum in London requires some elaboration. The room in question was the workshop of the late engineer James Watt. It was on the top floor of Heathfield, the house he had built for his family in 1790, and Collins was the man responsible for looking after the property. Born in 1736 in Greenock, Scotland, and dying in 1819 in Birmingham, Watt is best known for his work on the steam engine, which became a symbol of Britain's nineteenth-century industrial prowess, and he was the first engineer to be elevated into the pantheon of national heroes alongside soldiers and statesmen. He spent much of his time in the workshop after retiring from a long and fruitful career in 1800, and it contains a comprehensive physical record of the projects he undertook during that career. Upon his death in 1819, the workshop was locked up and preserved for 105 years. In 1924, Watt's associations with steam power, and his by then long-standing position as a revered historical figure, saw the workshop acquired by the Science Museum in London and re-erected for public display. It was during the preparations for the latter that Collins wrote to the museum about the dust.

As it happens, the Science Museum decided against acquiring the dust. In February 1925, Collins again wrote to Henry Lyons, 'I also am sending . . . a parcel containing . . . all the small articles found by me in the dust swept up from floor of Room, nails out of walls, also 1/2 dozen of the nails used to fasten down floor boards, these are rather interesting.'[5] This is a little disappointing because, if the reader will forgive the slight stretching of a scientific point, the dust would have represented the DNA, not just of the steam engine, but of the many other projects that Watt worked on as well: plaster of Paris for copying sculptures, chemical substances of different types, iron filings and turnings, maybe bits of brass and glass from scientific instruments. The dust represented the multifaceted nature of Watt's career.

The profusion of projects that Watt undertook is also reflected in the nature of the workshop's larger objects. They don't only represent the man Thomas Carlyle described as 'Watt of the Steam engine . . . this man with blackened fingers, with grim brow . . . searching out, in his Workshop, the Fire-secret'.[6] The fragments associated with the engine, hidden in the drawers and boxes, could be counted on the fingers of two hands. Rather, the workshop is filled with hand tools and materials of all sorts for wood- and metalwork and making scientific and musical instruments, chemicals, ceramics, sculpture, personal items, pottery, fragments of projects partly completed or gone awry and things set aside because of their personal associations or in case they might come in handy sometime. In one sense, the workshop was a personal museum for Watt as well as an active workspace. But above all, it is a shrine to making things.

This is a book about making things during Britain's Industrial Revolution, covering the period roughly from 1760 until 1820. Broadly, it will look at the making of goods associated with Britain's booming eighteenth-century industries, from scientific instruments and decorative metalware to cotton and pottery. Within those parameters, it will concentrate more particularly on the machine that became emblematic of Britain's Industrial Revolution: the steam engine. The book will explore the extent to which the engine developed alongside, and depended upon, a range of handicraft practices honed in those other industries, and in other trades besides, from chemistry to blacksmithing and foundry work. The engine was as much a cultural machine as a scientific one, and the culture it emerged from was in large part one of making (and possessing) things, not just thinking about them. The major point to be made is that, over the period in question, the transition from making by hand to making by machine was slow, piecemeal and not a done deal: manufacture by machine remained a promise to be fulfilled long into the nineteenth century, not during the eighteenth. For this reason we might call this book a craft history of the Industrial Revolution, or a prehistory of engineering.

Recent surveys of the Industrial Revolution have emphasized the creation in Britain of a 'knowledge economy', which succeeded because it could generate 'useful knowledge' and disseminate it to those who might exploit it commercially. In doing so, historians have created detailed theories of knowledge covering categories such as 'propositional' and 'prescriptive' know-how – the former concerning phenomena identified in the natural world, and the latter concerning how things work. And the processes by which the former crossed over into the latter have also been analysed in detail: the historian Joel Mokyr has described them as the centrepiece of an 'Industrial Enlightenment'.[7]

Having the infrastructure to support the widest possible flow of ideas was no doubt important to Britain's economy as it industrialized during the later eighteenth century. However, it seems counter-intuitive to place such a large emphasis on a single factor:

the relationship between theoretical knowledge and its shop-floor applications is difficult to define precisely. J. D. Cassini, director of the Paris Observatory, wrote that the inferiority of French scientific-instrument makers compared with the English 'comes from their profound theoretical ignorance; the Ramsdens, the Dollonds are geometers and physicists, our best makers are but workmen.'[8] It may also be possible to trace links between scientific discovery and technological practice for men like James Watt, his business partner Matthew Boulton and the potter Josiah Wedgwood. The historian Peter Jones has claimed for them the status of *savant-fabricants*, individuals bestriding both the scientific and practical communities, and their exploits are well documented.[9] But many other practical people, while they undoubtedly worked 'in a milieu in which the effects of the Enlightenment were pervasive', had little if any direct interest in science; or, at least, there is relatively little information to confirm that they did.[10] Watt, speaking of those he employed to erect steam engines in 1794, wrote how 'most of our Engineers who have not been regularly bred to the theoretical or practical part of the business, have been bred to analogous ones, such as millwrights, architects, surveyors etc. from which having almost all the previous learning it is easy to step to the other otherwise it must be uphill work'.[11] 'On-the-job' training produced skilled and knowledgeable men just as effectively as a more scholarly approach.

This is not to deny that scientific knowledge influenced how things were made. 'Science' remained a potent force in making and manufacturing artefacts: the instruments that measured with increasing precision, the detailed understanding of chemistry that underpinned pottery and the evolving understanding of the internal workings of the steam engine, for example. However, we will attempt to move beyond abstract, theoretical science towards science that depended on physically carrying out experiments – manipulating heat and materials, for example – often in ways that were distinctly 'industrial' in character. And we will also explore how science was just one of a number of factors that influenced how and why things were made.

First, however, we have to manoeuvre into a position from which we can see what those other factors could have been. The major issue to be addressed in moving beyond a purely scientific analysis is that, while new scientific facts and concepts were expressed in eminently portable form, written about and discussed in coffee houses, transmitted by lecturers and newspapers, so making things relied far more on the diametric opposite: *tacit* knowledge – what Joseph Moxon described in his *Mechanick Exercises* as 'cunning, or sleight, of Craft of the Hand, which cannot be taught by words, but is only gained by practice and exercise'.[12] This knowledge, encompassing 'dexterity . . . technical savoir-faire . . . experience, skills, and practical knowledge of energy and materials', could be conveyed only by lengthy hands-on training, and stored, not in written form, but in the minds of thousands of workers, craftsmen and artisans.[13] The question arises: can we get inside their minds to establish what they knew about the processes of making?

The answer is not quite as indecipherable as it might appear. Recent research by Celina Fox on the people and processes of eighteenth-century manufacturing has shown that model-making, drawing, societies and publications were basic tools of experimentation and invention in industrial processes.[14] One of Fox's main objectives has been to show that these 'scientific' ways of working owed a lot to 'the pragmatic methods of artisan culture', and it is implicit in this that artisans could be claimed as practical men with just as much validity as with which they could be appropriated as men of science.[15] This approach helps us begin to unpick the inner workings of the minds of those who made things. But concentrating on how artisans *communicated* ideas and knowledge to each other is, in a sense, still one step removed from establishing what people actually did and why, and it places the analytical emphasis *after* a project has progressed and has news to report to the wider world.

We can go further than this: as well as the sources that Fox draws upon, there exists a huge range of three-dimensional tools, materials and finished artefacts that craftsmen and artisans used and generated in their everyday working lives. These objects survive in abundance in museum collections and comprise almost the entire contents of Watt's workshop. The sheer profusion of tools and materials there and elsewhere illustrates both the huge range of artisanal experience in Britain's Industrial Revolution and the character of the Industrial

Revolution as being as much about simple tools, small machines and skilled labour as it was about steam engines and automatic processes.[16] As well as three-dimensional artefacts, there is also more information available about the processes of making than initially meets the eye. It is available in accounts across a range of subject areas: James Keir or Joseph Black in chemistry, Robert Campbell or Joseph Moxon in the handicraft trades and William Creighton, John Farey, Thomas Tredgold or Abraham Rees in machine making, for example. Sometimes it is contained in formidable multi-volume works of literature like Charles Holtzapffel's *Turning and Mechanical Manipulation*, published from 1843, and at other times it is scattered in all manner of technical proceedings, accounts, catalogues and trade literature. But it exists and has been drawn on for this book.

We can use these myriad sources on tools and techniques to delve into the world of making things during the eighteenth century. As Maurice Daumas has written regarding the construction of scientific instruments, it 'demands that the work of both scholars *and constructors* [my italics] be taken into account, for although the instrument itself might be based on theoretical knowledge its invention was only achieved when a craftsman succeeded in giving it material form.'[17] This neatly encapsulates the importance and power of those people in Britain who made things. It was in their work – on the bench, in the foundry or fitting shop and at industrial sites across Britain – that the abstract ideas, cultures and mentalities of science collided with the need to make and sell a tangible product. Watt's 'perfect' engine is a great example of this: it was an astonishing concept, a feat of experimental science, conceptual understanding and precision engineering, but that didn't stop the men erecting it on a windy cliff top in Cornwall, unloading it from a wagon by the simple expedient of just tipping the entire wagon onto its side.[18]

Exploring the world of making has two key questions, then. First, *how* were things made? In answering this, a number of interconnected strands recur throughout the book, and they are briefly summarized here. Artisans had to develop *products* which could be sold. In doing so they took into account both new knowledge and ideas, and also the needs of the markets they served. The range of products made was enormous, encompassing what we now class as industrial goods such as production machines, and consumer goods such as clocks or ceramic wares. The interplay between them turns up some interesting contrasts: how Matthew Boulton aimed to make steam engines in the same way as he previously produced buttons, or the relationship between clockmakers and factory-builders, for instance.

Artisans worked extensively to identify, acquire and find uses for new *materials*. Britain possessed an abundance of materials that could potentially be exploited: timber was supplemented and frequently superseded by cast and wrought iron and other metals, such as brass. Processes of making were often associated with the places where raw materials could most easily be accessed. In the Staffordshire Potteries, inhabitants had the right to extract clay wherever it could be found on common land – most often where the passage of vehicles had made deep ruts in the roads, which were immediately exploited, leaving dangerous 'potholes' behind.

Artisans *organized* production to work materials into finished products. Many trades developed a considerable division of labour, with each worker specializing in a particular job. This made them very fleet of foot, able to turn out established product lines quickly or switch to new products if necessary. The range of organizational possibilities was huge: from large concerns like Matthew Boulton's Soho Manufactory, which employed upwards of 500 people, to tiny one-man businesses operating from a garret at home. Although the long-term trend was towards the former, the latter proved extremely resilient, which is a tribute to the staying power of skilled practical people who survived on their wits.

Artisans innovated in the *techniques* used in their manufacturing processes, devising many new ones but often amplifying and re-inventing those that were well-established and applying them under new circumstances to new materials and products. Although histories of industrialization have often emphasized the increasing use of machines to make machines, considerable capabilities remained in the hands of individual craftsmen using relatively simple tools. At several points, we will explore the role of the senses in fields as diverse as metalworking, chemistry and pottery; no doubt others could be added to this brief list. And across a similar range of trades, one of the most valuable abilities was being able to accurately judge temperature by eye. Heat was not just a subject for scientific experimentation but comprised a practical workaday tool, too. Finally, where possible, the means by which techniques could be scaled up, from making scientific instruments to steam engines, for example, will be explored, as will the ways in which techniques could be transferred from one trade or industrial sector to another.

Lastly, artisans had to find a way to *market* their finished product. They might rely most on trade networks and word of mouth for work that was 'put out' or subcontracted from other makers. Alternatively, direct contact with customers could be best achieved by running a more high-profile retail operation. The importance of marketing was reflected in a profusion of trade cards, advertisements and directories, which were often illustrated and gave details of a producer's products and capabilities.

These five building blocks of making – product, materials, organization, techniques and marketing – suggest that artisans were as much endowed with entrepreneurial and commercial skills as they were with practical ability. Making things came hand in hand with managing debt and credit, keeping an eye on the bottom line, managing a possibly unruly workforce, seeking out customers and maintaining links in the trade. This high degree of innovation and resourcefulness went beyond that simply associated with new techniques.

The second key aspect of making things concerns not just the question of 'how?', but those of 'what?' and 'why?', too. This analysis has its starting point in the idea of 'path dependency', which contends that if, for example, Britain had plentiful supplies of coal and iron ore, it would be more likely to adopt new technologies which burned coal and smelted iron ore than those that exploited water power or timber resources. Proceeding down a particular path made future new technologies more likely to stick to that path. Path dependency has always been part of a formal analysis of economic trends as the economy industrialized. The intention here is to explore the influence not just of science but of culture on what things were made, and why.

The baseline for this analysis is that in Britain the practical contribution made by craftsmen and artisans was highly valued. In 1718 Guy Miege wrote of the English that 'None has been more industrious to improve the *Mechanick Arts*; and the World to this Day, is obliged to 'em for many of their useful Inventions and Discoveries.'[19] In the 1730s the art critic Jean-Bernard, Abbé le Blanc, commented: ''Tis not in great works alone that the English excel, the most common trades here seem to partake of the perfection of arts . . . The English artisan has the quality, extremely commendable, and peculiar to him which is, never swerve from the degree of perfection in his trade which he is master of.'[20] Jean Ryhiner, a Swiss calico printer, wrote in 1766 how 'Everyone knows this nation whose industry and stubborn patience in overcoming every kind of obstacle are beyond imagination. They cannot boast of many inventions, but only having perfected the inventions of others.'[21] In 1803 the economist and businessman Jean-Baptiste Say wrote how 'the enormous wealth of Britain is less owing to her own advances in scientific acquirements, high as she ranks in that department, as to the wonderful practical skills of her adventurers in the useful application of knowledge and the superiority of her workmen in rapid and masterly execution.'[22] These examples illustrate British workers' recognized prowess, not necessarily at generating original ideas, but at turning ephemeral ideas into tangible products.

Beyond the innate instinct for technological creativity that motivated these craftsmen and artisans, other factors as well as science influenced the paths that making things would advance along. The first is steam power. Paradoxically, despite it becoming an emblem of Britain's nineteenth-century industrial prowess, many, if not most, industrial processes were not steam-powered.[23] Until large-scale, steam-driven production became more widespread later in the nineteenth century, the engine was as much the product of a manufacturing process as any of the other products explored in the book. Rather than stimulating quantitative change in the economy, engines were the catalyst for qualitative change in how machines were built. By building them, machine makers worked out how to make other pieces of industrial mechanism more easily: production machinery for factories, self-propelled road vehicles, trains, steam at sea, were all in prospect. And in doing so they created a new profession of engineering from a diverse range of trades: clock- and instrument making, blacksmithing and millwrighting. The possibilities for new machines, and the opportunities presented by an emerging profession, spurred those who could make things to new endeavours.

The tremendous demand for consumer goods also influenced what products were made. People's material possessions were changing fast as the eighteenth century progressed. As the historian David Landes wrote, 'the Englishman of the 1750s was closer in material things to Caesar's legionnaires than to his own great-grandchildren.'[24] It was not just the quantity of possessions present in households that changed but their sheer range, the choice of materials and how they were branded, packaged and sold as well. Rather than being passed down from one generation to the next, many peoples' possessions were entirely new and modern, reflecting growing prosperity. A booming middle class wanted to display its affluence, and did so by spending money on things which gave an impression of distinction and newness, or modernity. The producer who could satisfy those desires stood an excellent chance of success.[25] It is telling that many of those industries that saw the greatest technological feats, and that inspired the most comment from those who saw them – cotton, ceramics and metalwares, for example – had the consumer firmly in their sights, and for this reason consideration of new consumer goods has to come alongside that of new technologies and ways of making things.[26]

The third factor influencing which things were made was a widely held fascination with precision. There was a considerable demand for products, both for consumers and producers, which were made as accurately as possible. The clockmaker John Harrison's chronometers were accurate to within one second every month, attaining unprecedented levels of horological accuracy given the limitations of existing technology. Matthew Boulton knew that, with his new coin-minting machinery, eight tuppenny pieces laid end to end would measure exactly twelve inches in length, providing a useful means of identifying counterfeits. From making steam cylinders accurate to 'within the thickness of an old shilling' in

1776, engineers progressed to measuring to one ten-thousandth and later even one-millionth of an inch.[27] Projects that exploited precision were more likely to progress than those that did not.

Finally, the classical world exerted considerable sway on the products that were made. Learning Latin, and the history and culture of ancient Greece and Rome, occupied a central place in education. Industrialists mined antiquity for inspiration: the potter Josiah Wedgwood made vases one of his main product lines, kickstarting what Matthew Boulton hailed as 'vasemania' – 'an epidemical madness . . . for vases, which must be gratified'.[28] In Watt's workshop there survive moulds for making plaster casts of antique figures. Classical influences were incorporated into designs for machinery; we can say that the steam engine became the first industrial machine to have as much attention paid to its aesthetic appearance as, say, one of Wedgwood's vases. Products which referenced the antique were desirable, indicating refinement and civility, and this influenced what things were made and why.

It is difficult to treat these factors in a linear way. For instance, exploration of the engine's development is most obviously about power, how it was harnessed and its applications; but Watt's engine was also a large precision machine, and it was developed within the context of manufacturing fashionable consumer goods like cotton wares and metal buttons. Similarly, consideration of Watt's early career as a scientific-instrument maker is most closely tied to the attainment of high precision – but it also took place against the backdrop of accelerating consumer demand for such instruments. We will sidestep debate over a causal relationship between consumer demand and technical innovation, except to say that the power of the engine and the power of consumers is the central motor of the narrative that follows. The relationship between the two was broadly underpinned by increasing precision in manufacture of all types and by the application of antique influences, in terms of how people were educated, but also with regard to what we now call product design. The relationship between these factors was dynamic, and to trace it over time, the book follows a rough chronology based around James Watt's life and some of the many projects that he was associated with. It is to Watt that we now turn.

James Watt's high standing was based on his personal reputation and that of the engine, and both are closely intertwined. For his nineteenth-century successors, Watt became the personal benefactor of the changes being seen across the country. At a London meeting in June 1824 to call for a public monument to commemorate Watt, the Earl of Liverpool wrote that

> by his steady perseverance, by the sagacity of his mind, by his patient thinking . . . he was enabled to apply the profoundest principles of science to the practical purposes of life; and . . . augment incalculably the resources of his own country, and even of the whole world.[29]

At the same meeting, the chemist and inventor Sir Humphry Davy proclaimed of Watt,

> If you seek his monument, look around you . . . Look round the metropolis; our towns . . . our dock-yards, and our manufactories; examine the subterraneous cavities below the surface, and the works above; contemplate our rivers and our canals, and the seas which surround our shores, and every where will be found records of the eternal benefits conferred on us by this great man.[30]

Such words quickly consolidated Watt's reputation as a colossus of Britain's Industrial Revolution.

The centrality of Watt and his engine has long continued to fascinate historians. In 1948 the engine was described by the historian T. S. Ashton as 'the pivot on which industry swung into the modern age', and more recently Watt was called 'a symbol of . . . everything that was progressive and innovative in Britain' during the eighteenth century.[31] Interpreting the nature of Watt's achievement has filled a library of books. For a long time the main focus was on Watt the craftsman and engineer, who 'affirmed the identity of those . . . who constructed and tended the machines of the workshop of the world'.[32] Most recently, Richard Hills's biography of Watt has made the most comprehensive assessment yet of his surviving papers and correspondence, David Miller has appropriated Watt as a chemist, Christine MacLeod has placed Watt within the context of the heroic age of the inventor in Victorian Britain and Peter Jones has tackled Watt as one small part of the wider Enlightenment movement. The Watt genre shows no signs of fading away; rather it is diversifying in its approaches and output.

How, then, to carve out a niche in this busy marketplace? The tendency has been to think about Watt in vertical slices: Watt the engineer, craftsman or chemist, or example. If the argument of this book is accepted, Watt was all of these things; they were not mutually exclusive. What underpinned all of these different identities was his ability not just to think but to *do*: to use tools, techniques and materials, to create tangible things across a range of activities. Rather than cutting the Watt 'cake' vertically, we are examining one of its horizontal layers. Britain depended for its movers and shakers on its doers and makers, and Watt stands for all of them, regardless of their specific trade or profession.

The major issue to be overcome here is avoiding what John Griffiths described as 'Wattolatry': the worship of Watt.[33] An element of this is unavoidable: the Science Museum has four Watt engines and his library in its collection, and his voluminous personal and business papers are preserved at Birmingham. The path dependency of how we write history depends on what sources have survived, and this is skewed heavily towards Watt rather than many of his colleagues. However, in writing about the hows, whys and whats of making things, I have tried to use Watt as a lens to focus on the question in hand, but then to peer over his shoulder, to find out what others were doing at the same time, calibrating one against the other. Watt was not alone in being inquisitive and resourceful, making his way, recording progress and what he found; quite the opposite. Alongside Watt we can read what many others thought of the new world of industry emerging before their eyes in Britain. Some commentators, like Josiah Wedgwood, John Robison or Matthew Boulton, Watt knew extremely well, and we have briefly touched on some of the practitioners whose writings can also be drawn upon. There are many others, from Daniel Defoe to Louis Simond, whose accounts help paint the bigger picture of a growing industrial economy. They are joined by a host of overseas travellers. Jabez Maud Fisher journeyed from North America, building links for his family business. Brothers François and Alexandre de La Rochefoucauld travelled to further their education but had a good eye for identifying and describing Britain's 'vital interests', which were often industrial in nature.[34] Johann Conrad Fischer was a pioneering Swiss steel-maker who made contact with many of England's eminent industrialists and manufacturers. Still others wrote broad and detailed accounts of particular towns and cities – James Gibson in Glasgow, John Aikin around Manchester and Sophie von La Roche in London, for instance.

What comes across from many of these accounts is the impact of the processes of making, and the products that were created, on the contemporary imagination.[35] The British military officer and author George Head wrote how there was no spectacle

more grateful to the heart of an Englishman than, viewing the interior of a manufactory of machinery, to observe the features of each hard-working mechanic blackened by smoke, yet radiant with the light of intelligence . . . and to reflect that to such combination of the powers of mind and body England owes her present state of commercial greatness.[36]

Later commentators agreed, including Ralph Waldo Emerson, who believed the English had successfully 'impressed their direct-ness and practical habit onto modern civilisation'.[37] The Industrial Revolution quickly came to be regarded as one of the great periods in Britain's history. One writer has it that Patrick O'Brien's naval stories of the Napoleonic Wars acquired a life of their own when he realized that they were 'the Englishman's Troy tales, as historically and mythically rich, and imaginatively exploitable as the story that produced *The Iliad*'.[38] And there is certainly something Homeric in Josiah Wedgwood's facing down of a competitive threat to his pottery thus:

Stand firm my friend, & let us support this threatened attack like Veterans prepar'd for every shock, or change of fortune that can befall us – If we must fall . . . let us not sell the victorie too cheap, but maintain our ground like Men, & indeavour, even in our defeat to share the Laurels with our Conquerors.[39]

This is more blood-and-guts stuff than the abstractions of science, economic theorizing and epistemologies of knowledge that seem to have tied up so much history of the Industrial Revolution: here is a bold new world filled with people, places and objects.

To return to the dust in Watt's workshop, it represented the long, multifaceted and highly productive career of one man. But it was upon such (metaphorical) dust that scientific and technological discovery depended. In workshops like Watt's, successive generations of skilled artisans, men, women and children, working in chemistry, ceramics, instrument making, engineering, the toy trade and countless other areas of endeavour, made a new world of material objects. The workshop and, by extension, Watt's work as represented within it give us a unique lens through which to explore that world. In asking ourselves whether we want the dust, the answer surely has to be – yes!

ONE

Sensible, Ingenious and Enterprising Men, 1736–56

THE CITY OF LONDON played a pivotal role in James Watt's early career. On 18 June 1755 he arrived in the city, having travelled on horseback for 470 miles from Greenock, Scotland. Tired and saddle-sore, he found himself transplanted from a maritime town of 3,000 souls 22 miles west of Glasgow into the heart of the biggest city on earth, 'a Prodigy of Buildings, that nothing in the World does, or ever did, surpass', containing one in eight of Britain's entire population, consuming every year 2,957,000 bushels of flour, 700,000 sheep, 238,000 pigs and 100,000 oxen, burning 590,000 tonnes of coal and drinking 7 million barrels of beer.[1] A day after arriving in the city, Watt ventured to Wapping in the East End to reclaim the chest containing his belongings, which had travelled separately. He described Wapping as 'an ugly and confused place. The streets here are most of them very crooked and dirty.'[2] Samuel Johnson also visited between 1767 and 1770, describing how 'men of curious enquiry might see in it such modes of life as very few could even imagine.'[3] And the German scientist Georg Christoph Lichtenberg had expressed in April 1770 how he 'could not possibly describe what strange figures' he saw, 'half-naked men and women, children, chimney-sweeps, tinkers, Moors and men of letters, fishwives and females in grand array'.[4] Wapping was an excellent place for Watt to encounter some of the wilder parts of eighteenth-century British society.

Wapping was a marine community, huddled on the north bank of the Pool of London, the centre of a global shipping network. The author Daniel Defoe counted the vessels he could see at any one time in the Pool and 'found about 2,000 sail of all Sorts, not reckoning

London in 1748, seven years before Walt's arrival in the city, as portrayed by Joshua Walker for the *Universal Magazine*.

Barges, Lighters, or Pleasure-boats, and Yachts; but of Vessels that really go to Sea'.[5] It contained timberyards, wharves, warehouses, victualling stores, brothels and gin shops. Perhaps, as he walked around, Watt's nostrils were accosted by the stench of the leather tanneries operating in Bermondsey, just south of the river, and his clothes were dirtied by the smoke of countless coal fires that led more particular inhabitants to change their linen twice daily.[6] But away from the quays and narrow streets frequented by out-of-work labourers, sailors, foul-mouthed watermen, prostitutes and street children, Wapping was also home to many respectable and successful mariners.[7] That the area, with its reputation for lawlessness, should also encompass middle-class affluence and relative prosperity indicates the polarized nature of the society Watt found himself living in.

The amount of drinking which went on, as recorded in accounts of the time, is amazing. The French author François de La Rochefoucauld noted in 1784 the 'fine inns where it is accepted that men go for prolonged bouts of wine-drinking'.[8] Samuel Johnson recalled that 'all the decent people in Lichfield got drunk every night, and were not the worse thought of.'[9] The German author Karl Philipp Moritz, travelling in England in 1782, observed that it was

not uncommon to see on doors in one continued succession, 'children educated here', 'shoes mended here' . . . and 'Funerals

Gin Lane, 1751, engraved by T. Engleheart in 1833 after an original by William Hogarth. The image came to symbolize the evils of the 18th-century gin craze.

furnished here'. Of all these inscriptions, I am sorry to observe, that 'Dealer in foreign spirituous liquors' is by far the most frequent.[10]

In short, much of the nation sought to be 'drunk for a penny, dead drunk for tuppence.'[11]

People's capacity for drinking was matched by their appetite for violence. In 1770 the Riot Act had to be read to quell rebellious pupils at Winchester College.[12] Moritz noted on his travels, 'We breakfasted at Dartford. Here . . . I first saw (what I deemed a true English sight) in the street two boys boxing.'[13] The chances of running into trouble were such that Horace Walpole commented, 'One is forced to travel, even at noon, as if one was going to battle.'[14] And if violence and drink often accounted for life being nasty and brutish, illness meant that it was frequently short. Complications in childbirth could spell the end for both mother and child. One in three children died before the age of five and life expectancy at birth was about 35 years. Infectious diseases such as tuberculosis, dysentery and typhus cut swathes through the population, and death could come from the most unexpected directions – even the lead used in cosmetics could finish off the fashionable.

Britain in the eighteenth century was, in many respects, a society of extremes. Samuel Pepys may have been an erudite diarist, but thought little of defecating in his own fireplace.[15] Marriage was for life, unless curtailed by death – highly likely – or, less likely, you could get a private Act of Parliament to have it annulled. A woman could only make a will with her husband's permission but he, if he chose, could have it rendered void after her death. In fact, Blackstone's *Commentaries* on English law, published between 1765 and 1769, noted pithily that 'In marriage husband and wife are one person in law, the very being or legal existence of the woman is . . . consolidated into that of the husband.'[16] A medical operation could transform genteel appearances into bloody horror. Failure of an erstwhile respectable business could mean financial ruin and destitution – a debtor owing more than 40 shillings could be arrested and imprisoned for up to twelve months purely on the word of his creditor.[17] The grim brick back-to-back slums of an industrial town might be punctuated by 'fine stone buildings with Corinthian columns', as if comprising 'a medieval town with the marvels of the nineteenth century in the middle of it'.[18] There were few, if any, safety nets to catch those who fell or faltered.

Watt's early encounters with this world, his upbringing and training in the rudiments of business offer a valuable insight into the infrastructure that facilitated Britain becoming the world's first industrial nation. Britain in the eighteenth century was an increasingly populous, mobile and highly interconnected society, and this was manifested in a number of ways. The surging population was underpinned by a range of physical networks and institutions. These supported a robust and enduring class structure, and to negotiate their way through this networked, class-conscious world, people had to master the tools of polite commerce. For all its polarities, British eighteenth-century society was a fertile place for young men like Watt to make their way.

It was a world which, broadly, didn't go hungry: Britain could feed itself. In 1700 only about one-third of Britons worked in farming. That this relatively small group of people could feed the nation suggests they were very productive – in fact, output per farm worker in 1705 was twice that in France, and had increased by 25 per cent by 1750.[19] There are many reasons for this. Crop rotation ensured that nutrient levels in the soil were replenished. Communal open fields were replaced by enclosure, consolidating land into bigger farms run more efficiently by a single farmer. And the amount of land actually being farmed grew, from 11 million to more than 14 million acres between 1700 and 1850.[20] All this paid dividends: corn output increased by almost half in the eighteenth century, and the number of sheep being reared more than doubled.[21] There were some periods during the wars against Napoleonic France when the nation briefly stared food shortage in the face. However, the scenario envisaged by the political economist Thomas Malthus – food supply rising arithmetically (1, 2, 3, 4, 5) while the population grew geometrically (1, 2, 4, 8, 16, 32) – was averted. Farming held its own and provided a firm foundation for industrial growth.

Britain's population was also growing rapidly – from about 6.5 million in 1700 to about 10.5 million in 1800 – with growth rates exceeding 10 per cent per decade from 1780 through to the end of the nineteenth century.[22] This increase was based on nuptiality, or the propensity for people to get married and the subsequent desire to start a family. The trend towards marrying earlier was based largely on the increasing availability of work opportunities, not just in farming but in new and expanding industries. People felt more secure financially, and because they no longer had to wait for their parents' demise to inherit their land, they married younger and were fertile for longer. More people meant more demand for products, more workers to be 'drilled into a supple labour force' and more people capable of devising new technological ideas.[23] All these factors helped sustain population growth once it had begun.[24]

The growing population was also increasingly mobile. Some people moved around to undertake apprenticeships – William Murdoch later walked from Scotland to Birmingham to join James Watt's engine making business, for example.[25] Others worked seasonally in farming, and navvies hopped from project to project digging canals. American traveller Louis Simond commented:

> You meet nowhere with those persons who never were out of their native place, and whose habits are wholly local . . . To go up to town from 100 or 200 miles distance, is a thing done on a sudden . . . In France the people of the provinces used to make their will before they undertook such an expedition.[26]

And the Romantic poet Robert Southey was struck by how travel 'is one of the pleasures of the English; and people . . . set out upon a journey of two hundred leagues to amuse themselves'.[27] That distance – over 1,000 kilometres – is certainly an exaggeration, but accounts do show that contemporaries thought little of walking tremendous distances. Robert Hamilton, for example, missed his coach from Fenton in Staffordshire to Birmingham one day in May 1796 and walked the 39-mile journey instead; in fact, he regularly walked or rode 20 miles every day around Birmingham and Staffordshire.[28]

So, eighteenth-century Britain was getting more populous, and its people were increasingly likely to travel in pursuit of work and new opportunities. It was against this background that Watt was born on 19 January 1736, at Greenock, on the estuary of the River Clyde. His father was a merchant, chandler and ship-owner, trading in coal, herring and salt, who built and owned shares in ships for both the ocean and coastal trade. He was also something of a local statesman – 'a member of the town council, a magistrate and a zealous promoter of the improvements of the town' – and an occasional inventor, constructing new pulley blocks for ships and Greenock's first crane for handling bales of tobacco.[29] His mother Agnes Watt was from a long-established Greenock family, 'a fine-looking woman, with pleasing, graceful manners, a cultivated mind, an excellent understanding, and an equal cheerful temper'.[30] In all, they were a respectable middle-class family.

Watt was the fourth child for Agnes and James Senior but the first to survive past infancy. Their first child died in April 1730 at only two and a half months. Then at the end of 1732 came a daughter, who died aged just over a year old, and a son who died at fourteen months in August 1734. With this catalogue of infant mortality, his parents must have been continually worried for James, who had a frail constitution as a boy, being troubled by poor health and migraines which made him 'languid, depressed and fanciful'. He subsequently received much of his education from his mother and tutors – Robert Arrol taught him the basics of Latin, and John Marr mathematics.[31] Young Watt absorbed himself in reading. He was fascinated by chemistry and mathematics and scribbled sums in chalk on his bedroom wall when he forgot his slate.[32] The breadth of Watt's reading is demonstrated by a portion of his book collection, which survives in the care of the Science Museum Library. Alongside

As his parents look on, the young Watt experiments with the steaming kettle. Herbert Bourne after Marcus Stone, *Watt's First Experiment*, 1879.

treatises on chemistry, such as Robert Dossie's *The Elaboratory Laid Open, or; The Secrets of Modern Chemistry and Pharmacy Revealed* (1758), Richard Brookes's *The General Practice of Physic* (1751) and David Fordyce's *Dialogue Concerning Education* (1745), can be found later additions, like John Croft's *Scrapeana* (1792), describing itself as 'A medley of choice bon mots, repartees, &c. to which is added, a large collection of Yorkshire anecdotes' – a reminder that Watt later became fond of some 'light amusing reading'.[33]

But he was not just content to read, and sought to expand from ideas into practice. His study of anatomy was accompanied, rather alarmingly, by being seen 'carrying off a child's head that had died of some uncommon complaint'.[34] There survives in Watt's workshop a set of Napier's bones, a basic calculating device, which was most likely made by Watt as a young man. It is rather crude and is covered with Watt's practisings of his signature. But it is the practical counter-point to his book study of mathematics. And because of his father's profession, Watt would have been surrounded by the stuff of running ships at sea: rigging, sails and sheets, blocks and tackle, capstans and more. He assembled his own set of tools, with which he built a model house and crane, and constructed a small forge for working metal. One acquaintance even recalled Watt retiring to the 'Old Mansion-house of Greenock' and there spending hours 'lying upon his back, to watch through the trees the wondrous movements of the stars'.[35] If this presents an image of a rather quiet, solitary boy, we are reminded that he 'was not wanting in sociability, but frequently entered into all the amusements of his school-fellows'.[36] Book learning was matched by a dry sense of humour, and Watt soon had a chance to put both to the test. He stayed in Greenock until April 1753 but, that month, set out for two years work acting as his father's agent in Glasgow. This was his introduction to the world of commerce.

Moving to Glasgow placed Watt at the commercial hub of west-ern Scotland. The quays lining the Clyde Estuary were crowded with bales of tobacco and boxes of herring, bar-iron, hemp for sails and nets, timber for boats and houses and salt for preserv-ing fish. Greenock became an embarkation place for emigrants sailing to America, and other ships linked the town to Ireland, the West Country and the Highlands.[37] Later, in 1790, a canal connected the Clyde to the Forth, linking the region to Edinburgh on a new east–west trade route.[38]

Watt Senior traded all sorts of goods around the Clyde. A letter he received from his son titled 'Invoice of goods bought at Glasgow' records tanned skins, padlocks, a quire of marble paper, two dozen pencils and more.[39] Young Watt's job was to source everything his father needed – from pencils to padlocks – and look out for commercial opportunities in the city. His uncle John Muirheid was on hand to show him the ropes. Perhaps one of the earlier things Muirheid may have taught young Watt was the need to project an air of respectability, and this can be seen in a list of clothes Watt took with him to Glasgow, including 'almost new' shoes, 'rufled' shirts, a number of Holland nightcaps, stockings, waistcoats, breeches and much else.[40] This is very much the wardrobe of a young gentleman about town settling accounts on his father's behalf, not just a workshop apprentice.[41]

In fact, his cousin Marion Campbell recalls that while in Glasgow, Watt

met with good society, and formed friendships with several intelligent and well-educated young men; they had frequent evening meetings to give or receive information. These gentlemen acknowledged and appreciated Mr Watt's superior abilities.[42]

This image of Watt and his young acquaintances offers a glimpse of the webs of contacts which coalesced in so many places across Britain, often based in the new coffee houses that were springing up everywhere. Watt was using one in Glasgow for his financial dealings in 1756, and London had more than 500 by 1739.[43] Their influence endures today: the insurance market Lloyd's of London started as a coffee house, and the layout of the trading floors remains based on the wooden booths and stools used by its eighteenth-century inhabitants. Luckily for Watt, and for us, the quality of the networks established over coffee was better than that of the coffee itself – Karl Philipp Moritz advised his readers in 1782, 'I would always advise those who wish to drink coffee in England, to mention before hand how many cups are to be made with half an ounce; or else the people

Coffee fuelled many commercial and philosophical transactions. In this recreation of a meeting between Watt and his friends in Birmingham's Lunar Society, the coffee pot sits prominently on the table.

will bring them a prodigious quantity of brown water.'[44] More seriously, in Watt's group we have a microcosm of a whole society which was tremendously *interconnected*. And this interconnectedness manifested itself in three ways: in the infrastructure of everyday life, in Britain's social structure and at the level of individuals. To use the analogy of human anatomy, the first comprised the body's blood vessels and nervous system, the second the skeleton and the third the individual living cells.

Watt and his acquaintances would have discussed many of the networks which aided and abetted their everyday lives, from the difficulties of travel to local government. Road travel could best be described as problematic. The most useable highways were old Roman roads which still had their original surfaces left, but even these were prone to subsidence, turning into ditches which became morasses of mud. The main road between London and Exeter could become up to a quarter of a mile wide in the winter as traffic took detours around really difficult stretches.[45] Others were rivers in all but name – witness the road from Hull to Leeds, which Daniel Defoe

31

recorded as lying in 'low, flat, miry country' flooded with rainfall from the surrounding hills which, 'for want of a proper current to carry such waters off, [inundated a] great part of the road, which is frequently under water'.[46]

One solution was to build turnpike roads, paid for by users. By 1770 there were 15,000 miles of turnpikes, centred around the most important industrial areas of the time – Shropshire, the West Midlands and the West Country.[47] In some places they were unpopular, it being reported that 'ill designing and disorderly persons . . . in several parts of this Kingdom associated themselves both by day and night, and cut down, pulled down, burnt, and otherwise destroyed several turnpike gate and houses.'[48] In fact there were turnpike riots in Herefordshire in 1732 and near Bristol in 1749, and opposition to toll roads around Leeds and Bradford erupted into a full-scale rebellion in 1753 which had to be suppressed by troops. However, improvements to roads profoundly affected communications. Practically nowhere in England could not be reached within four days.[49] Stagecoaches carried brief, scribbled 'intelligences' of the latest news and local newspapers began to carry the prices in London markets for the benefit of suppliers across the country.[50] A mail coach might make the journey from London to fashionable Bath in fifteen hours, and another hour would see it in Bristol.[51] By 1756 these unprecedentedly high speeds were being applied to a system of mail coaches to Plymouth and Swansea, and north to York and Newcastle. The emerging road network smoothed the flow of news, people and ideas.

If roads sped the passage of relatively portable things like news or ideas, more bulky items went by boat. By 1750 Britain had 1,500 miles of navigable rivers; by 1830 canals had added about another 2,500 miles and the older regional networks had been joined up by 'trunk' routes linking together the Thames, Mersey, Trent, Humber and Severn.[52] Well might François de La Rochefoucauld describe 'the water-circulation in England . . . as abundant as the blood-circulation in the human body'.[53] Canals were supplemented by coastal shipping. No part of the country is more than 70 miles from the sea, and the coastal trade became big business: three times more vessels were engaged in the coastal trade than took

Greenock in 1768, by Robert Paul of Glasgow. The town, where Watt was born and spent his early life, was an important port and maritime centre.

part in international voyages.[54] In 1774, 1,800 vessels hefted coal from Newcastle to London, while 900 more carried other freight – mainly raw materials, grain and other bulky items – and the size of each individual ship doubled in the 25 years after 1750.[55] Adam Smith calculated that up to eight men with a sailing vessel could transport 200 tons of freight which, if it went by road, would need 50 wagons, 100 men and 400 horses and take three times longer.[56] Efficient shipping was crucial to the industrializing economy.

Just as roads and ships knitted together Britain's internal networks, so the principal role of the government was to ensure the security of the whole and pursue expansion overseas. And, just as many British citizens liked a fight, so the country itself was extraordinarily pugnacious. Britain fought seven wars against France alone during the eighteenth century and was involved in overseas military operations for 75 years between 1692 and 1802. The main job of central government was to raise the money to pay for its war-fighting capability: financing war accounted for up to two-thirds of all government spending, and taxes rose eighteenfold in real terms over the course of the eighteenth century for that reason.[57] But beyond raising taxes, central government played only a relatively small role in Britain's domestic economy. As much as possible was administered locally; there were, for example, 23,000 Customs and Excise men keeping the tax revenue flowing to only 43 central Treasury officials.[58]

The 'hands-off' approach of central government was commented on by many overseas visitors, one of whom noted:

the greatest benefit which the government confers . . . is that of doing nothing at all: in the whole of this country there are no regulations . . .and, in the eyes of an impartial traveller, England has the appearance of being a hundred times richer than France.[59]

Another visitor was relieved that, while travelling around,

no stern examiner comes here to search and inspect us, or our baggage; no imperious guard here demands a sight of our passports; perfectly free and unmolested, we here walk through villages and towns, as unconcerned, as we should walk through an house of our own.[60]

At the local and national level, those representing the state remained accountable for their actions. As a young man in Glasgow, James Watt could complain about a local excise man, 'if he is in the wrong I shall find a way to represent the affair to his superiors. If such fellows are allowed to tyranise over the fair trader there will be no living here.'[61] The monarch couldn't raise taxes without Parliamentary approval – and Britain was 140 years ahead of France in having the people execute their king.[62] British people felt a particular freedom not experienced by those elsewhere.

The infrastructure of transport and information networks, and the state, provided Britain with her blood vessels and nervous system. And Watt described his friends at a Glasgow coffee house as 'much my superiors, I never having attended a College & being then a mechanick'. His awareness of his social position relative to his associates is suggestive of Britain's social structure, the skeleton or framework for the whole enterprise.[63]

Britain had a strong and durable social hierarchy. As early as 1709, Daniel Defoe had used his *History of the Union of Great Britain* to split the nation into seven distinct social groups, from 'The great, who live profusely', through 'The middle sort, who live well', to 'The miserable, that really pinch and suffer want'. These different social classes together formed an enormous pyramid, with the 186 'Lords Spiritual and Temporal' at the top, and the bottom comprising labourers, the poor and the destitute. Within each of these social strata the position of each individual was also closely delineated, and each was stoutly protective of his place; François de La Rochefoucauld explained how 'Everyone thinks he has a right to go first, and if one if placed beneath one's rank, one only hopes that whoever has affronted one did it by mistake.'[64] Social class even loomed large at the dining table, where 'strangers go first into the dining-room and sit near the hostess and are served in seniority in accordance with a rigid etiquette.'[65] Hierarchy was ingrained in everyday life.

T. Engleheart after William Hogarth, *Four Times of the Day: Noon*, 1833, engraving. In this scene, first published in 1738, Hogarth captured and commented upon the interactions between London's different social groups.

But while Britain's social structure was closely defined, it was by no means overly rigid. Class never became caste, and the German scientist Georg Christophe Lichtenberg could write that 'When I was in England, I lived sometimes like a lord, and at others like a workman.'[66] Rather, it was flexible – far more so than in France, Germany or Russia – and this helped Josiah Wedgwood query 'whether I am a landed gentleman, an engineer or a potter, for indeed I am all three'.[67] Although the cotton entrepreneur Sir Richard Arkwright started out as a wigmaker, for example, the movement wasn't just upwards. Skilled artisans could come from well-to-do families. Lewis Paul, a prominent figure in the early mechanization of cotton spinning, was a physician's son. Peter Ewart became a celebrated millwright, but his father was a clergyman and his brothers became a minister and a doctor.[68] The law of primogeniture, meaning that the oldest son inherited everything, forced younger siblings into the professions and trade. In the 1720s Daniel Defoe wrote that in the Home Counties 'there are several very considerable estates purchased and now enjoyed by citizens of London, merchants and tradesmen'.[69] Britain's social structure offered stability, but with the possibility of mobility for individuals if they sought it.

The close interplay between the classes facilitated industrial change. Jabez Maud Fisher wrote in the 1770s that even the booming industrial town of Manchester was 'seated in the midst of a rich and very populous Country . . . the Features happy for Prospect and beautiful with every Improvement; and its Neighbourhood crowded with Gentlemen's Seats'.[70] Indeed, sinking one's capital into industry was by no means ungentlemanly. Many of the great partnerships of the Industrial Revolution comprised 'an alliance of talent and money', partnering an ingenious mechanic with a gentleman eager to invest his capital.[71] Moving in the opposite direction, merchants and industrialists emulated the old landed gentry: cotton magnate Robert Peel moved into Drayton Manor and Arkwright lived at Willersley Castle.[72] The trend was picked up on by foreign commentators, one of whom noted in 1790 how 'Mr Boulton of Birmingham, Mr Wedgwood of Etruria . . . and other manufacturers of their standing, command such credit and respect that in the eyes of everyone they are on a level with the greatest in the land.'[73] It was possible in Britain, perhaps more than anywhere else, to reach the top of the social ladder by attaining success in industry.

If Watt and his young merchant friends in Glasgow aspired to ascend the social ladder, they sought to do so by meeting the demands of Britain's middle classes, the customers for many of the goods they would make and trade. Roy Porter has suggested that the amount the average eighteenth-century family spent on British-made goods quadrupled from 1688 to 1811,[74] and Josiah Tucker wrote in 1755 that

> the English . . . have better conveniences in their houses, & affect to have more in quantity of clean, neat furniture, & a greater variety such as carpets, screens, window curtains, chamber bells, polished brass locks, fenders etc . . . – things hardly known abroad among persons of such a rank – than are to be found in any other country in Europe, Holland excepted . . . almost the whole body of the People of Great Britain may be considered either as the customers to or the manufacturers for each other.[75]

Consumer spending was to be a motor for commerce and a stimulus for industrial change.

This acquisitive impulse came with some strings attached, however. Chief among them was the evolution of a system of law which protected property above all. On his travels around England, Karl Philipp Moritz stumbled across signs warning 'Take care! There are steel traps and spring guns here'.[76] What were the metaphorical traps and guns protecting the haves from the have-nots of eighteenth-century Britain?

First, the tax system was highly regressive – that is, the wealthier you were, the less tax you paid as a proportion of your income. No tax was levied on profits or business capital, and little on land or farm profits, benefiting entrepreneurs, merchants and landowners. Most taxes were placed on goods for which demand was high – beer, salt, glass, tea, sugar and tobacco – upon which the poor spent a much higher proportion of their income. So they were unfair, but freed up entrepreneurs' money for investment in new industries. Second, protecting property was one of the few formal roles of the state which was robustly upheld. The 'Bloody Code', as it became known, demanded the death penalty for 200 different offences against property. Of particular import to Britain's new industries, however, was the emergence of laws giving *ideas* the same legal protection as physical property – which were useful if, like James Watt, you were to become an inventor or a manufacturer with a new production process. The evolving patent system was expensive, complex and by no means infallible, and inventors often worked without recourse to using it. In fact, until 1852 it wasn't really a 'system' at all, but operated somewhere between being a means of bestowing patronage and a more formal system to give inventors legal protection for their work.[77] But it determined that a person should be rewarded if they invested time and money in something of value to the rest of society, and the possibility of that reward being substantial became an incentive to innovate.[78]

This, then, was the world Watt found himself entering as a young merchant with his commercial friends in Glasgow. It was a world of possibilities for advancement but, equally, Watt and his friends had to create those possibilities for themselves. They did so by developing their individual skills in applying the tools of politeness and civility.

In many aspects of life an informal code of behaviour supplemented the formal laws of the land. Daniel Defoe warned his readers to 'try all the methods of Gentleness and Patience which a forbearing Temper can dictate . . . before you proceed to Rigour and Prosecution.'[79] One of the motors driving this 'polite and commercial' society was the realization of those living in the new industrial towns that if they aspired to the life of landed gentry, they had to act like them, too. People also had to shift for themselves; because the state largely kept out of business, individuals expected to have to work in partnership with their fellows, and adhering to particular rules of conduct made for a smoother-running partnership.[80] Also, as we will see, many aspects of polite commercial society depended on trust – and without that, enterprise collapsed, with lasting consequences for all involved.

It is against this background that Watt left Scotland for the first time, in June 1755, and travelled to train as a scientific-instrument

Taking a Bargain, Northumberland, *c.* 1805, artist unknown. Many commercial transactions were carried out in small, informal groups like this.

maker in London. The precise motivation for this dramatic change is unclear, but he was now nineteen and needed to consider his longer-term prospects. While Watt was working in Glasgow for his father, he was introduced to members of the university there, including Robert Dick, Professor of Natural Philosophy. Perhaps Dick recognized Watt's talents as a merchant and potential as a practical man and persuaded him and his father that his talents could be best extended in the metropolis, as had Dick's own. Whatever happened, Watt found himself making the long journey south by horse to seek out a master. On his arrival he would receive a thorough grounding in the etiquette of polite commerce.

A basic premise of politeness was to maintain a respectable appearance. We have already seen how Watt, starting out in Glasgow, dressed as smartly as possible. This extended to how you travelled, too: Karl Philipp Moritz, walking from London to Oxford, was treated with outright hostility by those he met. Only afterwards did he realize that 'In England, any person undertaking so long a journey on foot, is sure to be looked upon, and considered as either a beggar, or a vagabond.'[81] Watt's long journey by horse rather than on

'The Mathematical Instrument Maker', from *The Book of Trades* (1824).

foot may have been as much about preserving appearances as practicalities.

Respectability went hand-in-hand with trustworthiness. On his arrival in the city, Watt needed someone to vouch for him and, luckily, he was not short of help in this respect: John Marr, who had accompanied Watt as he travelled south, introduced him to Mr Neale, a London watchmaker for whom Watt worked temporarily. Robert Dick in Glasgow also gave him a letter of introduction to James Short, a famous London telescope maker. Watt quickly began to build a web of contacts. And, once started, the web continued to expand almost of its own volition. Mr Neale in turn introduced Watt 'to some Gentlemen of the Instrument way in Westminster who will be more easily dealt with than those in town',[82] and James Short helped Watt to negotiate with the man who would undertake most of his training in London, John Morgan. Watt's subsequent activities were recorded in a long and detailed series of letters to his father in Greenock.[83]

Morgan, 'a man of as good a character both for accuracy in his business & good morals as any in his way in London', was based at Finch Lane in the City, between Cornhill and Threadneedle Street.[84] He agreed to teach Watt his wide knowledge of both technical and commercial aspects of instrument making. He showed Watt 'some fine new compasses of a new invented metal' and soon had Watt working at the brass parts of Hadley's quadrants, used for navigation.[85] This practical work came with careful instruction to Watt on 'the best methods of purchasing what instruments he may want and their lowest price among Tradesmen'.[86]

Morgan's manners were as important to his commercial persona as his technical ingenuity. Watt wrote that 'He is a very good natured man & is very ready to show me any thing I want to know.'[87] This was a widely accepted practice: when François de La Rochefoucauld visited a button manufactory in Sheffield during February 1785, the owner

not only showed us all his workshops, one after another, but he was careful to begin each with the workman explaining each process in the greatest detail; and as we were there with him five hours he invited us to take tea with his mother.[88]

Jabez Maud Fisher was pleased, on first meeting Edmund Radcliffe, 'the greatest Manufacturer in England', writing that he 'makes me very flattering offers of Interest and Introduction to his Correspondents in Spain, Portugal and France'.[89] Sharing knowledge and contacts in this way was considered to be commercial good manners.

Once Watt had established with associates that he was a respectable, trustworthy and well-mannered young man, he built his personal network through regular correspondence, letters of introduction and bills of exchange. Letters of introduction were crucial as a 'way in' for a newcomer to a community. Philipp Andreas Nemnich toured Britain in 1805–6 with no fewer than 1,200 letters of introduction to hand out.[90] In fact, a visitor couldn't do without them. Karl Philipp Moritz was eager to see the industrial wonders of Birmingham and had a letter of introduction to Benjamin Fothergill – but, on arriving, discovered that Fothergill had died eight days before. Poor Moritz recalled that 'without staying a minute longer, I immediately enquired the road to Derby and left Birmingham. Of this famous manufacturing town, therefore, I can give . . . no account.'[91] These letters were also significant because, in relying on a third party, they created webs of mutual obligation: once contact was established, it was maintained by regularly sending compliments, short messages and notes, and acknowledging them from others. Someone who provided an introduction and maintained contact like this might at some point expect a favour in return. As Watt prepared to return to Scotland at the end of his time working for John Morgan, he wrote to his father:

> Do you think that it is proper that I should write to Professor Dick at Glasgow (who recommended me to Mr Short without whose help I believe I would not have got a master) thanking him for his letter & to know whether there is any thing that I could do for him here before I come down?[92]

The involvement of a third party also characterized bills of exchange. These were written orders from one person, the drawer, to a third party to pay the bearer a sum of money on a specific date. It was very similar to today's cheque payment system but, whereas today the third party would usually be a bank, at that time it could be a commercial contact of the drawer with whom they had credit. This might explain why, for example, much of Watt's correspondence from London to his father in Greenock consists of accounts and details of debts owed and owing. Young Watt wrote on 1 July 1755, 'You'll please remember that you owe John Muirhead Junr 7/ for skins for lining your breeches & mine. I likewise owe Dr Muir in Glasgow for bleeding me twice & something I got to rub on my throat when ill in winter.'[93] An important part of Watt's commercial training would have been to establish how these credit webs worked. In fact he must initially have been rather discouraged because he found that in London 'the workmen being all so poor . . . they can't want the money a minute & a great many of the Wholesale dealers deal for so little profit that they cannot give credit'.[94] This is a reminder that the 'unofficial' finance system offered easy credit but was very fragile. One failure to honour a payment might start a domino effect as everyone tried to turn their paper credit into hard assets. As with letters of introduction, we see again the role of mutual obligation: debtors relied on creditors for cash, and creditors relied on debtors working hard to ensure they got their money back. For the system to work, everyone had to play their part.

Finally, letters encouraged a rich flow of information around Britain. At one level, Watt could write from London to his father at Greenock, 'I have had a fit of the Rheumatism which has been very troublesome to me – tho not so bad as to make me keep the House . . . In other respects I never had my health better since I remember.'[95] On another level, news of major events spread fast. Watt sent details to Greenock of a huge earthquake in Lisbon and told of concerns about a French invasion of the Kent or Sussex coast. He even breathlessly described the declaration of war against France in May 1756, noting, 'Their [sic] was the greatest mob fever saw which you can have no idea of unless you was acquainted in London.'[96] Watt also sent commercial intelligence, warning his father that competing merchant William McDowal 'has got some books draughts & other things . . . & am afraid he will be able to undersell you', as well as news of the latest fashions, which he had difficulty keeping up with: sending items requested by his father, he replied, 'I am sorry the handkerchiefs were not better but as it is a thing that I am no judge of I am the more excusable.'[97]

Britain, then, reverberated with news and views, bills of exchange and letters of introduction moving with travellers on land and at sea. An impression emerges of the strength of relationships between people, even when separated by hundreds of miles, and how their mutual obligation was a strong incentive to make a success of things. Watt's letters show his anxiety not to be a burden to his father for too long, for instance. He writes in November 1755, 'I am striving all I can to be the sooner able to be a help to you as I am in duty bound.'[98] The following April he reiterates that 'It gives me great pain to be a downdraught on you but hope shortly to be able to make you some amends.'[99] Watt was certainly becoming well versed in the ways of civil society but, to bring the story full circle, we return to his practical training as an instrument maker in London.

Watt's letters from London record the variety of his training. He worked on scales and rules for calculating and measuring, and Hadley's quadrants for navigation. In November 1755 he was making 'azimuth compasses for Eastindiamen' – the ships trading between Britain and the Indian Ocean – and the following April he was completing a brass sector for making calculations of scale and proportion, and a theodolite for surveying. Watt seems to have been a fast learner, proudly telling his father in August 1755 that he had made a better job of a quadrant than one of Morgan's apprentices of two years' standing. The variety of projects undertaken may be down to John Morgan making 'nothing but what's bespoke' – one-off pieces rather than items made in bulk.[100] This also contributed to the unpredictability of the work: Watt's letters record a series of rushes to fulfil orders, and he wrote in his letters how his hands shook from the work, and 'I have scarce time to write a letter now as we work to nine o clock every night except Saturdays'.[101] This was not unusual: long working hours were the norm. A visitor to instrument maker Jesse Ramsden's workshop in 1787–8 wrote that the workmen laboured for twelve hours between 6 a.m. and 8.30 p.m. for six days per week.[102] Men working for the ironmaster Ambrose Crowley worked from 5 a.m. until 8 p.m. with a half-hour break at 8 a.m. and an hour at midday, and had only Sundays off.[103] But in most respects Watt was lucky to be receiving a training which few people even in London could give him – in August 1755 he wrote, 'Very few here know any more than how to make a rule others a pair of dividers & such like.'[104] The following month he continued the theme: 'I now find there are not above 5 or 6 that could have taught me all I wanted.'[105] The thorough grounding in the practicalities of instrument making would stand him in good stead for the next part of his career, and he could write with some justification, 'I shall be able to get my bread any where.'[106]

By June 1756 Watt was preparing to return to Scotland. He had been in London for one year, less than the full seven-year apprenticeship usual at the time, but he had the makings of a 'sensible, ingenious and enterprizing Man, who plans and executes with equal Expedition' – a later description of Birmingham industrialist Matthew Boulton, but one which seems apt for Watt, too.[107] In short he had that blend of entrepreneurial skills – how to negotiate the social networks and structures governing everyday life and how to wield the tools of polite commerce – which characterized so many of Britain's artisans and craftsmen. To exploit what he had learned to its fullest extent, he needed now to be fully exposed to the great ideas and issues that were being hotly discussed – and this is what awaited him as he was appointed instrument maker to Glasgow College.

TWO

Artists of High Reputation, 1757–64

An invitation to James Watt's workshop at Glasgow College was highly prized among the college's students. The college faced onto Glasgow's High Street, and in John Slezer's *Theatrum Scottiae* (1693), John Sibbald wrote that the 'fore-part of it towards the City is of an excellent Structure being of hewen Stone'.[1] Behind this impressive frontage, more than 300 feet long, were two courtyards, entered through a gate 'elegantly ornamented with rustic work', later described as having 'not much regularity in their design, each part seeming to stand towards the other parts, in a state of independent crooked-ness and irregularity'.[2] And at the northwest corner of the inner yard, on the first floor, was Watt's instrument-making workshop, reached by a spiral stone staircase. Once inside the workshop, students found a room about 20 feet square, lit by three windows, filled with Watt's tools and scientific apparatus. It became a favoured meeting place: John Robison wrote how

> all the young Lads of our little place that were any way remark-able for scientific predilection were acquaintances of Mr Watt; and his parlour was a rendezvous for all of this description – Whenever any puzzle came in the way of any of us, we went to Mr Watt.[3]

For Robison and his 'young lads', Watt was someone to look up to both for his practical expertise and for other reasons: here was a man who had travelled to London and there dodged naval press gangs, witnessed the declaration of war against France and experienced the

James Scott after J. E. Lauder, *James Watt and the Steam Engine*, 1860. A dramatic reimagining of Watt at work in Glasgow.

excitement of the mob. As early as July 1757 Watt was writing to his father requesting '1/2 a Doz afternoon China tea cups a stone tea pot not too small a sugar box & slop bowl as soon as possible' so that he could suitably provide for his guests.[4]

Working at Glasgow College, Watt found that his interests were widely shared. The college was a centre of the great and unprecedented intellectual turmoil that took place in Scotland during the eighteenth century, and which has become known as the Scottish Enlightenment. Edinburgh, Glasgow and Aberdeen had their respective universities and a range of other intellectual organizations as well: Glasgow College was founded in 1451, and it was joined by a Political Economy Club from 1743 and a Literary Society from 1752. Like Watt's college workshop these institutions became centres of debate and bred a uniquely impressive array of thinkers. Foremost among them were Adam Smith, founder of the modern science of economics; David Hume, one of the most influential Western philosophers; Joseph Black, the chemist who discovered carbon dioxide (see page 49); James Hutton, who founded the discipline of geology; and Adam Ferguson, the founder of sociology. Such was the concentration of intellect that a Mr Amyat, living in Edinburgh, described how that city more than any other in Europe offered 'such a singular and such a noble privilege', of being able to stand at a point in the city centre and, 'in a few minutes, take fifty men of genius and learning by the hand'.[5]

Having learned his trade as an instrument maker, Watt found himself immersed in the Scottish Enlightenment and a new popular culture that was fascinated by science. Here we will examine how his workshop at Glasgow College became a focus for discussions, arguments and theorizing not just with Robison and his 'young Lads', but with other, more prominent figures as well, including Black and Smith. The diverse range of customers who became acquainted with Watt reflects the multifaceted nature of the demand for scientific instruments. Meeting his customers' needs led Watt both to pursue new ways of making instruments and to branch out into their retail. Although this kept the business afloat, making instruments would not sustain Watt in a long-term career, but it did provide the springboard for his next big project: working on the steam engine.

As Watt began his career making scientific instruments, he was launching himself into a culture where a vigorous 'taste for science, over all classes of men, in every nation of Europe . . . seems to be the characteristic feature . . . In no former age, was ever the light of knowledge so extended, and so generally diffused.'[6] In these circumstances a demand for instruments 'permeated the educated classes whether noble, gentle or merely respectable, in much the same way as a taste for music, cards, coaches or beverages'.[7] Watt was joining a trade that trebled in size during the course of the Industrial Revolution.[8]

The market for scientific instruments was multifaceted. Research by Alison Morrison-Low has identified six types of customer: dilettantes, practitioners, teachers, domestic users, scientific experimenters and the State.[9] The demands of each group varied, and their relative importance waxed and waned over time. Take the dilettantes, for example. Rich, and with leisure time to spare, they sought the very best instruments, specially commissioned to show off social standing and 'virtuosity' – the owner's knowledge of, and taste for, science, superb workmanship and life's finer things. Sometimes this interest appears to have been superficial: one writer recalled seeing 'how a

Joseph Black, chemist, lecturing. Black would enjoy a close relationship with Watt as he worked on the steam engine. Etching by John Kay, Edinburgh, 1787.

noble lord, taking a piece of string from his pocket, had measured off a row of books . . . and bargained for them by the yard or ell, without glancing at their titles or contents'.[10] But having the very best symbolized status, with a contemporary commentator noting 'the great number of persons whose wealth enables them to appreciate and to pay well for the best-constructed instruments'.[11] Instruments purchased included 'equatorial' telescopes whose advanced design allowed them to follow the rotation of the sky above, sold in some numbers by London's Jesse Ramsden, and the orrery, a working model

49

of the solar system named after the Earl of Orrery, the proud purchaser of the first one.[12] The king, George III, was a well-known instrument collector and his collection remains displayed at the Science Museum. This market was dominated by London-based makers who established enviable reputations for high quality and accuracy, but its relative importance declined as the eighteenth century progressed to be usurped by other groups – lecturers and practical users.

Lecturers occupied a strategic position in promoting science in the wider economy. Caleb Rotheram sold the subject in 1743 as 'one of the most usefull and entertaining branches of Learning, a high and refined part of Speculative knowledge, and of great importance in the common affairs of human life'.[13] In the early eighteenth century lecturers were itinerant. Three hundred pounds would purchase the kit required and, with luck, the proceeds from a single lecture course in coffee houses or instrument shops could recover the initial outlay.[14] Some delivered lectures alongside work as practical instrument makers: Benjamin Martin travelled from his London workshop to lecture across the West Country and Adam Walker combined wide-ranging work as an inventor with lecturing across the North of England.[15] They could be well equipped: Walker employed an orrery measuring 20 feet across. A lecturer visiting Birmingham in 1784 brought equipment weighing 30 hundredweight, comprising an orrery, globes, telescopes, air pumps for vacuum experiments, condensers, microscopes, barometers, prisms and magnets, and even an electrical machine.[16] Later more permanent institutions evolved: London's Spitalfields Mathematical Society ran lecture series seen by up to 500 attendees, and Mechanics' Institutes and Philosophical Societies established in many provincial towns. Some sneered at them – Edmund Burke described their gatherings as 'dens of bravoes and banditti [assuming] the garb and tone of an academy of philosophers'.[17] But others, like the engineer John Smeaton, defended 'the common Herd of conjuring Philosophers about Town' for their efforts reaching out to an audience hungry for science – and it was the instrument makers who provided them with the tools for the job.[18]

Alongside teachers and lecturers, there were others for whom instruments were very much a workaday tool: practitioners like navigators, surveyors and civil engineers. At sea navigators had to establish their precise whereabouts. On terra firma land had to be accurately mapped so that it could be enclosed for farming, improved, rented or sold. And as trade grew the best routes for roads and canals had to be determined prior to construction. Practitioners' demand for instruments could be considerable. By 1788 there were 12,464 ships registered in the UK, a number which would more than double by 1851. Each would need two octants or sextants, compasses and a chronometer.[19] On land new telescopes, quadrants, levels and compasses, and theodolites were developed for surveyors and civil engineers, and the number of new surveyors entering the profession every year doubled after the mid-1780s.[20] Practitioners at sea and on land offered a booming market for instrument makers.

Instrument makers stood at the intersection between practitioners' demands and new scientific discoveries. One of the best examples of this can be seen in sea navigation. On the one hand navigation errors of hundreds of miles were not unusual, and the cost of inaccuracy could be high: the Royal Navy warship HMS *Ramillies* found herself trapped against the Devon coast by faulty navigation in 1760, and only 27 men out of 800 survived the wreck.[21] On the other, the sheer size of the solar system was becoming apparent. Experiments in the 1760s established the sun as being 153,000,000 kilometres from the earth, and we now know that the moon, our nearest interplanetary partner, is 384,400 kilometres away. Creating the instruments able to take precise measurements from distant planets and stars presented a huge technical challenge. They had to be light, compact enough to be used on the heaving deck of a vessel at sea and able to measure an angle to within 30 seconds of arc – or 1/120th of a degree.[22] At sea, and on land, these practical and theoretical challenges were met with a series of new instruments.

It is against this background that Watt took his first steps, not learning his trade, but as a professional instrument maker. Of the potential markets open to him, that supplying teachers, professors and lecturers offered an early opportunity which Watt eagerly grasped: he was engaged to clean some instruments that had been bequeathed to Glasgow College by a trader in Jamaica. Following this project, in July 1757, he was appointed the college's instrument maker. Moving into his workshop on campus, he developed close links with the professors: he provided and repaired lecture equipment for John Anderson – 'Jolly Jack Phosphorus' to his students because of the demonstrations he undertook.[23] Joseph Black also became a customer, for whose chemical furnaces Watt manufactured doors, and who also purchased a digester (a pressure cooker which could be used as a basic steam boiler), moulds, pistons and even an alarm clock.[24] Watt was held in some esteem – Black was later to recall Watt as 'a young man possessing most uncommon talents for mechanical knowledge and practice, with an originality, readiness, and conspicuousness of invention, which often surprised and delighted me in our frequent conversations together'.[25] Both Anderson and Black were to play key roles in Watt's later career.

Watt developed a reputation within Glasgow College, then, as the 'go to' man for anything that needed making. Despite this, however, the business was a difficult one: making a broad range of products almost single-handedly made Watt a jack of all trades but master of none. In September 1758 he had a moment of appraisal. He wrote to his father:

> I have now had a year's trial here I am able to form a judgement of what may be made of this business & find that . . . there is little to be got by it as at most other jobs. I am obliged to do the most of them myself & as its impossible for one person to be Expert at every thing they very often cost me more time than they should do.

He ended gloomily, noting that if his venture failed he would have to 'fall into some other way of business as this will not do in the present situation'.[26] Watt adopted a two-pronged strategy. He would use his inventive abilities to make instruments in bulk at minimum cost, not for professors at the college but for bigger markets beyond its walls. To achieve this target he would establish a shop that would sell his own products and those purchased wholesale from others as well.

Mass-producing instruments meant that Watt aimed for the biggest market he could, and in Glasgow that meant the practitioners.

One of his principal products was the Hadley's quadrant. Developed by John Hadley in 1730, and further improved by him in 1734, it was intended for use at sea to determine longitude, measuring the distance between particular stars and the changing position of the moon as it moved across the sky. This 'lunar distance' could be used to establish the difference between local time and time at the Greenwich meridian, and hence the geographical position of the observation. This process required complex calculations but had the advantage of needing only a quadrant, which might cost a twentieth of the price of a chronometer, to establish the longitude.[27] Here was the big market that Watt sought: one of his early outlays was for 300 instruction pamphlets explaining how to use the quadrant. He expected to be able to make '14 dozen' every year or about three every week, and he was confident 'of selling more than I can get made'.[28]

Another of Watt's major products was a machine for drawing in perspective which he developed and sold from 1765. It ingeniously comprised a board to which paper could be secured, on three legs, so the whole stood up like an artist's easel. Looking through a peep-sight at the subject, and tracing a pointer around its outline, a complex jointed wood and brass frame transferred the image onto the paper with a pencil, complete with perspective. The machine's mechanism was delicate, and might not have survived outdoor use for long, but it employed some cunning features to make it compact and lightweight. The board holding the paper was formed by opening up a mahogany box, conveniently sized to fit into a gentleman's pocket, and the tinplate legs could be strapped together to make a staff to lean on.

Watt had set his sights on supplying a bigger market with a focused range of standardized products. As he developed these, he would have been acutely aware that instruments capable of reaching out any distance – a few hundred yards, say, for a perspective drawing machine, but across tens of thousands of miles for a quadrant – would only be as good as the tools, materials, and techniques used to make them. Watt wrestled with these challenges against the backdrop of great change in precision manufacture. Here we will explore whether he was up to the job.

For a long time, instruments were made of wood, but it could be a temperamental material. Charles Peale used a wooden 'polygraph'

Watt's perspective drawing apparatus, set up to produce an image of a house.

letter-copying machine during the dry American summer in 1803, but complained that when it rained, the mechanism 'swelled and tightened' so much that he could finish his letters only by unscrewing and loosening all the parts.[29] Hadley's quadrants could be big, measuring up to 18 inches in radius, and to reduce their weight, examples were built of mahogany, ebony and ivory. However, the flexing, expansion and contraction of the wood limited the instrument's accuracy.[30] Efforts were made to shrink it so it could be made of more durable metal without becoming too heavy.[31] Brass became preferred for its versatility: flat sheets could be bent, hammered, cut with shears and filed to shape. It could be formed into tubes to make telescopes, or joined by using a flame, molten metal solder and a blowpipe, for which the instrument maker needed a cyclical breathing technique, breathing in the nose and out of the mouth simultaneously to obtain a constant high-temperature heat.[32] It could also be cast in moulds to make into individual components or even complete single-piece instrument frames, releasing clouds of toxic fumes in the process. Finally, it could be highly polished, engraved and stamped, and given a coat of lacquer to protect the surface.

The quest for high-quality instrument mirrors and lenses similarly tested opticians' ingenuity. Obtaining pieces of glass that were free of imperfections was difficult, so reflecting telescopes used mirrors made of highly polished speculum metal. The refracting telescopes made from the 1760s used glass lenses instead, but these still needed to be accurately ground by hand, using progressively finer abrasive powders in a concave brass dish to shape the surface of each lens. It was difficult, laborious work, and the optician John Yarwell wrote to the astronomer Abraham Sharp complaining about his difficulties making the lenses: 'I must confess I have had more complaint from you *than from all the rest of mankind*, with the least profit, for the last you had.'[33] Watt's workshop contains boxes of semi-finished lenses, which he purchased from others with the aim of carrying out the fine finishing work himself.

Working brass and glass into precision instruments led to innovation in three key areas. The first machine that instrument makers needed was the lathe, designed to hold a piece of material and rotate it, so that different cutting tools could cut and shape it as it turned.[34] The lathe ranged in size from the tiny watchmaker's 'turns', small enough to be held in a vice and hand-spun to make watch shafts and spindles, to the 'great lathe', a bigger workshop machine powered by an assistant turning a hand capstan or working a treadle. The precision engineer Richard Roberts employed his wife for this duty, working in a bedroom while his wife drove the lathe from the basement.[35] Over the course of the century, the lathe went from being largely constructed of timber, and used to work wood, horn or ivory, to being a more robust iron-framed machine capable of standing up to the rigours of working metal. It has been described as the first engineer's machine – both because it was the first machine that could make the parts of other machines and because of its versatility: instrument components could be turned, bored and finished on it; glass lenses could be polished – and screw threads could be made.[36]

Screw threads – cylinders with an indented spiral running around the outside – were essential to successful precision instruments. They did not just hold components together, but were a valuable means of measuring: if a screw is an inch long and consists of twenty threads, rotating it ten times will move it axially by half an inch. Knowing the number of threads on a screw, and making them as fine as possible, meant screws presented new means of accurately measuring tiny angles and distances. At first they required highly skilled hand work. Exactly measured diagonal lines called transversals were drawn on a strip of paper, their length matching the circumference of the thread needed. Then the paper was glued onto the rod and, if done carefully, the ends of the diagonal lines linked up to form a spiral along its length. Using the spiral line for guidance, a narrow, pointed hand file started the thread. This was deepened with a larger triangular-section file, and then it was finished with a chaser, a tool with three or more teeth of the profile needed for the completed thread, which was pressed into the thread as it rotated.[37] London instrument maker Jesse Ramsden later built a number of special screw-cutting lathes, and their output was used to make fine adjustments in all sorts of instruments – some later threads were employed in measuring devices claiming an accuracy of within one-millionth of an inch.

Another use of screw threads was to make, or 'divide', graduated scales. Navigation instruments needed to be smaller and lighter, but the barrier preventing this was being able to produce a small enough scale by hand. This entailed securing the scale on a 'dividing plate', calculating the position of each graduation by geometrical means using compasses and then marking each with a steel blade before polishing to produce a clean finish. The work was so delicate that some London makers kept their tools and the scales at a near-constant temperature to avoid distortions caused by thermal expansion, only working in early mornings during the spring and autumn.[38] And, as he had devised ways of cutting screw threads, between 1768 and 1774 Ramsden also cracked the problem of making scales by machine. He designed and constructed a 'dividing engine' (see page 59): the scale to be graduated was fixed to a large horizontal wheel with teeth cut around its circumference, which engaged with a finely cut screw thread that, when rotated, turned the wheel through minutely controlled angles. The engine was straightforward to operate, and Ramsden's apprentices, and sometimes his wife, used it.[39] A complete, immensely accurate scale could now be made by relatively unskilled labour, not in a matter of days, but in half an hour.[40]

Making the best use of these new materials and techniques determined the organization of the instrument trade.[41] It was structured into two broad groups: mathematical and optical instrument makers.[42] A company might position itself in either one of these areas and specialize in making a particular type of instrument. For example, James Short of London made reflecting telescopes only and John Cuff made only microscopes. Many confined themselves to making only the most critical parts of each instrument, putting the rest out to subcontractors. As Campbell noted, the optical instrument maker 'himself executes very little of the Work, except the grinding the Glasses . . . The Cases and Machinery of his Instruments are made by different Workmen, according to their Nature, and he adjusts the Glasses to them.'[43] Some makers – 'out of doors' workmen, 'Chamber masters' and 'Garret masters' in London – worked in their own homes with a small number of employees, selling products to the public retail outlets of Martin, Adams, Dollond, Ramsden and others.[44] In Sheffield 'Little Mesters' rented space in a factory and sold their output to its owner.[45] And finally, within each company each individual might have a particular specialism: grinding lenses, making instrument frames or finishing and lacquering.[46]

A consequence of this complex trade structure was that the name engraved on a finished instrument was a 'brand' name – that of a businessman and designer in overall charge of the manufacturing process but responsible for physically making few of the components. Such a man was required 'to have a pretty good Education, and a penetrating Judgment . . . and must be a thorough Judge of such Work as he employs others to execute'.[47] What was the 'Watt' brand? And how did Watt organize and equip his business to make it?

Far from being a solitary craftsman, Watt assembled a team of employees. In February 1758 he was looking for 'any lad that can file tolerably well' and thereafter the workforce expanded to a maximum of fourteen trained workmen and apprentices.[48] Only one of them, John Gardner, was with Watt for the long haul – in fact, he became Watt's right-hand man and took over the instrument making business in about 1770. The others worked as required on a variety of different projects. The men had their own areas of specialization: Alex Gardner worked on lenses and James Couper mainly made quadrants, for example – but the range of output demanded meant they often turned their hands to anything required. Robert Allan, for example, was employed making parts for quadrants in 1760, but in the following two years was making violin bows and guitars.[49]

Having developed his team, Watt also remained closely linked to the instrument making trade in London. He was well acquainted with Jesse Ramsden: he had his business correspondence sent to Ramsden's shop and they also corresponded about a telescope Watt developed, which survives in his workshop, that could be used to measure distances. The close links between Ramsden and Watt endured: Watt's later colleague John Southern was present as Ramsden was taken to be buried in December 1800, and he wrote, 'My feelings were considerably hurt this morning at the sight of poor Mr Ramsden's coffin, in which he was descending the stairs for the last time, just as I called in.'[50] But in technical terms there was a gulf between the world of making instruments in London

Jesse Ramsden alongside his dividing engine, J. Jones after Robert Home, 1790.

and Glasgow, and explaining this requires consideration of the materials and techniques Watt used in instrument making.

Both brass and glass can be found in quantities in Watt's workshop, and references to many other materials can be traced in his ledgers. The deep brown of cocoa-wood from the West Indies made it popular for flutes.[51] Black ebony from India or Mauritius, and mahogany from the Caribbean, tended to warp and twist less than other woods, and were often used for the frames of scientific instruments, with graduated scales to take measurements added in brass. Later brass replaced wood entirely. Green ebony and boxwood could be made into rulers or turned in a lathe.[52] Plane wood (called 'plaintree' by Watt) was used in musical instruments, while John Williams of Newcastle provided Watt with 'tubes and cylinders of glass'.[53] Steel was used in tiny quantities for pinions and pivots, which had to withstand considerable loads – and Watt squirrelled away broken table-knives as a useful source of tool steel.

To work these materials, Watt used hand tools extensively and drawer upon drawer of them remain in his workshop. He would have been familiar with them from his training in London, and a list he sent his father prior to travelling from London to Scotland in June 1756 gives the things which he deemed 'absolutely neces-sary'.[54] It includes among much else a 'standing vice' – probably a leg vice to fit on the side of a workbench – hammers and anvils in different sizes, files for shaping metal, cast and plate brass, screw plates for cutting threads on metal rods, dividers and compasses, an iron brace and bits for drilling holes, a selection of hardwoods, tortoiseshell and mother-of-pearl for instrument making and even 'an alphabet of letters' – letter stamps for marking wood or metal. By October 1759 the tool list had expanded considerably to include a 'great turning lathe', as well as draw plates for making metal wire of different diameters, and 'patterns for casting brass'.[55] Later the noted toolmaker John Wyke of Liverpool supplied a clockmaker's vices and files, screw plates, dividers and more, and the workshop devoured a huge range of other consumables, from half a hundred-weight of emery powder for polishing to cat gut, copper wire and varnishing brushes.[56]

Many of Watt's tools can be matched against contemporary descriptions of workshop equipment. Some, for example, can be identified in Joseph Moxon's *Mechanick Exercises*, the grandfather of all modern DIY books.[57] Others can be spotted in the details of the sale arranged when the watchmaker Larcum Kendall died in 1790.[58] Many of the basic tools are similar, and these are a counterbalance to the emphasis on mechanization, lathes and dividing engines in instrument making. But among them are Kendall's 'curious' tools – 'a box containing curious models', 'a curious deepening tool', 'a curious engine for cutting spirals' and even 'a very curious unique engine for cutting horizontal wheels'. These are the special-purpose tools designed to give Kendall a technical edge over his competitors. What were Watt's equivalent 'curious' tools, and how successful were they?

Prominent among Watt's early specialized tools were printing plates for making the scales on quadrants and other instruments. Two plates for printing the scales for barometers on paper still exist in Watt's workshop. One has two scales depending on the temperature: 'Dry/Very Dry; Set Fair/Set Frost; Fair/Frost; Changeable; Rain/Snow; Much Rain/Much Snow; Stormy', which is suggestive of the ferocious Glaswegian weather, about which Watt could describe to a friend the '100 people I see just now running by wett to the skin, no doubt cursing god in their hearts. I believe the [rain] drops are an inch in diameter.'[59] Alongside these plates there is also a beam compass with interchangeable heads, for making scales on instruments. One of the heads consists of a small 'comb' with eleven sharp points on it that, pressed against a brass sheet and

An instrument makers' workshop, 1849. Although of a later date, much of what can be seen would have been very recognizable to Watt.

dragged in a radius across it, would scribe eleven lines at once – much quicker than making each individually. That Watt was making barometers with printed paper scales, rather than engraved brass ones, and speeding up production by scribing multiple lines at once, suggests that he was making a cheaper product for the lower end of the market.

It may also be that these more ingenious techniques are not as novel as they appear at first sight. For instance, in Moxon's *Mechanick Exercises* there are details of a method of 'laying moldings either upon metal, or wood, without fitting the work in a lathe'.[60] This called for the use of a 'strong iron bar' – a beam compass – with a centre-pin on one end, and fitted with 'a tooth of steel with such roundings and hollows in the bottom of it, as I intended to have hollows and roundings upon my work' on the other. With the point placed in the centre of the workpiece, he

employ'd a labourer, directing him in his left hand to hold the head of the center-pin, and with his right hand to draw about the beam and tooth, which (according to the strength) he us'd, cut and tore away great flakes of the metal, till it receiv'd the whole and perfect form the tooth would make; which was as compleat a molding as any skillful turner could have laid upon it.

Watt's scriber for making multiple lines at once is a simpler form of what Moxon describes here.

Historian of mechanism Michael Wright has even suggested that one of Watt's projects appears to have gone subtly wrong. Resting on one of the shelves in Watt's workshop sits a wheel. It is cast brass and 15 inches in diameter.[61] Shallow teeth have been cut around the circumference, indicating that it is a dividing plate, a small version of those made by Ramsden in London and used to make the scales for instruments. But it hasn't been used much, and some detective work shows us why. The teeth around the outside would have been cut by placing the edge hard up against a worm screw whose leading edge was nicked to make it cut into the metal. As the screw was rotated it would have turned the plate through

360 degrees, cutting teeth all the way round as it progressed – three or four complete rotations would have been needed to make the teeth deep enough. Because the accuracy of any instruments divided on the plate depended on the positioning of the teeth and hence on the accuracy with which it was rotated, a careful instrument maker would painstakingly check the position of the teeth, using a magnifying lens, against marks determined by geometrical means – and there are some marks made with compasses, showing some attempt at carefully laying the whole thing out. But in making the plate, Watt didn't check against these marks, and though there are supposed to be 360 around the circumference – one per degree of rotation – there are only 359. Because of this carelessness, any instrument Watt made using the plate would have been correspondingly inaccurate.

If Watt's attempt at constructing a dividing engine went awry, he had more success making screw threads. He wrote to his friend William Small in 1773 that 'My dividing screw can divide an inch into 1,000 tolerably equal and distinct parts on glass' – meaning he was using it to mark the scales on glass thermometer tubes.[62] A year later, he wrote again to Small, 'I had occasion to use my last dividing screw for the first time the other day . . . It did not err the 1/200th of an inch in the whole 9 inches.'[63] Watt could do fine work if he put his mind to it, but a question mark rests over whether the bulk of his work actually required him to do so.

The London instrument makers were an acknowledged elite and their capabilities do not necessarily reflect those elsewhere. This is not to denigrate those makers based outside London, like Watt. But precision was subjective: what might be an impressively accurate work of precision to a shopkeeper buying an instrument to amuse his family might be sniffed at by a dilettante used to the output of the very best London workshops. The standards of precision the London makers achieved were something for the others, including Watt, to aspire to. Watt certainly followed the trend for theoretical learning to underpin practical instrument making. He took a copy of Nicholas Bion's *The Construction and Principal Uses of Mathematical Instruments*, translated into English by Edmund Stone, with him when he returned from London to Scotland. Also in his library were Gregory's *The Elements of Astronomy, Physical and Geometrical,* Desaguliers' *A Course of Experimental Philosophy* and Smith's *Compleat System of Opticks.*[64] And he borrowed Gravensande's *Elements of Natural Philosophy* from his father.

But whether Watt's business demanded that he pursued such a theoretically grounded, precise approach is doubtful. Instrument making on a tight budget required a more pragmatic approach – like copying the work of others, for instance. Watt wrote to his father, 'If you can get a good well shaped Davis quadrant that has been approved by some experienced seaman send it up. I shall return it in a week at any rate send the best you can get.'[65] He also wrote, 'I wish you would send up a pair of each sort [of brass dividers] . . . as I am getting a boy who I intend to set making them . . .'.[66] Three months later, he wrote again, 'If you'll please send up a Binacle [sic] compass & the exact measure of all the different sizes, I shall get you some made.'[67] As Watt copied his peers' work, others did the same to him. Watt sold 80 of his perspective drawing machines in total.[68] But George Adams, the prominent London instrument maker, pirated its design as his own invention 'for taking the true perspective of any landscape, building, gardens, &c.', selling it for the considerable sum of six guineas.[69] And rather than the latest precision methods, other ruses were frequently employed. John Rabone later told how the straight rules 'in general use by mechanics' were made

> by placing the article to be divided and the original pattern side by side, then passing a straight-edge with a shoulder fixed at right angles to serve as a guide, along the original, and pausing at each division; then a corresponding line is made on the copy by the dividing knife . . . This method, in skilful hands, admits of much accuracy.[70]

So for some instrument makers, 'good enough' was preferable to 'the best', and satisfied their customers.

Concentrating on making instruments that were just good enough did not preclude innovation and awareness of the latest new theories in other areas, however. Brief mention of Adam Smith has been made above, and we return to him now: Watt's workshop at Glasgow College was a 'favourite resort' for Smith during his tenure at Glasgow College.[71] Watt and the older professor established a sufficiently strong rapport for Watt, in retirement after 1800, to manufacture a portrait bust of him, a privilege most often retained for Watt's closer friends and acquaintances.[72] Of more immediate import is how Smith's theories of how the economy worked relate to practices inside Watt's workshop. In his most famous book, *The Wealth of Nations*, published in 1776, Smith wrote how labour, not land, was the source of wealth and prosperity, and organizing labour as efficiently as possible by having a high degree of 'division of labour' would enable wealth to be maximized. This meant taking workers from making an entire, finished product from scratch and giving them specialized jobs, each based on a single part of the overall process. The example Smith chose was of a factory making pins, where ten specialized workers operating together might make 48,000 pins per day, compared to 200 if they had each to undertake the entire process from a length of wire to the finished pin.[73]

There survive objects from Watt's Glasgow workshop that embody this revolutionary approach – the theory that would underpin the rise of the factory system in Britain. And they are associated with one of Watt's more surprising business ventures: making musical instruments. This might seem peculiar given that he had 'an absolute deficiency of any musical ear', and he was later wary of employing a colleague because he enjoyed playing the violin, which he thought 'the source of idleness'.[74] But commercially they were in much demand, and the tools and techniques needed to make them differed little from those needed to make scientific instruments. Watt could add another string to his bow, so to speak, with relative ease.

The range of tools in Watt's workshop matches closely those needed for flute making as described in Louis Bergeron's *Manuel du Tourneur* of 1816.[75] There is a complete set of long reamers for making the hole down the centre of each flute, a mandrel for the sections of each instrument to be held on a lathe so that its outside surface can be smoothly finished, and a pair of boring collars to hold the flute parts so that the joints between each can be fitted together tightly. Watt's other innovations suggest attempts to speed

Watt's flute tools laid out on the bench in his workshop.

up and simplify each part of the flute making process in line with Smith's doctrine of the division of labour: the box containing many of the tools already described also contains short lengths of wood with pins driven through at a 90 degree angle. These were used to mark the positions of the finger holes on each flute more quickly than marking each individually. Having been drilled, the finger holes were finished with a 'fraise' tool, a rotary cutter with teeth that looks like strawberry (in French, a *fraise*). And to 'undercut' each finger hole – that is, to make the place where it met the bore running inside the length of the flute a little wider – Watt developed a special tool with three spherical cutters positioned along a single spindle which could be put inside the bore to undercut three holes at once. Using these tools it would have been possible to pass each flute from one workman to the next, each able to quickly undertake his part of the overall process. Watt was also applying these ideas to manufacture of his perspective drawing apparatus: in one corner of his workshop sits a wooden box packed with the incomplete remains of a number of these, as well as many components awaiting assembly. Comparing them suggests that different parts were supplied by different workmen in batches that could be passed from one to another. Specialization was taking off rapidly in instrument making, so Watt

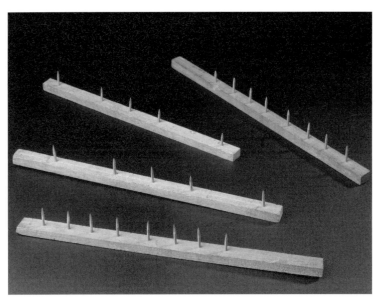

Some of Watt's pin gauges for marking the positions of finger holes on flutes.

Watt's special tool for undercutting three finger holes on a flute at once.

was not unique in this respect, but the survival of such artefacts given Watt's association with Adam Smith makes them significant.

Significant in another way is one final artefact illustrating Watt's business practices. It is a stamp for marking figures on wood, consisting of four letters: 'T Lot'. Lot was a renowned Parisian flute maker, raising the question of whether Watt was marking his own flutes as those of Lot and charging more for them.[76] The surviving pieces of Watt's flutes are not of the best quality – he pressed one unfinished piece into service in the workshop as a handle to hold glass lenses while polishing them – so the ruse, if that is what is was, would not have fooled the discerning flautist. But perhaps the fashionable young gents who would be Watt's potential market in Glasgow were not too discerning.

Watt wasn't just making flutes. He was connected to Charles Clagget in Dublin. Clagget became a major customer, purchasing instruments and tools to the sum of £164, including guitars, violas da gamba and even 'a set of wheels for wiring strings'.[77] He proposed a business partnership with Watt that would involve Watt relocating to Dublin, ultimately to no avail. In 1776 Clagget patented a number of improvements to the violin. His plan was to divide the fingerboard into two interlocking parts. One could be lowered to enable the other, shaped like a miniature ladder, to form raised frets that guided the trainee violinist's fingers. When not needed any more, the moveable piece could be raised to create a normal, smooth fingerboard. It seems a complicated way to do things: tying gut strings around the fingerboard in the right places would have the same effect.[78] But from the heap of unfinished fingerboards in Watt's workshop, it would appear that Watt saw some promise in the idea and may have been commissioned to make them by Clagget before he obtained his patent.[79] But of greater significance are marks on the surviving fingerboard pieces that suggest that they were cut using a circular saw; small round saws survive in the workshop. This is the earliest known evidence for the use of what remains a widely used woodworking tool.[80] Watt's musical instruments may not have won prizes, but making them helped him show off a canny talent for invention that a London instrument maker would have been proud of. And in being a branch into a new business for Watt, they

The 'T Lot' stamp from Watt's workshop.

point to something that Watt and his London counterparts did have in common: not just making instruments but having a shop to sell them, too.

Watt's shop strategy reflects the scale of the market for instruments that could be used at home. Many people loved to observe and record the weather, that great British preoccupation, and they purchased good-quality thermometers and barometers to help them. The naturalist Gilbert White recorded thermometer, barometer and even wind readings in a ready-printed diary by Benjamin White of Fleet Street, London, and his observations contributed to his *Natural History of Selborne*, a pioneering holistic study of the environment he lived in.[81] Thomas Turner, a Sussex grocer, purchased scientific toys for his family: 'I entertained my sister Sally, and my brother's wife, with the sight of the Modern Microcosm, which I think is a

69

Robert Sayer, *Astronomy*, c. 1790, engraving. In depicting some wealthy buyers of scientific instruments, it suggests the affluent market that instrument makers could tap into.

very pretty curious sight, for we see the whole solar system move by clockwork, in the same manner as they do in the heavens.'[82] It wasn't just Turner who liked scientific devices. Later in his diary he records, 'There being at Jones's a person with an electrical machine, my niece and I went to see it, and though I had seen it several years ago, I think there is something in it agreeable and instructing, but yet at the same time very surprising.'[83] Domestic users were encouraged by publications that introduced the subject to them, like Henry Baker's best-seller 'The Microscope Made Easy' of 1742, which was intended 'for the instruction of such . . . as desire to search into the WONDERS of the *Minute Creation*, tho' they are not acquainted with *Optics*'. Not all instrument users had earnest scientific discovery in their sights, however. Attending a sermon at St Margaret's Church, Westminster, Samuel Pepys entertained himself with a 'perspective glass up and down the church by which I had the pleasure of seeing and gazing a great many fine women'.[84]

To launch himself fully into the world of instrument retailing, Watt entered business partnership in October 1759 with John

Craig, a Glasgow-based merchant and architect. Watt and Craig complemented each other well: Craig injected more than £700 into the business, roughly £50,000 in today's money, and looked after the finances.[85] Watt provided contacts and expertise, visiting London to buy stock wholesale and securing space below his first-floor workshop to sell it in. The new shop must have been quite a sight, as Watt moved beyond instruments to retail everything from chess boards, necklaces and earrings to thimbles, watch chains, coffee mills and buckles.[86] In December 1763 the venture's success led Craig and Watt to relocate to bigger premises on Glasgow's Trongate, a long, broad street lined with colonnaded buildings that comprised the main, fashionable shopping centre. Watt could proudly write to his father, 'my shop does very well.'[87]

Watt was following a retail trend already established elsewhere. Many manufacturers would often keep a large stock ready for sale, some made by themselves, but more purchased wholesale from others. This reflected the fact that customers did not want to wait weeks for an instrument to be built but wanted it straight away. Gradually the divisions between mathematical and optical instruments disappeared – both types sat side by side on the shelves, awaiting customers. In 1768 Jean Bernoulli wrote of George Adams's London shop that as well as the globes Adams was well-known for, it was 'provided with a prodigious number of instruments for physics, mathematics, dialling, astronomy, &c.'[88] The appearance of the shops must have been amazing, as Bernoulli recalled:

You have certainly heard of the richness and brilliance of London shops, but I doubt that you have realised how much Astronomy contributes to the beauty of the spectacle: London has a great number of opticians, their shops are full of reflecting and refracting telescopes, octants, &c. All these instruments, properly displayed and arranged, please the eye as much as they impress by the reflections to which they give rise.[89]

Shops were places where an astute instrument maker would unashamedly show off his wares: to demonstrate his telescopes, John Marshall had his name painted in white on the roof of a house twenty houses away from the shop, and prospective telescope purchasers were encouraged to spot it.[90] Shops, then, were places to meet like-minded company, browse, and exchange news and ideas.

But Watt's expanding business empire also shows us how vulnerable an artisan-entrepreneur could be to financial problems and competition. The famed London telescope maker Benjamin Martin overcommitted himself and plunged into bankruptcy.[91] When the microscope maker John Cuff gave up his London shop because he worked too slowly to sustain the business, he found that even in Norwich there were 'several persons who sell Optical Instruments of an inferior sort and of late, Riders are imployed . . . who comes to seek out Customers & get orders'.[92] And John Gardener of Glasgow, who started out as an apprentice with Watt, began a family business making scientific instruments that went bankrupt four times in 75 years.[93] Instrument making was not a trade without risks, and this was certainly the case for Watt.

Looking through the accounts of Watt and Craig's partnership suggests that the business was not sustainable.[94] In the first year of the partnership Watt's expenditure was about £261 (about £20,000 in today's money), but he brought in only around £73. This might be expected as he got things up and running. The following year, 1760–61, income rose to over £170 and Watt made a profit of £83 – but he borrowed £133 from Craig. In the third year, the income was £290 but outgoings totalled £481 – a loss of £194 and, again, £135 was borrowed from Craig. The business costed more to run than it brought in, and all the time the debt to Craig mounted steadily. How it was to be repaid is unclear.

Watt also had competition in Glasgow. George Jarden was another blacksmith and mathematical instrument maker active at the same time as Watt, but in 1757 Watt commissioned him to divide the scales on some instruments for the surveyor John Gray, suggesting the two had an amicable relationship.[95] A more serious rival was John Carlile, an established general merchant with an enormous product range that comprised over 120 different product lines listed in a 1755 advertisement, with a promise of more 'particularly mentioned in his printed catalogue'.[96] Carlile must have been a daunting competitor to relative newcomer Watt, who seems only slowly to have appreciated the value of catalogues, trade cards and instruction books to boost sales. He did have some catalogues printed for his shop in 1766, but by then it would seem more of a last-ditch attempt to bolster flagging sales than a proactive attempt to build business.[97] In 1765 Watt faced a new threat: John Craig died, and the money he had lent to the business needed to be repaid.

Watt's foray into the world of instrument making brought mixed results. He had links to makers in London and aspired to the levels of precision they attained. However, although many aspects of his work were highly ingenious, and he must have received a thorough grounding in running a business, Glasgow was a limited marketplace, which brought financial difficulties and meant that Watt's ambitions outran what he could achieve there. That Watt was himself aware of things going awry is reflected in a letter to his father of 1766 in which he wrote of acquiring 'a stock of Experience *that will soon pay me for the trouble it has cost me*'.[98] It was fortunate for Watt that, even as his business ran into trouble, he was able to draw on his contacts in Glasgow College. Rather than diffusing Watt's efforts, as they had done previously, the college community was to help him focus on his biggest project ever: steam.

In the winter of 1763–4 a model engine was brought to Watt by John Anderson. Anderson found that the model would only work for a short time before coming to a halt. Watt was ideally placed to effect a repair, and this came at a propitious moment for the engine. As Watt dismantled Anderson's model, the engines used in Britain were 'atmospheric', a type first developed by the Dartmouth iron-monger Thomas Newcomen in or before 1712. Newcomen's engine had a large, open-topped metal cylinder, inside which a piston could slide up and down. The piston was connected by chains to a heavy wooden beam, which pivoted at its mid-point, and the opposite end of which could be connected by long rods to water pumps deep underground. To make the engine work, the cylinder was filled with steam. When it was full, the steam supply was cut off and cold water was sprayed in. This condensed the steam, creating a partial vacuum beneath the piston. Because the top of the cylinder was open, atmos-pheric pressure pushed the piston down into the vacuum beneath

The model engine belonging to John Anderson that Watt repaired in the winter of 1763–4.

it, rocking the beam and operating the pumps attached to its other end, lifting water from deep underground. Then, the weight of all the pumps and rods hanging on the end of the beam returned it to its starting point and the cycle began again.

Newcomen's atmospheric engine was simple, robust and reliable. But it had a single, big drawback: it consumed an enormous amount of coal fuel. This didn't matter so much if the engine worked at a coal mine, burning unsaleable 'slack' coal, small pieces and dust. But the engine was uneconomic to use anywhere that coal was not cheap and plentiful, like Cornwall, where the metal mines employing the engine had to ship coal from South Wales at great cost. Watt's upbringing as a Scottish Presbyterian had engrained in him an austere view of waste and economy. It offended his sensibilities that Newcomen's atmospheric engine wasted so much fuel. For him it was as much a moral project as a scientific one to make it less wasteful. After more than a year's work Watt had a solution which would not just cure Anderson's model, but had the potential to transform the steam engine.

This story was narrated by John Robison, a student at Glasgow College who had a curious ability to find himself present at some of the eighteenth century's defining moments. He accompanied General Wolfe to the battle of Quebec in September 1759 which secured Canada for Britain, and travelled with John Harrison's marine chronometer on its trial voyage to Jamaica in 1761–2, verifying its phenomenal accuracy. He can even take the credit for introducing Watt to the steam engine, having had a plan for an atmospheric engine published in the *Universal Magazine* in November 1757. Robison and Watt struck up a close friendship: Robison ransacked the library in search of textbooks on steam to help Watt, and together they studied the latest findings from authors like Belidor and Desaguliers. Expecting to find Watt just a workman, Robison instead discovered 'a Philosopher, as young as myself, and always ready to instruct me. I had the vanity to think myself a pretty good proficient in my favourite study, and was rather mortified at finding Mr Watt so much my superior.'[99] As Watt's instrument-making work was underpinned by a great deal of reading and study, so his insights into his workbench projects went beyond what a more ordinary mechanic or instrument maker might have diagnosed. As Robison claimed for Watt, 'everything became science in his hands'. This approach was applied to Anderson's model engine in the winter of 1763–4.

Watt eventually returned the model to Anderson; he had already sawn its pump casing in half, for example, and even more radical measures than Anderson would have countenanced were needed to make it work to Watt's satisfaction.[100] But it had started him on a new research trajectory which would bear fruit in a way encapsulated during an encounter in the summer of 1765. John Robison walked without ceremony into Watt's parlour to find him seated before the fire with 'a little tin cistern' resting upon his knee. He was recollecting a previous conversation they had had about steam when Watt abruptly put the tin cistern on the floor at the foot of his chair. He replied to Robison, 'You need not fash yourself any more about that Man, I have now made an Engine that shall not waste a particle of Steam.' While doing so he looked complacently at the cistern, half-hidden by his foot. But seeing Robison try to ascertain what it was, he briskly hid it away beneath the table, and met Robison's questions with 'rather dry answers'.[101] The tin cistern represented a major leap of imagination by Watt: it was his first model of what he called the 'separate condenser', the use of which made the engine as sparing as possible in its use of heat and fuel: its efficiency compared to the old atmospheric engine rose threefold.[102]

The separate condenser was possibly the greatest single improvement ever made to the steam engine. But now, the death of his Glasgow business partner John Craig meant the loss of a key supporter just as Watt had to scale up his discovery into a full-size industrial machine. It was in large part Watt's gifts as an instrument maker – the 'go to' man of Glasgow College – that presented him with the opportunity to make this major breakthrough. Instrument makers were at the heart of a new and expanding scientific culture that was as much commercial and practical as it was philosophical, and the technicalities of instrument making were solid foundations for the business of building steam engines.

Instrument makers were early on resolving the problems of making artefacts in metal that were as robust as they were accurately made. Their designs incorporated useful attributes like bracing and careful proportioning that prevented the instruments being deformed by use, and which could be applied on a larger scale with industrial machines. They took the first evolutionary steps in refining those 'tools to make tools' that would be invaluable in the new industries: lathes, metal-cutting machines and precision machine tools. The processes of manufacturing instruments could be expanded onto

Trade advertisement for the instrument makers Chadburn Brothers of Sheffield, 1851. Among the instruments can be seen a number of model steam engines.

an industrial scale. Making brass tubes for telescopes already took serious effort: a brass sheet would be formed into a rough cylinder and this was then squeezed between a steel mandrel and a die (the former forming the inner and the latter the outer surfaces) using a force of several tons, to give it a precise diameter.[103] The old way of making a screw, cutting the thread by hand, was later used (albeit with some modifications) by one of Matthew Boulton's smiths to make a huge wrought-iron screw for a press 6 inches in diameter and 7 feet long.[104]

Watt was also early in what became a longstanding relationship between instrument makers and steam engines. Anderson's model, repaired by Watt, had been built by Jonathan Sisson in London, better known for surveying instruments and his 'great Skill, Accuracy and Fidelity'.[105] As late as 1851 a picture of Chadburn Brothers of Sheffield's instrument shop includes, among the barometers, telescopes and globes, fine models of stationary and locomotive engines, and instrument makers were being commissioned to make fine-quality models into the 1860s.[106] Instrument making offered valuable insights into building larger industrial machines. Now, for Watt, the challenge of scaling up his engine meant he had to master the dynamics of the steam and heat contained inside it.

THREE

Looking for a Living, 1764–74

THE BROOMIELAW QUAY WAS the trading heart of the city of Glasgow. On the north bank of the river Clyde, its quarter-mile length was a hive of activity: ships were prepared to sail for the Baltic, Mediterranean and Caribbean oceans laden with goods ranging from almonds to yarn.[1] Still more departed for North America carrying bales of linen, returning up to eighteen months later, laden with tobacco from Virginia, Carolina and Maryland.[2] Often the ships were also involved in the transportation of slaves between the west coast of Africa and the Americas. As the ships and lighters moored alongside the quay presented a forest of masts and sails to observers, so the quayside itself was a mass of cranes and hoists, barrels and stacks of goods: oatmeal and strong ale, glass, Muscovado sugar, linen textiles and tobacco. The last of those was a particularly lucrative trade – in 1775, more than 13,000 cubic metres were imported through Glasgow and Greenock, around half of the total amount entering Britain.[3] The tobacco lords became a wealthy elite and their influence and commercial power was expressed in the shape of new buildings that subdivided the older medieval city with well-planned new streets, both broad and handsome. For Daniel Defoe, Glasgow was

the emporium of the west of Scotland . . . It is a large, stately, and well-built city, standing on a plain, in a manner four-square; and the four principal streets are the fairest for breadth, and the finest built, that I have ever seen in one city together . . . it is one of the cleanliest, most beautiful, and best-built cities in Great Britain.[4]

'A First View of Practical Chymistry', published in the *Universal Magazine* (December 1747). Chemical workplaces like this were important for Scotland's industrialization, and Watt's future career.

Glasgow became, then, a prosperous reflection of Scotland's growing industrial and commercial power.

We have already explored Watt's instrument making business, and his introduction to the steam engine, within the context of a burgeoning scientific culture. Now we can look in more detail at the interconnections of that scientific culture with the wider world of industry and commerce as represented by the Broomielaw Quay – a relationship that was particularly strong during the Scottish Enlightenment.[5] A distinct emphasis was placed on building links between chemistry and its applications, which proved to be a major stimulus to the Scottish economy, was closely associated with growing prosperity and new trends in consumption, and also formed the immediate background to Watt's work developing the steam engine. The engine evolved alongside other projects founded upon Watt's interest in chemistry, which had its most prominent output in his work for Glasgow's Delftfield Pottery. And as chemistry depended in large part upon the manipulation of heat, so it was also fundamental to Watt's understanding of how the engine worked, underpinning its evolution into a machine on an industrial scale.

The Scottish Enlightenment saw close bonds forged between the universities in cities such as Glasgow or Edinburgh, and partners in industry. This union can be summed up with a single word: improvement. Rather than concentrating on attaining abstract knowledge about humankind and the natural world within a purely academic setting, improvement was a motivation for tangibly bettering humankind's situation and, as the earlier philosopher Francis Bacon had described it, helping in 'the relief of man's estate'.[6] In Glasgow, for example, John Anderson founded a series of informal lectures, intended for a broad public audience, and as Watt's workshop at Glasgow college had become a favourite meeting place for students and staff, so Anderson regularly visited the workplaces of the city's artisans, 'giving them such information as was likely to benefit them in their respective arts, receiving in return a knowledge of those which he could not otherwise have obtained'.[7]

Anderson's lectures were in demand because, after 1750, Scotland was home to a broad and strengthening range of industries. The output of her coal mines more than quadrupled over the course of the eighteenth century.[8] Linen production stretched across central Scotland and much of the output was sold in English markets, reflecting the importance of the Act of Union of 1707 in bringing political and economic integration with England. Profits from lucrative trades such as the import of tobacco were invested in other sectors, including marine stores for shipping, glass, bleaching and metals. And even when the tobacco trade collapsed after the American War of Independence, merchants quickly strengthened links with the Caribbean to import sugar and took advantage of an extant and highly skilled workforce to establish cotton mills alongside those already weaving linen.

This resilient industrial base provided particularly fertile ground for the application of new philosophical research in chemistry.[9] William Cullen, distinguished professor at Glasgow and then Edinburgh until 1789, had declared,

Does the joiner want a particular glew [sic]? Does the mason want a cement? Does the dyer want a means of tinging a cloth of a particular colour? Or does the bleacher want the means of discharging all colours? It is the chemical philosopher who must supply these.[10]

But it was Cullen's student and assistant Joseph Black who most fully devoted himself to building bridges between research and its industrial applications. Black was rigorous, preferring to stick strictly to the facts and considering 'every hypothetical explanation as a mere waste of time and ingenuity'.[11] He was also a lover of quiet contemplation, described by Watt as 'a Gentleman of great modesty', and another acquaintance recorded how 'Disputes he shunn'd, nor car'd for noisy fame; And peace forever was his darling aim'.[12] It may have been his reticence that made him reluctant to write much down: he would not publish his important research on heat, for example, and it only became public when a pirated version of his College lectures appeared, unauthorized, in 1770.[13] But for all his reluctance to publish, Black acquired an enviable reputation as consultant to industrialists working on a very wide range of projects including 'sugar refining, alkali production, bleaching, ceramic glazing, dyeing, brewing, metal corrosion, salt extraction, glass making, mineral composition, water analysis and vinegar manufacture'.[14]

Black's consultancy illustrates the fruitful flow of ideas established in Scotland between philosophical science and its industrial applications. The civil engineer Thomas Telford wrote of being 'very deep in chemistry', having obtained a 'copy of Dr Black's lectures . . . I am determined to study with unwearied attention until I attain some general knowledge of Chemistry as it is of Universal use in the [practical] arts.'[15] From 1798 the metallurgist David Mushet was inspired to narrow the gap between practical iron founders and 'metallurgical philosophers' by publishing a long series of papers exploring how chemistry could be applied to iron production. He developed a detailed knowledge of the characteristics of iron ores, identifying a huge reserve of high-quality ore in Scotland to supply the foundries there.[16] If these examples suggest that the flow of ideas was only in one direction, this was not quite the case: Alexander

John Anderson, c. 1775. Anderson forged strong links between university teaching and industry, and the institution founded after his death survives today as Strathclyde University.

Wilson, later professor of astronomy at Glasgow, started out as a type founder.[17] And James Hutton's interest in geology, which led him to describe the earth's geological processes as having 'no vestige of a beginning – no prospect of an end', stemmed from his industrial and agricultural interests: he had a chemical works making sal ammoniac (which was used as a flux by tinplate makers, dyers and brass workers), and inherited two farms, which focused his attention from chemistry, quarrying and land drainage schemes, to the composition of the earth beneath his feet.[18]

Philosophical chemistry and its industrial applications were, then, two sides of the same coin, and Black was at the forefront of a community which encompassed both. One of the major examples of their research interests in Scotland was in manufacturing alkalis, chemicals with caustic properties that had a wide variety of uses, from bleaching textiles to making glass. In the 1780s Scottish weavers produced over 7,000 miles of cloth every year.[19] Before it could be dyed or printed, it had to be bleached white, which was a major production bottleneck. The woven cloth was cleaned with an alkaline mixture of water and ashes from burned kelp seaweed or barilla before any traces of this 'lye' were removed by soaking in a dilute acid, most often soured milk. It was then laid out on one of 250 huge bleachfields to whiten by the oxidizing action of the sunlight over a period of months.[20] Making this process more reliable and faster received the attention of chemists including William Cullen and Joseph Black. They devised ways of making synthetic alkalis from salt to replace alkali derived from seaweed, and stronger acids and, later, chlorine as substitutes for bleaching by the sun. In doing so they reduced bleaching from a process taking weeks or months to one that could be completed in hours or days.[21] And they also forged links with others like John Roebuck, who had established an industrial plant for making sulphuric acid near Edinburgh in 1749, and James Keir, raised in Scotland but working in England, who turned synthetic alkali manufacture into a commercial process for the first time.[22] Together this coalition of theoretical and practical talents refined the chemistry of manufacturing textiles, but also of soap, glass, acids, brewing and dyestuffs. Scotland developed a prospering chemical industry that stands as a counterbalance to concepts of the Industrial Revolution as traditionally dominated by textiles manufacture and the application of steam power, for example.[23]

This new industry had two key characteristics. First, it stimulated economic growth, as remarked upon by Justus von Liebig in 1843, when he noted, 'We may fairly judge of the commercial prosperity of a country from the amount of sulphuric acid it consumes.'[24] This prosperity was reflected in the expansion of Glasgow: the city grew from 23,000 to 42,000 inhabitants between 1755 and 1780, and

The Bleacher.

'The Bleacher', working on one of the enormous fields where cloth was bleached white by the sun; from *The Book of Trades* (1824).

the population's character changed, too. The historian James Gibson recorded how 'hitherto an attentive industry, and a frugality bordering on parsimony, had been the general characteristic of the inhabitants of Glasgow'.[25] But increasingly

> the ideas of the people were enlarged, and schemes of trade and improvement were adopted, and put into practice, the undertakers of which, in former times, would have been denounced madmen; a new stile [sic] was introduced in building, in living, in dress, and in furniture; the conveniences, the elegances of life began to be studied [and] luxury advanced with hasty strides every day . . . every person is employed, not a beggar is to be seen in the streets, the very children are busy.[26]

Second, this newfound economic stimulus found physical form in a new culture of consumption. Contemporary historian James Denholm described a

> great change . . . in the manners, dress, &c. of the inhabitants of Glasgow, more especially since the rapid rise of the manufactures, which have diffused wealth more generally among the people than before, has occasioned a consequent alteration in their dress, furniture, education, and amusements.[27]

New consumer goods, as demanded by the denizens of Glasgow and across Britain, were not simply material possessions but signified membership of a new, refined social class defined by prosperity and an awareness of the latest tastes. This consumer culture was expressed in a profusion of shops, shopping and new products. The German writer Sophie von La Roche, visiting London in 1786, was amazed by the city's profusion of 'watchmakers, silversmiths, china-shops, confectioners without equal, and the goods so elegantly displayed behind those fine glass windows'.[28] Professor Georg Christoph Lichtenberg, visiting from Germany in 1770, found himself distracted by 'silversmiths, shops of Indian wares, instruments, and the like'.[29] Britain stood on the brink of possessing a prosperous market for consumer goods that was national, and even global; as one historian describes it, 'Birmingham buckles on French shoes, Sheffield forks and knives in Connecticut and Barbados, Staffordshire tableware on Anglo-Indian tables'.[30]

It was against this background that James Watt met his wife. Margaret Miller, or Peggy, as Watt called her, was one of his cousins, and they were married in July 1764. Peggy brought to the fore Watt's 'gentle virtues, his native benevolence, and warm affections', helped run his shop and managed the household.[31] It is uncertain how much they could partake of the fruits of consumption available around them. Although it is traditionally stated that they lived in a house on Delftfield Lane, just to the west of Glasgow's city centre, Watt and Peggy seem to have moved or 'flitted' several times around Glasgow.[32] Those possessions that do survive from Watt's early life – such as a silver George II 'skittle ball' teapot, named after its shape, silver spoons, a sauce boat and mugs – appear mostly to have been inherited from his father, who died much later, in 1782.[33] Watt's biographer notes, then, that the Watts 'practiced housekeeping, from necessity as well as choice, on a very humble scale'.[34] And while Watt's marriage was affectionate, if short of money, it was also fraught with loss.

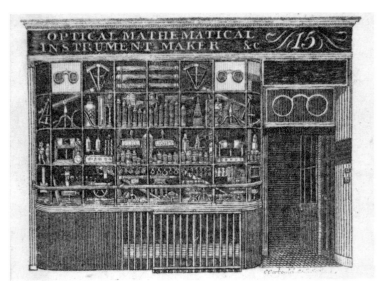

The shop frontage of A. Mackenzie, mathematical and philosophical instrument maker, taken from his trade card, c. 1816. Shops like this were part of a retail industry selling all kinds of consumer goods.

A first son was born in July 1765, but died aged only four months. In the summer of 1767, a daughter, Margaret, was born, who lived until September 1799. And on Christmas Eve 1770 a second daughter arrived, named Agnes, who died in February 1772. Only James, born in February 1769, outlived his father. Such levels of child mortality were not unusually high, but constituted a tragic background to Watt's career.

The world around Watt and his family was shaped by increasing prosperity and the rise of a consumer culture which prized material possessions. It was a world that Watt himself did not partake of immediately, but it provided the context within which philosophical chemistry and its industrial applications could evolve. As Clow and Clow suggested in their book *The Chemical Revolution*, chemistry was in large part a 'social technology', and had effects far beyond the purely technical: the clothes that people wore, the beer that they drank, the soap they washed with, were the products of chemical processes. But equally, broader social and economic forces like consumption and prosperity mediated the relationship between philosophical chemistry and its industrial outcomes. One example of this is the interaction between consumer demand for pottery and the development of new ceramic wares. Another, of more immediate import here, is in John Roebuck's pressing need for an engine to work at his coal mines.

Roebuck had attended the lectures given in Glasgow by Joseph Black and was a speculative investor in interests that included acid manufacture, the iron foundry at Carron and coal mining. With his mines beset by underground floodwater, he needed a sure way to keep the deep workings pumped dry and profitable. Watt, it seemed, was his man. Joseph Black introduced the two men and, from 1767, Watt and Roebuck were in partnership. Roebuck paid off Watt's debts to the estate of John Craig, who had financially supported his shop in Glasgow, and offered the use of the Carron works and his home at Kinneil as a place to get the engine working away from prying eyes.

Watt's partnership with Roebuck involved extensive work improving the engine's design. Its overall form changed extensively; early versions had the steam cylinder turned upside down with the piston rod pointing downwards and arranged to raise and lower a large weight as it operated. This was replaced with a design that had the cylinder standing upright, and which matched more closely the long-established atmospheric engine. The condenser changed as well: from being immersed in a cistern of cold water to condense the steam, to using a jet of water injected inside. The piston design was also modified extensively to ensure that it was a good, close fit inside the cylinder as it moved up and down. The most immediate outcome of this work was that Roebuck was convinced of the 'justness of the Principles' of the engine, encouraging him to invest further and, in return for an agreement that he would receive two-thirds of any income derived from the project, he paid for Watt to obtain a patent on the separate condenser. Watt acquired the patent in January 1769, and it became the foundation of his entire future career, thanks to his being persuaded by future business partner Matthew Boulton and his friend William Small that he should patent the condenser's principles and not the means of *applying* those principles. A great many practical improvements to the engine by Watt and – controversially – by others would be covered by the terms of his patent, giving him and Roebuck legal domination of state-of-the-art engine design.

With the patent obtained, Watt's tests on a full-size version of his engine continued at Kinneil until April 1770. They were not as successful as he would have wished, and strained his relationship with Roebuck to breaking point. Roebuck desperately needed a reliable machine to keep his mines dry, but Watt wanted nothing less than perfection. To recall his earlier words to John Robison, he wanted the engine to 'not waste a particle of steam'. Meeting Watt's high expectations meant overcoming countless technical problems, but these continually knocked his fragile confidence. In October 1768 he recorded his 'natural inactivity, want of health & resolution'. Later he claimed to 'have met with many disappointments . . . I have now brought the engine near a conclusion, yet I am not nearer that rest I wish for than I was 4 years ago . . . Of all things in life, there is nothing more foolish than inventing.' On 30 October 1768 Roebuck wrote to Watt, 'You are letting the most active part of your life insensibly glide away. A day, a moment, ought not to be lost.'

It was to no avail: as late as February 1770 Roebuck could complain that 'a single step has not been advanced towards the engine'.[35]

As Roebuck's coal mines filled with water, and his money seeped away, Watt faced a dilemma. The engine offered the chance of long-term success and wealth, if only he could fully comprehend what was going on inside it, so as to perfect its performance. But he also had a growing family to support, and feared 'growing grey without having any settled way of providing for them'.[36] In the nine years from 1765 until 1774, he spent only two periods of three years in total, in 1765–6 and 1768–70, actually working on the engine.[37] As we will see, when Watt did grasp the internal workings of the engine, he saw it as a chemical machine. But until this happened, his circumstances forced him to pursue a range of projects that enlarged and exploited his knowledge of chemistry.

The scope of Watt's chemical interests is indicated by the contents of his workshop, which is a veritable storehouse of practical chemistry. One corner houses 66 chemical storage jars, drawers contain tiny individually wrapped or boxed samples of substances, and upon shelves sit brown paper parcels containing chemicals purchased in bulk, tied with the original string and labelled in Watt's hand. Fifty different substances comprise ingredients most closely associated with pottery, both the manufacture of glazes and the ceramic bodies they were applied to. Twenty-three, including gamboge, tragacanth, 'cochenilla' and turmeric, found use in dyestuffs. Twenty more, including vermillion umber and 'Precipitate of Prussian Blue', were employed in artists' colours. 'Benzoin', Epsom salts and 'Chinese Carthamus' had medicinal uses, reflecting Watt's role as family doctor as well as husband and father.[38] The range of substances, 140 in all, reflects that Watt cast his net widely depending on what particular projects he had in mind. As early as 1765 he was working with Black to produce alkali from sea salt. In 1784 he was researching the composition of water, while in parallel he was devising a means of chemically copying letters, employing 'iron cement' to seal joints in his steam engine and, later, working on plans to bleach textiles with chlorine for the first time in Scotland.[39] This was not a systematic but more an opportunistic approach to chemistry.

Watt's workshop, Birmingham, 1924. Here we can see jars of chemicals, pestles, mortars and bowls, scales for measuring, and even Watt's apron, hanging on the right.

That is not to say, however, that Watt's chemical interests were not philosophical. As David Miller has written, 'the theoretical Watt and the "cookbook chemist" Watt', as illustrated by the contents of his workshop, 'were the same person'.[40] Similarly, Joseph Black's lectures were written, according to John Robison, 'in the clearest, simplest, and most intelligible . . . Language; such that any sensible dyer or Blacksmith or druggist will understand completely' – yet Black was also regarded as the foremost chemical philosopher of his time.[41] Theory and practice enjoyed a close relationship, and Watt soon had the chance to put his knowledge of both to the test in one of chemistry's most high-profile outputs: in 1768 he became a potter.

The Delftfield Pottery had been established by four business partners in 1748, and was based just west of Glasgow city centre, quite close to the Broomielaw Quay. Its original product was Delft-ware, clay fired in a kiln at relatively low temperature which was allowed to cool off and then dipped in a glossy white tin glaze. It was dried before having patterns painted on, often in blue – a fashion that had originated in Delft, Holland. But Delftware had a thick, soft body, making it fragile – boiling water could cause cracks – and liable to scratch easily. Even as the Delftfield Pottery was founded, the popularity of Delftware was beginning to wane. If the pottery's founders, businessmen with little practical pottery experience, appointed Watt to turn its fortunes around, he was quick to realize the importance of making a more durable product, and began to research what this might be and how it could be made.

There were two possible paths that Watt could pursue: to make Chinese porcelain or improve Britain's existing domestic pottery. Porcelain was immensely sought-after throughout Europe in the eighteenth century, and in 1721 alone, 2 million pieces were imported into Britain.[42] Originating in China, porcelain was made from kaolin, a fine, soft white clay. It was mixed with other ingredients which, in England, might include glass or bone ash, from which is derived the term 'bone china'. When fired at a very high temperature, these ingredients fused together to produce a fine, durable product with a translucent, glass-like finish. Learning the secrets of this manufac-turing process was a project played out across Europe: it was first mastered in Dresden in 1709 under conditions of tremendous secrecy, and became a preserve of royal factories making luxurious tablewares for monarchs and their courts. British porcelain makers were established later on, at Bow and Chelsea in London, at Worcester and Derby, among other places. These producers imitated oriental styles in products like tablewares and decorative figures intended not just for the very wealthiest customers, but for those of more modest means as well.

The alternative to a new domestic porcelain industry was to develop the already extant British earthenware trade. The English potteries had long been 'a more or less rustic art, remarkably skilful but always very near the people, simple . . . and reflecting the country life of the time'.[43] Louis Simond wrote of the 'common-ware' widely used in France as well as Britain that it was 'coarse and heavy, with the glaze scaling off, or full of cracks crossing each other in every direction, like lace-work, and retaining in their interstices the various juices of a hundred successive dinners'.[44] But earthenwares evolved quickly to ultimately produce a new ware described by John Aikin in 1795 as 'the source of a very extensive trade, [which] may be ranked amongst the most important manufactures of the kingdom': creamware.[45]

Creamware imitated porcelain in appearance but took advantage of locally available materials and techniques. It was produced by firing 'ball' clay mixed with ground flints at a low temperature to produce a light-coloured body that could be coated with lead glaze. After a second firing, this was 'smoother, warmer in colour, and better adapted for utilitarian purposes'. Production began in Britain in the 1740s, and it proved to be at once durable, cheap and good-looking enough to appeal to a large, discerning market.[46] Despite difficulties in obtaining a consistent colour and quality of finish, it gradually usurped the older Delftware, giving rise to a commerce

so active and so universal, that in travelling from Dunkirk to the southern extremity of France, one is served at every inn upon English-ware. Spain, Portugal, and Italy are supplied with it; and vessels are loaded with it for the East-Indies, the West-Indies, and the continent of America.[47]

The name most closely associated with this new trade was that of Josiah Wedgwood. He devoted enormous efforts to establishing the scientific basis for its manufacture: it took 411 attempts to obtain the perfect chemical recipe for his creamware glaze, for example. But Wedgwood matched patient experimentation with skill in marketing his products: convinced of its 'real utility & beauty', in 1766 he sold a cream-coloured table service to Queen Charlotte, naming it 'Queen's Ware' in her honour, a name that was widely adopted.[48] In other aspects of his business, a network of agents across Europe drove sales, catalogues and hand bills were used to excite demand, and showrooms in London and Bath presented 'a thousand lovely forms and images; vases, tea-things, statuettes, medallions, seals, [and] table-ware'.[49] But even with his Staffordshire workshops producing over 600,000 pieces of ware yearly, Wedgwood could not keep up with demand – in fact, he found it 'really amazing how rapidly the use of it has spread allmost over the whole Globe, & how universally it is liked'.[50] Although he retained his position as a leader in the pottery industry, over 100 other potteries in Britain also made creamware.[51] Included among them was Watt's Delftfield Pottery.

Watt faced significant barriers in his pottery work. Potters treated the ingredients for their wares as trade secrets, so there was extensive duplication of effort. Watt was also isolated from the main pottery industry in England, explaining that his 'insulated manufactory has much to struggle with'.[52] However, despite a tendency to mix reports of progress with complaints, the company prospered on the back of his chemical work. As early as January 1769, Watt wrote to his friend William Small that 'Our pottery is doing tolerably . . . I am sick of the people I have to do with. Tho' not of the business, which I expect will turn out a very good one.' Almost three years later, he claimed that 'our pottery does very well tho we make damned bad ware'.[53] Some of this bad ware, rejects that would usually have been thrown out, appears to have ended up in Watt's workshop to store his chemicals in.[54] By May 1773 an advertisement in the *Glasgow Journal* could announce that Delftfield had 'now learned the art of manufacturing yellow Stone or Cream Coloured Ware . . . They are thereby enabled to serve their customers at lower prices than formerly, and they flatter themselves with better ware.'[55] Later, surplus wares found ready buyers in North America, at New York and Charleston.[56] Delftfield thus provided Watt with much-needed income – £70 every year (about £5,000 in today's money) – just when he needed it to support his family.[57] The company's success depended upon Watt's researches into the composition of the wares and the glazes used.

Watt's experiments on the bodies of his pottery wares were diverse. Early in his research, he tried replicating porcelain manufacture, writing to Joseph Black in 1768 that 'I found that [pipe] clay may be burnt as white and hard as any porcelain', and some of the containers for chemical samples in Watt's workshop have recipes for soft-paste porcelain written on their lids in Watt's hand.[58] These experiments came alongside development of dense and impermeable new 'stoneware' products, and the workshop also contains a whole drawer of small test firings of pieces of cream-coloured clay, accompanied by notes from Watt recording that they were fired 'by 55 degrees' and 'by 80 degrees' of 'Wedgwood's thermometer'.[59] In sourcing these materials, Watt's often peripatetic life, travelling on business, paid dividends: he found good-quality killas clay near Falmouth in 1782, and his workshop contains a wooden box filled with mineral samples, as well as a small amount of 'Asbestus' in rock form, and even three human teeth and part of a jawbone, with a note that they were from the battle of 'Louearly Field fought 1160'.[60] While travelling to Birmingham in 1774, Watt also conscientiously noted that the 'stone grows softer and gravel harder'; he certainly developed a canny eye for potentially useful materials to employ at Delftfield.[61]

Work on clays was accompanied by research on glazes. Watt began devising mixtures of lead and tin for stonewares, and his investigations of a source of cobalt give us the earliest account of any of his chemical experiments.[62] Later, he looked into sought-after creamwares too: the glaze used lead as a primary ingredient, producing a yellow finish. To make it paler, cobalt could be included as well; Watt's workshop contains a number of samples of this, and the raw materials from which it could be extracted, as well as manganese, used to remove any green tinges from the glazes,

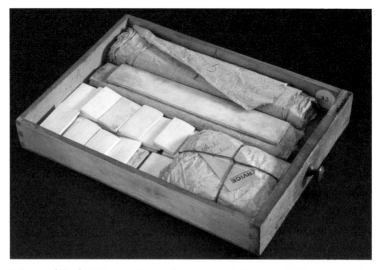

A drawer full of Watt's experimental ceramic test pieces, 1768–80, preserved in his workshop.

all carefully preserved in packets and boxes.[63] The success of Watt's chemical work is suggested by the Scottish potter Robert Muirhead, who described one of his recipes for a fine, white glaze as 'an entirely new art . . . not discovered & practised by any other persons in Britain'.[64]

Turning the clay and glaze ingredients into a finished product depended on them being fired in a kiln, and Watt turned his attention to this, too. He found the Delftfield kilns fuelled with wood; the wares within were exposed to the flames and smoke, which often spoiled the glaze with black marks, and the heat from the fire was unevenly distributed, so that wares placed in some parts of the kiln took longer to fire than others. He changed the shape and internal layout of the kilns so they became more evenly heated, replaced wood fuel with cheaper coke or coal, and changed how the kiln's furnace was stoked with fuel to reduce smoke and prevent ashes contaminating the wares.

Watt's work on the Delftfield kilns, the better to bake hard the clay wares and finish the glazes, is a reminder that understanding the nature of heat, and how best to manipulate it, was a central concern to all those engaged in chemistry. It was also central to

Watt's developing understanding of the steam engine when he eventually returned to it. Many accounts of the engine point to Watt as a thermodynamicist, pioneering the application of a science of heat that was formalized in the early nineteenth century. However, Watt's understanding of heat was far different from that of his successors. Rather than being a form of energy, Watt and his colleagues regarded heat as a chemical compound of heat and water. By extension Watt saw the engine as a piece of chemical apparatus where the chemical elasticity of the steam within drove the piston and made the vacuum generated in the separate condenser perform useful work.[65]

This interpretation of the engine, rather than placing a division between Watt's work on the engine and, say, his research at the Delftfield pottery, sees them as closely related. Watt was also extremely well-placed to be carrying out that work while in contact with Joseph Black, the foremost researcher on the nature of heat.[66] That said, it is difficult to quantify exactly how far Watt's work at Delftfield was informed by philosophical considerations about heat. Although details of particular experiments can be traced in his correspondence, he did not systematically record his working practices and their outcomes but, as David Miller has commented, 'it would be surprising if . . . his ideas about heat as a transformative agent were not involved.'[67] Certainly, some of what we know about Watt's pottery is gleaned from his letters to Black, which is telling in itself. In establishing how different fuels heated the kilns, for example, Black helped Watt with a vivid description: 'A kiln which is heated with flaming fuel may be said to be heated by means of a torrent of *liquid fire* which flows through it, but I am persuaded that cokes act mostly by radiation like that of the sun.'[68] As for Watt's detailed ways of working, he wrote of picking up from Black what he called 'the correct modes of reasoning and of making experiments'.[69] And Watt's personal seal, an emblem of an eye with the initials 'J.W.' below, was surmounted by a single, bold word: 'OBSERVARE', 'to observe', suggesting his skills in methodical observation, measurement and record-keeping.

If Watt's working practices at Delftfield were informed by strong philosophical elements, as seems likely, then he was not alone.

Pottery was recognized as offering excellent opportunities 'for the exercise of ingenuity and research' and was an attractive career for 'persons of observant habits'.[70] Simeon Shaw, in his history of the Staffordshire potteries, wrote how Enoch Wood of Burslem 'had such a judicious arrangement that it presents all the appearances of a most extensive Laboratory and the machinery of an Experimentalist', and Thomas Minton was 'possessed of extensive information of the chemical properties of the earths', for example.[71] And the close integration of theory and practice that pottery relied upon suggests the existence of a shared set of practices and concerns for chemists of all backgrounds. A broad framework for this discussion is provided by Joseph Black's 'general doctrines of chemistry', of which 'the more general or universal effects of heat' stood out prominently.[72]

The furnace was at the heart of much activity in philosophical laboratories. It provided the heat to distil liquids inside glass retorts or alembics which sat on top of the fire while resting inside a bath of iron filings, melted tin, lead or even mercury to ensure that even heating took place.[73] Some furnaces were brick-built structures not dissimilar to a blacksmith's hearth, but Joseph Black designed a portable furnace, 22 inches high and 20 in diameter, mounted on castors so that it could easily be moved about. If a specially designed furnace was unavailable, more domestic alternatives would work equally well. One author noted that 'a complete furnace, *capable of being worked in a parlour chimney*, may be had, which will create little trouble, and will require no assistance from the bricklayer.'[74] Certainly, the stove in Watt's workshop served as a means of cooking and heating but was also pressed into service for experiments requiring heat; it is accompanied by crucibles to contain liquid substances – some of which still contain the solidified contents of their last experiment – tongs, leather aprons and glass spectacles to protect the eyes.

Just as the laboratory chemist spent much time labouring over the furnace, so great 'bottle' kilns, named after their shape, loomed large in the working lives of potters. Firing was the most risky part of the pottery process: wares were placed in the kiln packed inside saggars, containers made of fire-clay positioned to allow heat to circulate around them, and left for 50 hours or more. Some of Wedgwood's work, 'the cameos, intaglios, bas-reliefs, and the majority of the vases, lamps, and candelabra', only needed a single firing.[75] But other products, including the creamware, were referred to only as 'biscuitware' after its first firing because of the colour, porosity and absorbent qualities attained. After the first firing, the ware would be covered in glaze, a mixture of chemical ingredients, and then fired a second time. This time, the pieces were each separated with tiny stools or 'spurs' so that the glazed surfaces would not fuse together. And rather than a long, gentle cooling period, the kiln had to be opened at exactly the right moment to obtain the best effect from the glaze as its chemical constituents were transformed by the heat. Now the firemen rushed in, at risk of serious burns, and the wares were removed while still at high temperatures to be cooled, placed in storerooms and then packed, ready for dispatch to customers.

All applications of heat shared the problem of how precisely to measure the temperatures attained. A pottery kiln might have an eye-hole set into its wall, and by peering through it at the colour of the fire an experienced potter could gauge whether the temperature was right. The terms for describing the look of heat – 'red, bright red, and white heat' – were 'indeterminate expressions' with 'numerous gradations, which can neither be expressed in words, nor discriminated by the eye'.[76] But gauging the temperature wrongly could be costly: in firing his 'Jasperware' pieces, Wedgwood at one time suffered a 75 per cent loss rate, and the roads of the Staffordshire potteries were routinely repaired using misfired wares from the local kilns.[77] Observations had to be within very close tolerances: Wedgwood once remarked of a firing, 'Every Vase in the last Kiln were spoil'd! & that only by such a degree of variation in the fire as scarcely affected our creamcolour bisket at all.'[78] And the same temperature had to be obtained repeatedly. Wedgwood complained that

we are told . . . that such and such materials were changed by fire into fine white, yellow, green or other coloured glass; and find, that these effects do not happen, unless a particular degree of fire has fortunately been hit upon, which degree we cannot be sure of succeeding in again.[79]

Accurately gauging temperature by eye under these conditions was a skill only obtained by hard-won experience over a period of years.

The problem of measuring temperatures was solved in philosophical chemistry by, for instance, using thermometers of the type made by Daniel Gabriel Fahrenheit from 1724, or by Anders Celsius from 1742. James Watt made them for Joseph Black, and lent him the dividing plate that he used to quickly mark them with graduated scales.[80] However, delicate glass-and-mercury thermometers would not survive for long in a pottery kiln, where temperatures routinely passed above 1,000°C. Instead Josiah Wedgwood developed his 'pyrometer', which measured the amount clay will shrink as it is heated. Round clay tablets, each an inch across, were placed in a kiln alongside the wares being fired. At intervals, tablets were removed and placed in a scale consisting of 'two pieces of brass, twenty-four inches long . . . divided into inches and tenths, fixed five-tenths of an inch asunder at one end, and three-tenths at the other, upon a brass plate'.[81] The scale was calibrated for temperature on the basis of careful experiments; as each tablet would decrease in diameter by as much as one-quarter during a firing, the diameter read against the pyrometer scale told the fireman what the temperature inside was: the smaller the diameter, the higher the temperature.[82]

Wedgwood's pyrometer embodies an interest in attaining the highest possible levels of precision across chemical experiments and processes. The need for precision extended beyond just the measurement of temperature. Equally careful attention was paid to recording changes in mass. As Black undertook experiments in the period from 1752 to 1755 which would lead to his discovery of carbon dioxide, he employed a balance that carefully measured the mass of the substances used to the nearest grain, or 64.8 milligrams.[83] Henry Cavendish, working on the chemical composition of water in the early 1780s, could weigh small quantities to within six milligrams.[84] The materials of pottery were also the subject of intense scrutiny. The old way of working, with wares made from clays 'of the coarse yellow, red, black, and mottled kind . . . the body of the ware being formed of the inferior kinds of clay, and afterwards painted or mottled with the finer coloured ones mixed with water, separately or blended together', was no longer adequate.[85]

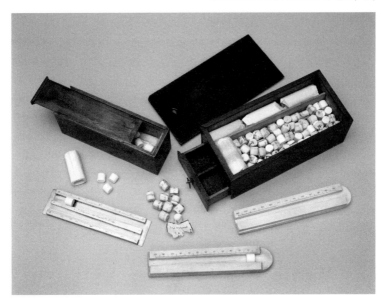

A Wedgwood pyrometer set, 1786.

There was now a move towards carefully obtaining the best available; Wedgwood specified precisely that clay obtained from Pensacola in North America 'must be got as clean from soil, as if it was to be eat, & if they were to get several parcels, at different depths, & put them in separate Casks, properly number'd, I could by that means easily ascertain what depth of the mine is best for our purpose'.[86] And chemists could play a key role in validating the quality of such materials; as William Cullen wrote, 'the philosophical chemist is the assay master to arts in general. He brings all new projects to the test, & . . . works trials in small for their improvement.'[87]

Although new means of precision measurement were becoming available, their use required more trust to be placed in those instruments than their users were sometimes willing to give. Michael Combrune introduced thermometers into brewing, publishing an account of how he did so in 1758, but his father objected to such 'experimental innovations' and Combrune had to keep the offending instruments hidden away.[88] The senses remained the chemist's preferred diagnostic tools across a spectrum of potential projects.[89] In his 'Brief Analysis of Water by Precipitants' (1810),

George Smith describes how 'Good water has no smell; such as abounds in aerial acid, diffuses a penetrating odour. Such as contains any sulphur, yields a smell resembling that of rotten eggs.' Taste was also employed:

Acid occasions a gentle pungent acescent taste; a bitterness accompanies those waters which contain . . . nitre, or magnesia; a slight austerity proceeds from lime and gypsum; a sweet astringency from alum; a saltishness from common salt; a lixivious flavour from alkali; a bitter astringency from copper; and an inky taste from iron.[90]

When Watt and Black corresponded about corrosion inside a pumping engine caused by the water, Black concluded that 'the Water . . . contains a quantity of fixed air tho only a small quantity . . . it is perceptible by . . . a person who has a delicate taste'.[91] The senses were amplified by specialized laboratory equipment, but they remained the foundation of much chemical work into the twentieth century.

In this respect the experience in pottery matched that in philosophical chemistry. The success of pottery really was in the hands of the potter; after being away from the wheel for even a short time, the 'essential smoothness and flexibility' of his hands was lost, and it would take them a number of days to become reacquainted to the feel of the clay.[92] Pressing delicate relief detail, handles and decorations onto a piece of pottery without applying too much pressure took a well-trained, delicate touch. Even the process of applying glazes depended entirely on the dexterity of the dipper, immersing each piece up to his or her elbow, remembering the rule that 'the portion of the article which enters first shall come out first, so that each portion shall receive the same amount of glaze.'[93]

This is not entirely to play down the role of new chemical equipment. Antoine Lavoisier's laboratory contained around 6,000 pieces of glassware alone, for example, and improved apparatus was manufactured in both glass and ceramic, able to withstand corrosive substances, sudden changes in temperature, contain 'elastic vapours' and even bear violent heat 'without melting or being otherwise injured'.[94] Alongside his vases and dinnerwares, Josiah Wedgwood made a popular range of 'Useful Wares' for chemists: pestles and mortars for mixing and grinding purposes, evaporating pans, basins, funnels, siphons, retorts and tubes.[95] Watt's workshop contains some of these; beneath the central workbench rest long earthenware tubes used for experiments in which gases were passed over red-hot solids, and a pair of jasperware mortars sit on the open shelves.[96] The manufacture and use of this apparatus also suggests further crossovers between experimental chemistry and industry of a more robust nature: the mechanical means by which chemical solids were broken into fragments or ground to powders in the laboratory involved 'mortars, sieves, files, the hammer & anvil, &c.' 'Cementation' of materials – laying them layer upon layer so that they reacted together – was named after a 'resemblance between the arrangement of the materials, and the laying of bricks in mortar'.[97] And the capabilities of industrial workshop practice impinged directly onto the manufacture of some experimental apparatus. Joseph Black complained about having to make his portable furnace 'of the simplest rectilinear shapes, because workmen find great difficulty in executing curved and uncommon forms; and not one of a score of them will do it with accuracy'.[98]

Just as there were extensive crossovers between the practices of philosophical and industrial chemistry, so the equipment used by Watt and Black in their experiments on heat bridged both worlds. Watt's work on the engine required his models and small full-size prototypes, as well as some specially commissioned instruments to measure the quantity of heat contained within steam, for example. But in addition to these, he employed readily available chemical balances to measure the amount of fuel burned and water evaporated, thermometers and barometers for measuring temperature and air pressure and, most prosaic of all, a 'common tea kitchen' to generate steam for his experiments, while Black's laboratory at Glasgow 'extended little beyond basic apparatus such as furnaces, stills and glassware'.[99]

To summarize, then, chemistry in many areas of experimentation and application was based on the accurate manipulation and measurement of heat. These techniques evolved from being based on the senses – although this tradition would long endure in other aspects of chemistry – to being approached in a more carefully quantifiable way. Though these developments were played out in potteries and chemical laboratories, they were of profound significance to the development of the steam engine, and the key players in realizing this were Black and Watt. Having outlined how heat was seen as a chemical substance by both men, and their contemporaries, we will assess their perceptions of its properties and how they could be applied to the engine.

Although their philosophies of the chemical nature of heat were similar, Black and Watt approached the nature of heat from subtly different starting points – Watt with the particular objective of making the engine work, and Black from the perspective of explaining philosophically how a substance absorbs heat. Black carried out his research before Watt, who referred to Black to validate his findings. But this is not to say that the two had a 'master and pupil' relationship. Far from it: Watt's ideas about heat progressed beyond Black's.[100] The historian Arthur Donovan claimed that Black's move from Glasgow to take up a post at the University of Edinburgh in 1766 was 'the end of his career as a creative philosophical chemist'.[101] Black wrote to Watt in March 1772, 'I have no chemical news, my attempts in Chemistry at present are chiefly directed to the exhibition of Processes and experiments for my Lectures, which require more time and trouble than one would imagine.'[102] Black's interest in heat, despite his close associations with industry, would always remain *primarily* an interesting subject for lectures and debates. By contrast, in 1766 Watt was only a short way into the engine project.[103] He would make a much greater personal commitment to understanding the engine, and stood to lose out in a very real way if his understanding faltered. As he later wrote, 'I, having become the father of a family, and loaded with cares of many kinds, had less time for mere philosophical conversations.'[104]

Black had begun his research on heat in 1755 when he was first appointed to the college at Glasgow. It is traditionally said that he first turned to heat as a fruitful area of research after considering that snow is not melted instantly on a sunny winter's day but lingers for some time, and that an overnight frost does not immediately cause ice to form – both phenomena that would be widely visible during a Glaswegian winter.[105] His observations showed that while ice melted, its temperature remained constant, and this raised uncertainties over the relationship between temperature and heat: if the former did not necessarily reflect the latter, how could the amount of heat absorbed by ice be measured? Black devised an experiment to find out in December 1761: he placed two glasses in front of a fire, one filled with water at a temperature of 33°F and the other with ice. With the room temperature standing at 47°F, the water temperature reached 40°F, exactly halfway between its original temperature and that of the room, in 30 minutes. The ice, however, took over ten hours to reach the same temperature, during which time, Black calculated, the extra heat it absorbed would have heated the water by 140°F. Black called this considerable increment the ice's *latent* heat. Black then turned his attention from melting ice into water, to turning water into steam. Noting that it takes longer to entirely boil off a quantity of water than it did just to raise it to boiling point, he found that a pan of water with a temperature of 50°F took four minutes to reach boiling point, but then another twenty minutes to boil off entirely – and this time the latent heat of the steam generated was calculated as being 810°F. Black quickly realized that steam was a tremendously effective medium for storing heat.

Watt's experiments with engines led him to similar conclusions. The atmospheric engine used a piston that could slide up and down inside an open-topped cylinder. Steam was injected beneath it, and the piston rose. Then cold water was injected below, and atmospheric pressure pushed the piston down into the partial vacuum thus created underneath. When working on Anderson's model engine, Watt found that at each working stroke, the amount of steam required amounted to several times the volume of the cylinder, and that 'an enormous quantity of injection water' was needed to subsequently condense it and create the working vacuum.[106] This latter was, Watt subsequently concluded, because of the immense amount of heat that the steam contained: he found that one volume of water turned to steam could boil six times the initial volume of water.

As for the amount of steam required being considerably more than the volume of the cylinder, this brings us to the capacity a body has to absorb heat, or its *specific* heat. As Watt described it, 'all bodies are sponges in respect of heat and some bodies can contain more of it and some others less.'[107] A long series of experiments with his model and prototype engines showed Watt that excessive steam consumption was caused not, as he initially thought, by heat escaping through the cylinder walls, but by the metal cylinder itself having to be warmed prior to every working stroke. Because the cylinder of a steam engine could easily consist of several tonnes of cast iron, it had the capacity to absorb a large quantity of heat that was wasted as soon as cold water was sprayed inside the cylinder to form a vacuum.

The nature of specific heat had also been explored through smaller-scale experimental means. Daniel Fahrenheit had found that when equal volumes of water and mercury were mixed together, if the mercury was initially hotter than the water, then the temperature of the mixture was less than the average of the two, but if the water was hotter then the opposite was true. Scottish physician George Martine had also found that when two glasses of equal volume, one containing water and the other mercury, were placed in front of a fire, the temperature of the mercury rose faster. Black solved the puzzle posed by both experiments by suggesting that mercury had a lower capacity to absorb heat than water, meaning it could be heated and cooled more rapidly.

Watt's responses to the nature of specific and latent heat shaped the design of his steam engine. His initial approach to the heat wasted by the metal cylinder being alternately heated and cooled was to propose that it be built from a material that would absorb less heat, like wood. But later he realized that the problem could be entirely avoided by condensing the steam in a vessel separate from the cylinder – the separate condenser. This way, the cylinder could be kept at a constant high temperature, reducing the waste of heat to an absolute minimum, and the condenser could be kept as cool as possible to create the vacuum that the engine depended upon to operate. As for the movement of the steam between the cylinder and condenser, Watt appreciated that steam, perceived as a chemical compound of water and heat, was an elastic substance – more so as the amount of latent heat was increased.[108] He realized the implications of this while walking on Glasgow Green in May 1765, later writing how 'the idea came into my mind, that as steam was an elastic body it would rush into a vacuum, and if a communication was made between the cylinder and an exhausted body [containing a vacuum], it would rush into it, and might there be condensed without cooling the cylinder'.[109] With the benefit of hindsight, we can say that Watt had grasped the principle which every condensing steam engine subsequently built would depend on.

With progress made in his understanding of the engine, the way forward for Watt lay in refining it as a truly practical industrial machine. But now a range of other factors determined where, and when, this would happen. Industry in Scotland, although expanding, rested on uncertain financial foundations: capital to invest had been in short supply and, in 1769, the Bank of Ayr was established to provide funds for industrial expansion. But it proved over-liberal in its allocation of money, and Scotland's industrial economy overheated. A brief surge in production and speculation was followed by realization that new markets for extra output were not emerging as quickly as hoped, a glut of unsold goods, falling prices and the collapse of economic confidence. In a single fortnight during June 1772 ten banks failed across Britain.[110] The Ayr Bank, which had lent so much in so short a time, was the subject of particular attention from customers seeking to exchange banknotes for gold. By 25 June it had collapsed with liabilities of more than £1 million (£1.3 billion at today's prices), triggering two years of trade depression in Scotland and the evaporation of funding sources for Watt's work on the engine.

With the finances of the engine project uncertain, Watt also faced changes in his personal life. His friends and supporters Joseph Black and John Robison had moved on, Black to a new teaching post in Edinburgh and Robison to pursue his career, albeit temporarily, in Russia. And there was one further, tragic matter to deal with. Travelling on business in Scotland's Great Glen during September 1773, Watt received a desperate letter: his wife was expecting a child and was dangerously ill. He set off for Glasgow as fast as possible, but, having stopped overnight at Dumbarton, he was intercepted by his brother-in-law, Gilbert Hamilton. As Watt later recalled, 'by his black coat & his countenance I saw I had nothing to hope.'[III] The child had been delivered stillborn, and Peggy, his wife, had died afterwards. The black figure of Hamilton stepping down from the coach heralded the end of Watt's dreams of a career in Scotland. Already a new start was being promised in Birmingham. Little did Watt know that the partnership he would form there would become one of the greatest of Britain's Industrial Revolution.

FOUR

Gentlemen of Merit and Ingenuity, 1765–81

ON MONDAY 11 MARCH 1776, *Aris's Birmingham Gazette* carried an account of how 'a Steam Engine constructed upon Mr Watt's new Principles' was set to work at Bloomfield Colliery, near Dudley in the Midlands. The engine began work in the presence of its proprietors, who were accompanied by 'a Number of Scientific Gentlemen whose Curiosity was excited to see the first movements of so singular and so powerful a Machine: and whose Expectations were fully gratified by the Excellence of its performance'. The Bloomfield engine was the first full-size engine built to Watt's design for a customer, and this was the first time mention was made of it in the press.[1] Compared to the model Watt began his steam career with, it was immense, standing almost 30 feet tall, with the steam cylinder alone measuring 50 inches in diameter. Its physical size was matched by its cost – £2,000 in total,[2] or over £125,000 in today's money – and by the impressiveness of its operation. It was certainly an exemplary piece of mechanism: its workmanship was widely commented on as being 'unparalleled for truth', the engine made fifteen working strokes every minute, driving a pump 300 feet underground via an elaborate system of strong wooden rods, but using only one-quarter of the fuel that an atmospheric engine would have required to do the same job. Gone was the older engine wheezing steam from every joint, or even teams of patient donkeys arduously driving round an endless chain pump to lift the water. With each end of the great working beam scribing a 7-foot arc through the air during each stroke, the metronomic action of the lever and rod gear controlling the flow of steam into the cylinder, and the periodical gush of water lifted

Matthew Boulton's Soho Manufactory, by Francis Eginton, 1773.
This centrepiece of Birmingham's manufactures played a prominent
role in the history of the steam engine.

from the mine, pouring into a wooden launder to flow away, here
was a new order of machine which aroused the acclamations of the
scientific gentlemen as well as the 'number of joyous and ingenious
Workmen' who accompanied them.

The engine built by Watt as business partner to Matthew Boulton
of Birmingham was a landmark machine in the history of the
Industrial Revolution and, in the aspirations for how it would be
constructed, was unlike anything that had gone before. But the
way that it was actually built remained rooted in the manufacture
of metalwares for consumers and in well-established craft metalworking skills: the engine did not bring into being radically new ways
of making machines – or not immediately, anyway. Here we will
explore how the engine's development played out within the context
of the city of Birmingham, its environment and culture, Matthew
Boulton and his Soho Manufactory, and the manufacture of one of
Birmingham and Boulton's most important product lines: buttons.

First and foremost, the engine was a product of the metalworking capabilities of the city of Birmingham. In the eighteenth century
Birmingham had the largest concentration anywhere of expertise in
metal manufacturing. Arthur Young called it 'the first manufacturing
town in the world' in 1791, and what historian J. R. Harris has called
today's 'global metal-bashing industries' are all to some extent its

descendants.[3] This primacy was based on plentiful supplies of coal and iron ore, which could be transported on an efficient canal network linking Birmingham to the Black Country, the seaport at Bristol, and even Hull and Liverpool via the Trent and Mersey navigation. By 1780 six coaches every day made the journey to London, and mail coaches also travelled to Bristol, Shrewsbury, Liverpool, Manchester, Sheffield and Nottingham.[4] The town also had few of the restrictions on trade which could be found elsewhere. One author wrote, 'No trades unions, no trade gilds, no companies existed, and every man was free to come and go, to found or to follow or to leave a trade just as he chose.'[5] With growth unrestricted, good infrastructure and the materials to produce metal goods close at hand, Birmingham became the third largest town in England.[6]

As a metalworking centre Birmingham was home to over 50 distinct trades, and this unprecedented concentration of industry attracted visitors anxious to see the sights. Georg Christoph Lichtenberg visited in 1774, describing the 'very large and thickly populated town, where almost everyone is busy hammering, pounding, rubbing, and chiselling'.[7] This relentless industry had a considerable effect on the atmosphere of the town and its people. François de La Rochefoucauld wrote in his travel diary:

> The town of Birmingham is vast, handsome and well-peopled, its roads broad and straight . . . But the great smoke created by the steel and plate manufacturers makes the whole town sombre. It's impossible to keep the windows clean for a single week.[8]

And Robert Southey was 'dizzied with the hammering of presses, the clatter of engines, and the whirling of wheels . . . the devil has certainly fixed upon this spot for his own nursery-garden and hot-house'.[9]

These conditions, so vividly imprinted on the memory of those who witnessed them, were the product of an industrial culture that emphasized the transformation of ideas into practical schemes. While nearby cathedral towns like Worcester or Lichfield wanted 'polite' science, Birmingham people demanded instruction in subjects applicable to the town's day-to-day manufacturing economy: physics

William Sharp after William Beechey, *Matthew Boulton*, 1801.

and mechanics, hydraulics, pneumatics and hydrostatics. The lecturer John Warltire ran courses in metallurgy and mineralogy, as well as providing tuition in the scientific method.[10] The drive to innovate was also reflected in the number of patents acquired by those based in Birmingham, which was ahead of all other towns in Britain except London – until 1819, Birmingham men took out three patents for every one acquired in that other great manufacturing town, Manchester.[11] William Hutton could with some justification write of Birmingham that he 'was surprised at the place, but more so at the people. They were a species I had never seen . . . I had been among dreamers, but now I saw men awake.'[12]

At the forefront of Birmingham's industries stood Matthew Boulton. Born in 1728, he took over and expanded the family business working in the 'toy' trade. Toys were not playthings for children but a wide range of decorative metal products: gold and silver toymakers produced items such as trinkets, tweezer and toothpick cases, smelling bottles and snuff boxes. Steel makers created corkscrews and buckles, sugar nippers, watchchains and snuff boxes. The trade was immensely valuable: John Taylor and Samuel Garbett, two of the other leading toymakers, claimed in 1759 that their output was worth £600,000 every year – about £45 million in today's money – and Edmund Burke christened Birmingham the 'Toyshop of Europe'.

By 1768 Boulton's business was prominent enough for him to be described as the 'most complete manufacturer in England, in metal'.[13] His success was based on the construction of the Soho Manufactory, a little more than a mile northeast of the city centre, which he claimed upon completion as 'the largest Hardware Manufactory in the world', a wonder of the new industrial age employing more than 400 people: 'SOHO! – where Genius and the Arts preside, Europa's wonder and Britannia's pride', as it was described by James Bisset.[14] The output of the Soho workshops was huge. A single pattern book from 1775–90 catalogues over 1,400 different product designs being made.[15] With this manufacturing capability, Boulton realized that the Manufactory itself was a potent marketing tool. He capitalized on visitors drawn to this breathtaking scene, building them a tea house to refresh themselves and a shop in which to make purchases. Even the shop was an experience, like a 'Cabinet of Curiosities, splendid magnificent and gaudy; more like the costly pageantry of some Eastern Court than the Toys of a Birmingham Shop'.[16]

Boulton's success was also based on an astonishing ability to network and exploit the connections of the world of polite commerce.

He showed visitors around Soho himself, and Samuel Johnson recalled 'Tuesday Sept. 20th [1774] . . . went to Boulton's who with great civility, led us through his shops . . . Twelve dozen of buttons for three shillings! Spoons struck at once!'[17] In his diary for another day, Boulton recalled:

> We had Prince Poniatowski, the nephew of the King of Poland, the French, the Danish, the Sardinian, and ye Dutch Ambassadors . . . and only yesterday I had the Viceroy of Ireland. Not a day passes but we have some Nobleman or other.[18]

Boulton's friend William Small jested with him about his networking prowess: 'I hope the King and Royal Family, the nobility and the Ministry and your other friends are well.'[19]

With his manufacturing capabilities, and the networks of contacts at his disposal, Boulton was 'an iron chieftain, and . . . a father to his tribe'.[20] He and Watt first met in September 1768, when Watt was returning from London while securing his patent on the separate condenser. He was enthralled both by Boulton and the Soho Manufactory. Reciprocally, Boulton was drawn to Watt by friendship but also, tellingly, by 'love of a money-getting ingenious project'. Even as he consolidated his reputation, and moved in increasingly exalted circles, Boulton's business finances staggered from one crisis to another. By 1777 the Soho Manufactory was surviving thanks only to a series of bank loans, and it continued to run a huge deficit until at least 1777.[21]

To stabilize his finances, Boulton needed a new, successful business opportunity. Watt's engine offered the best chance he had of obtaining one. However, Watt remained under obligation to John Roebuck in Scotland who, having invested heavily in the engine and desperate for progress, kept Boulton at arm's length. He offered Boulton a licence to make engines for the Midlands, but Boulton turned him down, commenting, 'It would not be worth my while to make for three counties only, but I find it very worth while to make for all the world.' Boulton was content to play a long game and in 1773 made his move: work on the engine had been stalled for three years, and it lay cold and rusting at Kinneil. Roebuck could no longer meet his financial commitments and was heading for bankruptcy. Boulton acquired Roebuck's two-thirds' share of the partnership and, in May 1773, Watt quickly dismantled the engine and shipped it to Birmingham. With four years of Watt's original fourteen-year patent on the separate condenser already passed, Boulton sought an extension to enable him to make a return on his initial investment. Watt was dispatched to London and in May 1775, despite determined opposition, secured an extension of the patent until 1800. The way was clear for Boulton and Watt to press ahead with their partnership building engines.

With his boldness and connections, Boulton was the perfect partner for the more retiring Watt. James Keir reflected that 'his successes and his failures were all on a grand scale', and he certainly strove to ensure the engine was successful, engaging in detail with how it would be made.[22] In an early letter he explained to Watt how, by having an engine manufactory filled with 'excellent work-men', with 'more excellent tools than would be worth any man's while to procure for one single engine', he could build engines 20 per cent cheaper, and with 'as great a difference of accuracy as there is between the blacksmith and the mathematical instrument maker'.[23] This was a direct appeal to Watt's practical abilities and sensibilities about the engine. But in another, later, letter Boulton went further, explaining, 'We are systematising the business of engine making as we have done before in the button manufac-tory.'[24] As Watt had his leap of the imagination in devising the separate condenser, here was Boulton's equivalent: to precisely make engines en masse, just like making buttons. So how actually were buttons made? And how did the firm of Boulton & Watt build engines?

The manufacture of buttons was, like many of Birmingham's other products, driven by the demands of fashion. The design of shoe buckles, for instance, underwent

every figure, size and shape of geometrical invention: it has passed through every form in the whole zodiac of Euclid . . . The ladies also, have adopted the reigning taste: it is difficult to discover their beautiful little feet, covered with an enormous shield of buckle; and we wonder to see the active motion under the massive load.[25]

From reaching the height of their popularity in the 1780s, the vagaries of taste meant that, by 1791, 20,000 people working in the buckle trade were petitioning the Prince of Wales claiming distress.[26] In support of their claims, the *Birmingham Gazette* in May 1790 contrasted the 'Manly buckle' and 'that most ridiculous of all ridiculous fashions, the *effeminate* shoestring'.[27] Buttons matched buckles in fashionable circles; one cartoon of 1777 shows a young gentleman effecting a 'coup de bouton' on a well-dressed young lady who shields her eyes from the dazzling light reflected off his cut-steel buttons.[28] Another has a stylish young man proclaiming 'I am the thing!', with a mass of steel buttons effacing his coat, and one even incongruously taped to the top of his hat.[29]

To satiate the heavy demand for buttons, their manufacture very quickly developed into a carefully organized and efficient process, which became one of the highlights of Soho. Abraham Rees wrote that there was 'no manufacture which includes such an infinite variety of operations as that of the button-maker'; it employed 'a little Army of all ages', and the scene of them hard at work was, for Jabez Maud Fisher, 'too great for Description. Tis wonderful, astonishing, amazing.'[30] In 1770 buttons were being made in a range of materials, from silver and glass to horn, ivory and pearl.[31] But out of these the most popular was steel – so popular, in fact, that often cheaper glass was polished up to imitate it. Boulton ordered steel from Benjamin Huntsman in Sheffield but also carefully recycled 'cuttings and scraps', melting them down into cast steel for new uses. There was also a trade in old sword blades and even horseshoe nails, which would be used for the tiny studs in steel buttons.[32]

Turning this steel into the finished product took a whole range of techniques, which were perfect candidates for the application of simple machine tools like presses, stamps and lathes. An Italian traveller wrote in 1787 how these helped workers in 'binding, twisting, shaping, pointing, cutting, marking, and turning the metals with wonderful quickness'.[33] First, a 'blank' for each button was

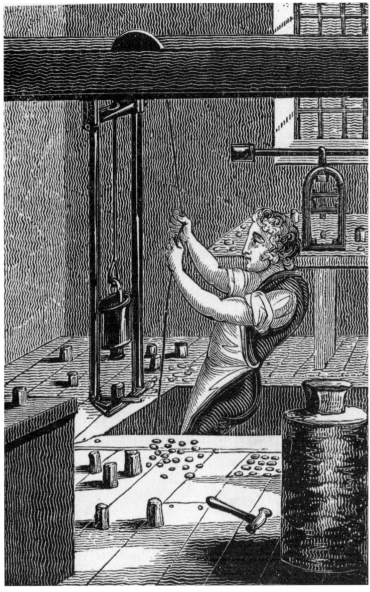

'Button Maker', from *The Book of Trades* (1824). He is working a drop-stamp and is about to raise the upper die ready for striking.

cut out of a sheet of metal using the fly-press. The press was 'composed of a smooth cylindrical punch of steel, which is pressed by the screw into a hole, corresponding in size to the stamp. In this way a small circular disc is pressed out.'[34] Press workers were in almost perpetual motion, swinging the flys (the large, weighted levers that gave the press its working impetus) from 14,000 to 20,000 strokes a day.[35] Usually the blanks were formed as shallow cups, with 'cramps' around the outside which could be turned over with the use of pliers to hold other, decorative material in position. Next, a drop stamp was used to apply decorative shapes or patterns to the button. The stamps had two dies: a lower one, which was concave and engraved with the pattern, and the upper, which was convex and attached to a large iron weight. The upper die was hoisted up by a rope and block between two vertical posts. When it dropped, guided by the posts, it formed the blank into the desired shape. Metals could be inlaid into each other using stamps, which was a particular Soho specialism. Alternatively, tiny individual pieces of polished steel could be set into a blank by hand. This required a steady hand and a good eye, often making it a child's job. Then an edging lathe would smooth the circumference of each button, removing the rough surplus material or 'burr' left around the edge. Sometimes a special engine-turning lathe could be used to produce elaborate geometric patterns on the front of buttons, the lathe mechanism turning in a way reminiscent of a modern child's spirograph.

With the button's shape and decoration finished, it would need mounting on a 'shank', a shallow hook, so it could be fixed to clothing. Even in the 1820s Abraham Rees was describing a shank making machine as 'a very curious engine', suggesting the technical wizardry that went into making even this simple component. But all the equipment of button making was capable of high precision: drop stamps had a catch which secured the upper die after it had fallen, to avoid it bouncing and damaging the button, and the lower die was accurately positioned by four screw adjusters.[36] And engine-turning lathes, already being used by Josiah Wedgwood to create complex designs on ceramics at Etruria, would be refined to produce the un-forgeable geometric patterns on banknotes. Wedgwood employed a mathematical instrument maker to construct and maintain equipment in his Etruria factory, but the job of making the lathes fell to an 'ingenious & indefatigable smith'.[37] That an instrument maker could make an industrial machine, and a blacksmith a high-precision one, is testament to the practical skills held within these respective trades.

Choreographing all these techniques required careful organization, and each worker came to be an expert in a single, tiny part of the overall process. A commentator remarked how, in preparing the button blanks, 'A small boy makes the blanks red-hot in a small furnace. Another boy puts them under the punch, one by one. The third picks them out of the punch and greases the upper mould between each punching with a greased brush.'[38] A visitor to Soho admired how this approach made the faculties of those involved 'more expeditious and more to be depended on than when obliged or suffered to pass from one to another'.[39] The same visitor recorded how each button 'passes through fifty hands, and each hand perhaps passes a thousand in a day; likewise, this work becomes so simple that, five times in six, children of six to eight years old do it as well as men'. Although the division of labour was extreme, there was still some latitude for those involved to exercise

considerable artistic skill, or educated art, as in closing, tool making, burnishing, and in the turning of pearl and other buttons, and where so high a degree of workmanship is not necessary, there is still a certain variety of labour and careful attention to be given to it that involve some exercise of the mind as well as the mere *physique* . . . so that a certain kind of sharpening of the wits goes on, more than exists in many other kinds of labour.[40]

Some button makers estimated that this way of working was twenty times faster than when each individual item was made by a single worker.[41]

The button making workforce consisted of men, women and children. Women tended towards specific parts of the process, particularly polishing the finished steel buttons with 'the combined oxides of a mixture of lead and tin . . . mixed with water or proof spirit' until a fine black shine was produced.[42] Patent agent Thomas Gill went so far as to note that 'no effectual substitute for the soft skin which is only to be found upon the delicate hands of women, has hitherto been met with.'[43] How long their hands remained delicate while being immersed in metal oxides and alcoholic proof spirit is questionable. Children worked largely in the unskilled side of the button trade; they included among their number the 'nut crackers', 'little lads who are engaged in breaking the outer shells off the vegetable ivory nuts [the seeds of palm trees] ready for the workman who saws them up. Every little rascal who is too wild for steady work can be set to do this, their destructive propensities being happily utilised in the manner described.'[44]

Button making contributed, then, to the industrious atmosphere of Soho that so exhilarated visitors. 'The front of this house', wrote Jabez Maud Fisher,

is like a stately palace of some Duke. Within it is divided into hundreds of little apartments, all which like Bee hives are crowded with the Sons of Industry. The whole Scene is a Theatre of Business, all conducted like one piece of Mechanism, Men, Women and Children full of employment according to their Strength and Docility. The very Air buzzes with a Variety of Noises. All seems like one vast Machine.[45]

We can almost hear the heave and thud of the drop stamps, the tinkle of the button blanks falling from the presses, the whirring treadles of lathes and the thunder of feet as children raced boxes of materials from one workshop to the next. This is how Boulton systematized the button manufactory. From 1774 the challenge for Boulton & Watt was applying these concepts to the business of making steam engines.

The basics of engine manufacturing were well established. To build a Newcomen engine, the customer would contract with an engineer to erect the engine, and with different metal foundries and other suppliers to provide the components and materials needed. The cylinder and pumps would usually be delivered ready for use, and some of the smaller iron parts would be ordered from local suppliers for ease of delivery, but everything else had to be manufactured on site, for which purpose the engineer assembled a team of smiths and plumbers, masons and carpenters. This was broadly the path Boulton & Watt followed, albeit with some significant differences. They were careful to specify particular suppliers of each part to ensure their high standards were met. John Wilkinson of Bersham, Shropshire, became their favoured supplier of engine cylinders and pistons, pumps and condensers. Izon's foundry in West Bromwich, Wilkinson's other works at Bradley, near Birmingham, and the city's Eagle Foundry manufactured many of the smaller metal components, and piston rods were made by Jukes Coulson of Rotherhithe, who had a well-established reputation for making ship's anchors.[46] Importantly, then, beyond the very specialized parts like the 'nozzles', which controlled the flow of steam in and out of the cylinder, Boulton & Watt did relatively little of the physical work of engine-building themselves.

This was a canny move: the partners realized that manufacturing Watt's improved engine and exploiting it commercially were not necessarily the same thing. The former, with the possibility of technical difficulties in getting the engine to operate as required, and needing engineering facilities, foundries and workshops, would require huge investment and carry heavy risks. The latter, obtaining revenues from the engine's users, was where the potential profits were. So Boulton & Watt, rather than building engines from scratch themselves, designed them, carried out the necessary calculations, produced working drawings and provided an 'engine erector' from a pool of appropriately skilled men to oversee the day-to-day execution of each engine's construction. But the bulk of the work of physically creating the parts for each engine was given to others.

What, then, of assembling engines like buttons? This was a powerful piece of rhetoric, suggesting Boulton's formidable persuasive abilities and shining a light on the close interconnections between machine making and a wider world of manufacture and consumption. But things would not work out that way in reality; no one had built engines on the scale Boulton & Watt wanted to before, and they needed to establish working practices that minimized the risks involved. As Boulton had bided his time to form his partnership with Watt, now he played a long game to ensure the success of the engine business. 'Making engines like buttons' was a statement of intent, perhaps intended to overawe his competitors. But the process of getting there was complex.

This complexity dogged Boulton & Watt from the start because of the location of most of their likely customers. They were not in the more easily reached new manufacturing towns or on coalfields, because these generally had sufficient supplies of water power, or enough cheap coal to run inefficient but adequate atmospheric engines. A key market for the pumping engine was to be Cornwall, where metal mines extracting valuable tin or copper ores needed more power as they dug deeper underground, but were reliant on coal supplies shipped at considerable expense from South Wales. Both these factors meant the Cornish miners sought the most efficient engine available; they needed to replace 75 atmospheric engines, which were struggling to cope with pumping huge volumes of floodwater just as their owners' finances were stretched by their prodigious coal consumption.[47] Boulton & Watt offered an ideal solution to the difficulties faced.

While we have considered the actions of steam and heat inside the engine, we have not yet explored the engine as a physical artefact that had to safely and efficiently exploit those properties, the construction of which was the major challenge that now confronted Boulton & Watt. The engines they made were big 'house-built' machines, working inside a building that provided support to the major components, and mainly used to pump water for canals, mines and water supply. The heart of the engine was its cylinder, which was mounted vertically on a strong foundation and measured 4 feet or more in diameter. Within was the piston, a large disc which filled as closely as possible the cylinder bore. The piston was attached to a piston rod that passed through the top of the cylinder via a 'stuffing box', which kept the steam inside while allowing the rod to go up and down. Steam was only injected into the cylinder on top of the piston, driving it downwards on its working stroke and making it a 'single-acting' engine. The piston rod was attached to a beam, which usually pivoted on top of one of the engine house walls, and the outer end, protruding outdoors, was connected to the pump rods that might extend hundreds of feet underground to drive pumps that moved water wherever it was needed. Inside the engine house a plug rod hung from the beam: this moved synchronously up and down with the piston, and pegs on it hit levers that opened and shut the engine's 'nozzles'. Engines on this scale, in the form of Newcomen's atmospheric engine, had been built since about 1710. Now Boulton, Watt and their workforce faced the demands of making a similar-sized machine requiring the precision of instrument making.

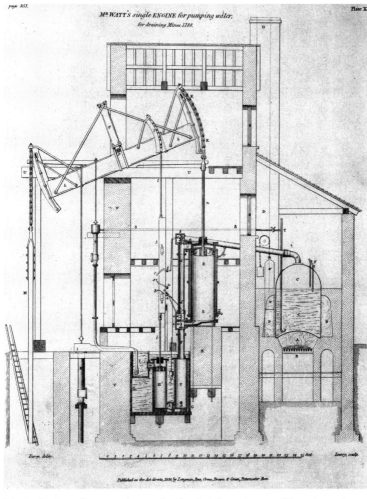

Watt's single-acting pumping engine for draining mines, 1788, as drawn in John Farey's *Treatise on the Steam Engine* (1827).

Much of each engine was made of timber. The engine beams were huge logs of oak or deal, several feet square, more than 15 feet long, and reinforced with braces and iron straps to withstand the strains placed upon them. Inside each engine house the engine's moving parts were supported by a robust wooden frame. Engine builders worried constantly about the supply of large pieces of timber, particularly as the needs of the Royal Navy became increasingly pressing during the wars of the last quarter of the eighteenth century, and its cost rose. And the relative ease of working timber, following long-established techniques, had to be balanced against the difficulties of using it in a machine, like Watt's engine, that required high precision. Daniel Treadwell wrote how 'A machine constituted of wood, subject to constant swelling and shrinking, and warping with every change of the atmosphere, is always liable to derangement. Indeed it can be said to be hardly capable of preserving its identity!'[48]

So, there was some impetus to use different or new materials. Watt's Kinneil engine had a cylinder made of block-tin, solid tin blocks heated to melting point and then poured into a mould to form the correct shape upon cooling. Tin wasn't strong enough to withstand the vacuum within and the cylinder collapsed, to be replaced by one cast in iron.[49] And it was iron that became the engineer's main material. Giant blast furnaces in South Wales or Shropshire produced cast iron 'pigs', rough iron ingots named after the moulds the molten metal was poured into from the furnace, resembling a sow with piglets suckling at her side. The pigs were transported to Soho and other engineering centres and melted again to be turned into finished products. Alongside cast iron came wrought iron, supplied in bars that had been heated in a specially designed 'puddling' furnace to remove the carbon and any impurities, then shaped by massive hammers and squeezed between rotating pairs of rollers until it was very fibrous in composition, which quality helped give it great strength. Iron was durable, strong and capable of being precisely finished. Building steam engines required new parts to be made from iron in two ways: by casting and by forging. And the means of carrying out these processes 'were rude, and the machinery imperfect . . . Nearly all depended on the individual workman's skill.'[50] Those skills were in employing a range of hand techniques.

Take casting iron, for instance. First, a wooden model or 'pattern' of the required component had to be made. The pattern maker's tools were similar to those used in fine joinery or cabinetmaking, and he worked in deal, pine or mahogany, carefully dried so that it would not warp, screwing the pieces of wood together so they could be easily altered if need be and using a plane for fine adjustments.[51] The pattern maker had to understand the entire casting process: he had to avoid sharp internal corners, which could lead to cracks in the cooling metal, and surfaces were always tapered, not quite parallel or square; if they were, there was a worse chance that they would stick in the sand mould, damaging its surfaces. Some allowance also had to be made for the metal contracting as it cooled, and the thickness of the metal was kept as constant as possible, so it cooled evenly.[52]

The patterns would be placed in huge beds of sand, which was packed around them so that, when they were lifted out, a perfect negative copy was left behind for molten metal to be poured into. The tools for this were simple trowels and shovels, and mauls to ram the sand in closely to the pattern. But the composition of the sand was critical, and depended on the moulder's skill: it needed to be damp, or 'green', to form a good impression, but this carried the risk of an explosion if the molten metal contacted too much moisture, or, if gases could not escape, a 'blown' casting with areas of spongy, porous metal that would be much weaker than the surrounding material.[53] And prior to the molten metal being poured, the details of the mould would be carefully prepared with tools: copper spoons for removing sand, trowels to smooth surfaces and round-ended tools to make sharp corners smooth. 'Runners', the channels in the mould to convey the molten metal as quickly as possible to where it was needed before it began to cool and lose its liquidity, were also carefully laid out.[54] Finally, with the metal poured and cooled down over a period of days, the casting would be taken from its mould, cleaned up and prepared for further work.

Alongside casting, forging the iron to shape was an important part of steam engine construction. Wrought or 'malleable' iron was supplied to the Soho Engine Manufactory by Isaac Spooner of Birmingham, and Watt also specified use of 'the best tough scrap

'The Iron Founder', from The Book of Trades (1824). He is pouring molten iron from a ladle into a box mould for making small castings.

iron from Wednesbury' or 'the best gun barrel iron'.[55] Often the fibres of this high-quality metal were treated the same way as the filaments of spun cotton, and twisted as they were worked to avoid the outer surface becoming marred by dirty, longitudinal seams or 'spills', which could spoil inferior ironwork.[56] Forging these bars to the required shapes needed the use of a smith's furnace to raise them to the right temperature, from a black-red just visible in daylight, to a bright red at which most work was performed, and white-hot and burning with vivid sparks for welding pieces of iron together.[57] From the furnace the pieces of iron were hastily transferred to the blacksmith's anvil and there, with tongs, hammer and a range of other tools, they would be worked to the required shape: 'drawing down' reduced the thickness and increased the length of a piece of iron; 'upsetting' it made it thicker and shorter; and 'building up' saw pieces welded together.

These three main processes were central to the manufacture of many parts of the engine, and would have comprised much of the work carried out at Soho. The centrepiece of the Engine Manufactory was a blacksmith's shop with two great hearths for heating the iron, and at least one lathe – probably a great lathe with a hand capstan to drive it, given the size of some of the components that might be turned there: the largest of these might be the piston rod that attached the engine piston to the beam. This was made by taking a bundle of smaller rods, the central one round in section, the outer ones comprising angular 'mitre iron', all heated until they began to emit sparks, and then welding them into a single mass under the blows of a team of men wielding sledgehammers under the guidance of the foreman, indicating where he wanted the hammer strokes to fall with a long wooden wand.[58] At the other end of the scale of forge-work came the making of smaller items like nuts and bolts, demonstrating the versatility of the smith engaged in engine manufacture.

With foundry and forge work highly dependent on the hand skills of the foundryman, pattern maker or smith, the only part of the engine that required a dedicated, highly accurate machine tool was the cylinder. This reflects that much of Watt's frustration with the engine arose from being unable to make a piston and cylinder

'The Blacksmith', from *The Book of Trades* (1824).

A model of John Wilkinson's mill for boring steam engine cylinders, 1775. The cylinder is held down on its side with chains, and sectioned so that the cutter working inside can be seen.

that were a close fit to each other; if there was any gap between the two, steam would leak through and the engine would come to a halt. Finding a suitably elastic but durable 'packing' material to fill the gap between piston and cylinder while still allowing the former to move up and down caused major delays to the engine's development; Watt experimented with cork, pasteboard, leather and linseed oil. Later he even resorted to 'horse-muck' and 'paper pap mixed with flour paste'.[59] Finally, the piston had rope wrapped around its circumference, compressed tight by a 'junk ring', and this worked well.[60] But the best strategy was to make the cylinder as accurately as possible and, for this, Watt depended on the ingenuity of John Wilkinson who, in 1775, made a cylinder-boring machine. A cylinder, cast from iron as a tube open at both ends, was secured on its side upon the machine and a boring bar was placed along its axis, also supported at both ends. The bar supported a cutter that was advanced along the bore by a rack, rotating as it went and cutting the cylinder straight and perfectly true. The degree of accuracy Wilkinson acquired using this machine was unequalled in its time; Watt boasted that 'Mr Wilkinson has bored us several cylinders almost without error, that of 50 in. diameter . . . does not err the thickness of an old shilling at any part.'[61] The cylinders on Watt's experimental engines, at 18 inches' diameter, might vary in diameter by around 1/8 of an inch. With Wilkinson's machine, a cylinder almost three times larger could be machined to a maximum error of around 4 millimetres.[62] Here was precision manufacturing scaled up from scientific instruments to steam engines.

Having made the unfinished components, and the cylinder, it was now time to fit them together. The first step was to gather all the engine parts at the site where they would be assembled. As far as possible, heavy parts like cylinders were moved by water, from Birmingham by canal, from Wilkinson's Bersham works via the River Severn, and then around the coast until as close the final destination as possible. But after that the final leg was completed by road, with huge teams of draught horses, supplemented by teams of men if, as in Cornwall, the mines were perched on cliff-tops or on rugged moorland.

The arrival of all the parts on site marked the first time the complete engine would have been united at a single location. The engine erector and his team had the first chance to inspect everything, and parts would often be missing, or the wrong size. Erecting the engine was not just a matter of final assembly, but of completing a major part of the actual manufacturing process. Assuming the engine house walls were in place, the first step would be to install the engine beam, lifting it about 18 feet to the top of the engine house using pulleys and ropes, first raising one end, then the other, and then placing it approximately in position.[63] The next major step was to fit the cylinder and align it perfectly on its foundations. This needed careful use of a weighted plumb-line to achieve perpendicularity, wedges for adjustment and long bolts to hold the whole securely. With these two main parts positioned, the rest of the engine could be assembled. It might take four or five weeks to complete, and came with attendant risks to the men involved – Boulton wrote home from Cornwall in 1779, 'Tom Bowden has had two of his fingers burnt one quite broke off James Darlestone his hand much hurt, so that out of seven we have but four that can work.'[64]

The opportunities for injury reflected the nature of the engine-erecting process. Fitting the components together would emerge in time as a distinct trade. Much of the fitter's work would be concerned with the accurate cutting and shaping of metal components using a range of basic hand tools: hammers, chisels, files and drills. Hammers and chisels were used to chip away metal. The chisel was up to 8 inches long, with a convex cutting edge. It was used to make a series of cuts across the surface to be removed, about one-thirtieth of an inch deep. The first layer of cast iron chiselled away could be the most difficult, as it would be impregnated with sand from the moulds it was cast in, which destroyed the chisel's cutting edge.[65] If a lot of metal had to be removed, huge 'flogging' chisels, over a foot long, were used, with one man gripping the chisel in both hands and another wielding a sledgehammer.[66] Tallow, rendered from mutton or beef fat, would be used to lubricate the chisel's motion and protect the cutting edge, but the hammer and the end of the chisel were kept scrupulously clean to avoid blows glancing

The View of Botallack Mine by Philip Mitchell, 1840. Botallack was famous for its precarious position, and the workings extended some way under the sea.

off and causing injury.[67] Having chipped off as much as they could, engine erectors then reached for their files to complete the surface to a fine finish. Even in the 1820s, the cost of producing a perfectly flat cast-iron surface was twelve shillings per square foot – one of Boulton & Watt's engine erectors in Cornwall might earn nine shillings per week.[68]

Drilling holes in metal was equally time-consuming and labour-intensive. For the size of work needed on a steam engine, the brace would be the most effective tool, made of metal as opposed to the wooden braces used by carpenters. The brace would turn a flat drill rather than the spiral fluted twist drill used today; the flat drill had a pair of cutting edges meeting in a point, and worked not by cutting the metal but by scraping it. To assist in this onerous task a lever or heavy weight could press down on the top of the brace to apply pressure onto the drill, but often two men would be needed to turn the brace, sometimes spooning linseed oil into the hole formed to cool the drill.[69] A larger hole could be made by drilling through a number of times and rounding out the hole with a file; or, more commonly, it was easier to cast a hole bigger than needed and then use wedges to secure whatever passed through it into position.

Watt would have been acquainted with the techniques of foundry, forge and fitting even before he began his partnership with Boulton. From 1765, as well as making scientific instruments in Glasgow, and his experimental engine at Kinneil, he had built a small number of atmospheric engines for customers in Scotland. And as the engine grew from a benchtop model to an industrial machine, Watt grew as well, noting in 1769, 'I am not the same person I was four years ago when I invented the fire engine . . . the necessary experience in great was wanting; for acquiring it I have met with many disappointments.'[70] By 'in great', Watt meant the ability to build a full-scale machine, and this ability was now to be tested to its fullest extent: between 1776 and 1778 orders for 22 engines came from Cornwall, along with almost the same number again elsewhere across Britain, and the practical burden of constructing them fell on Watt's shoulders. Such were the calls on his time and expertise that he wrote to Boulton in February 1778: 'I fancy I must be cut in pieces and a portion sent to every tribe in Israel.'[71]

The physical and mental exertions of erecting engines placed Watt under enormous pressure; here was a man who had previously admitted he would 'rather face a loaded cannon than settle an account or make a bargain'.[72] But the pressure to design and build machines, struggling against the limitations of tools, materials and workmen, and working under adverse conditions a long way from home, also told in Watt's family life. In July 1776 he married his second wife, Annie McGrigor, daughter of a Glasgow-based bleacher – illustrating Watt's continued associations with the chemical industry. The opportunity was taken to move into a bigger house in Birmingham, and bring from Scotland Watt's children from his first marriage, Margaret and James. Their mother was dead, they had been left with relatives when aged only six and four respectively, and now they faced losing their father again as he drove forward the engine business in Cornwall. Two new children arrived: Gregory in October 1777 and Jessy in May 1779. But with their father often absent from home, and Annie vociferously advancing her own children, Watt's family life thereafter would not be happy. By 1785 Watt's relationship with his elder children had broken down: Margaret married without his consent in 1791 and moved to Scotland, having four children of her own but dying in childbirth in June 1796. She had not heard from her father for two years. James junior remained on difficult terms with his father, finding Matthew Boulton a more supportive figure, culminating in a period of rebellion, the context and consequences of which will be explored later.[73] Any consolation from the presence of younger Gregory and Jessy would be short-lived: Jessy succumbed to tuberculosis in 1794 aged only fifteen, and a decade later that disease also claimed Gregory, a promising and talented young man intended to follow Watt into the engine business. It is likely that Watt could at least have salvaged his relationship with Margaret and James, if only he had been a more permanent presence in their lives; such could be the cost of making machines.

Matthew Boulton was also heavily engaged in Cornwall. He rolled up his sleeves and dived into the fray, writing to Watt that 'of all the toys and trinkets which are manufactured at Soho, none shall take the place of fire engines in respect of my attention'.[74] He could be found greasing the piston on an engine, complaining of a pair of engine erectors being 'drunken, idle, stupid, careless, conceited rascals', even delving into the technical detail of how to build the engines more quickly: 'We are desirous if possible to lessen the expense of fitting up our nozzles, which at present is very considerable . . . we are at present obliged to chip and file a great deal.'[75] Presently Boulton and Watt appointed William Murdoch as their chief representative in Cornwall, his technical skill and ability to take on fractious Cornish miners with his fists if so required – an option hardly open to the reticent Watt – giving him considerable authority, and freeing Boulton and Watt for other activities.[76]

For Watt this meant working at his home in Birmingham with an assistant on calculations, correspondence and drawings, and only occasionally venturing onto the shop floor. This way, he could play to his strengths, leaving the outward-facing part of the business to Boulton, and turning his attention to some of the other innovations that would support the engine making process. The main challenge facing Watt was that, unlike making buttons, building engines remained dependent on a relatively small, multi-skilled group of men. Good mechanics were scarce: Watt told his engineer friend John Smeaton that he wished he could 'find operative engineers who can put engines together according to plan, as clockmakers do clocks – we have yet found exceedingly few of them'.[77] Watt's use of clockmakers as an exemplar is interesting, because in clockmaking one man still made a complete clock from start to finish – unlike buttons, there was little, if any work specialization.[78] So Boulton & Watt's men tended to be jacks of all trades, and they were expected to excel in all of them, producing 'the well-known "Soho workmen", whose services were sought directly or indirectly wherever their fame had spread'.[79] Ensuring that these men could work as effectively as possible required a range of supporting tools and techniques, and this became Watt's preserve.

This comes with a caveat, however. Although Watt has received the credit for many of these improvements, we should not forget that others were the responsibility of his relatively unsung colleagues on the shop floor at Soho and elsewhere. For example, William Murdoch had quickly become Boulton & Watt's leading pattern maker before being sent to Cornwall, and there his abilities led him to make small, largely unauthorized adjustments to the engines as they were built – often to Watt's irritation. Later the success of Boulton & Watt's engine for driving factories as well as pumping water depended on Murdoch, as did much of the machinery required to build engine components at Soho. With men of this calibre engaged by the company (and Watt described Murdoch as 'the most active man and best engine erector I ever saw'[80]), there was a constant flow of changes that did not necessarily begin life in Watt's hands.

First came new paper systems. In 1779, Watt wrote his *Directions for Erecting and Working the Newly-invented Steam Engines*. This was the first book anywhere devoted to the steam engine, and it codified all the practical experience of engine making acquired over the previous three years. It was intended to counter a steady flow of enquiries from engine men working across the country, and came with printed checklists of engine components to use when working on site – Watt later used spare copies to wrap up delicate items in his workshop. Printed forms also detailed which iron founders would supply which components for each engine, with room left for dimensions and other notes and comments.[81]

Of particular importance was Watt's method of letter copying. In order to record the voluminous correspondence that building each engine entailed, everything had to be copied longhand. Now, to save time and effort, Watt developed the first practical office machine, which he patented in 1780, and which Joseph Black praised for its 'neatness and propriety'.[82] Its working premise was simple: a letter was written using ink specially formulated by Watt. Then thin copying paper was laid over the top, and both were squeezed between rollers, after which the duplicate could be read through the back of the thin copy-paper. The ink was formulated to stay wet for around 24 hours so, in theory, several copies could be taken from a single original. In practice this relied on the ink being very carefully prepared, and often the original might be smudged when first copied. The copying press was hugely successful, simplifying the administration of the engine-building business. A copy made by Watt, and preserved in his workshop, records that 'Time, labour & money are saved, dispatch & accuracy are attained, and secrecy is preserved by this newly invented art of copying letters and other writings.'[83]

Roller press for copying letters, by J. Watt & Co., 1818.

Boulton and Watt formed a subsidiary company marketing the press to others; 630 were sold in its first year. Well might Watt claim that 'Every gentleman engineer must now wear a pocket rolling press.'[84]

Paper processes were matched by technical improvements to the engine itself. There was a move towards using standardized parts, which meant quicker initial construction and easier provision of spares in the event of a breakdown. Boulton realized that otherwise, 'if any misfortune should happen' and, for example, the pumping engine for a mine was halted, floodwater might drown the workings, which 'might be ruined before a piston rod could be made'.[85] Even a standard design of engine house was adopted. Quality was ensured by making at Soho all the wooden patterns which might be used for casting iron components, even if the casting itself was carried out elsewhere.[86] And improvements were supported by careful experimentation. For example, there survives from the firm of Boulton & Watt a set of four models of engine beams of different designs, which appear to have been tested to determine which was the strongest. Two have reinforcing wooden 'queen posts' and iron straps, together with over-scale hooks or rings to hang weights on, and the other two are wooden latticeworks, one of which actually broke during the course of experiments.[87]

Finally, making measurements associated with the engine led to the development of new precision instruments. The first of these was the micrometer, reputedly made and used by Watt from *c.* 1776, which used the rotation of a fine screw-thread to measure to within 1/1,900th of an inch.[88] The instrument had originally been developed by William Gascoigne for astronomical use, both measuring the diameters of stars and the angular distances between them. Its adoption in engineering suggests the degree of accuracy to which Boulton & Watt aspired. The second instrument points to the business model they adopted to make and sell the engine: it is a revolution counter. Remember Boulton & Watt's distinction between making the engine and exploiting it. Despite their best efforts they made very little money from the former: just a few late-arriving components, or a faulty casting, could turn a profitable job into a loss-making one. Exploitation was where money could be made: Boulton & Watt's engine was more efficient than the equivalent-sized atmospheric engine, so the partners charged a royalty for its

Watt's engine counter, *c.* 1781. An early batch of the counters was made by John Wyke of Liverpool, who had sold Watt instrument making tools earlier in his career.

use, initially a flat rate based on the saving in coal fuel consumed. However, this caused disputes between Boulton & Watt and their customers, because engine use fluctuated: for instance, a mine pumping engine might stand idle in the summer when groundwater levels fell. Boulton complained: 'It is rather hard to work without profit and then not get paid.'[89] The answer was to record the number of working strokes made by each engine and then send a bill based on that, for which purpose Boulton & Watt had built a number of engine counters. They sat on the engine's beam and, as it rocked up and down, a pendulum inside clicked back and forth, its movements captured by a set of dial wheels. The box was tamper-proof, and only Watt's agents had a key. Here was an early application of power metering, the idea of which remains in use today.

It is tempting to say that Boulton's declaration that he was making engines like buttons was canny marketing. But it was not empty rhetoric: he had to take a bold leap in the engine business for it to succeed because no one had undertaken such an ambitious project before. That leap had to be attended with measures to minimize risk. Returning to that first engine, erected at the Bloomfield Colliery, the newspaper report of it beginning work breathlessly noted, 'All the iron foundry parts were executed by Mr Wilkinson; the condenser with the valves, pistons and all the small work at Soho by Mr Harrison and others, and the whole was erected by Mr Perrins conformable to the plans and under the directions of Mr Watt.'[90] Wilkinson was at Bersham, Harrison at Soho, Perrins at Bloomfield and Watt at his house – separated by miles, but all working on the same project. Boulton created what we will call a 'dispersed factory', and it was what a business analyst today might call 'scaleable': once the basic infrastructure was in place, it could be expanded as circumstances dictated, without a detrimental effect on Boulton & Watt's core interests. This was no mean feat – in fact, it cannily exploited the fact that locally made components were cheaper than those made at Soho and could be shipped out to where they were needed.[91] By 1800 Boulton & Watt had built 440 engines, each of which, with its attendant boilers for raising steam, was the size of a modern detached house. And by going out and hustling for the engine, Boulton freed up Watt to do what he could do best – working on the practical innovations that the business depended upon. We can close this chapter in Watt's career by returning to those practical matters which took up so much of his time, and that of his colleagues.

First, just as Watt was intrigued by heat, and measured it with thermometers, mechanics used heat to work metal, and measured it by the metal's colour. They hardened and tempered their tools to give them a good cutting edge by heating them to a pale straw yellow for lathe tools, or a yellow tinged with purple for chipping chisels and saws.[92] Foundrymen needed the right temperature to pour molten metal – too hot and the mould would be damaged; too cool and the metal would not pour smoothly: they watched for the sparks dancing atop crucibles of molten iron, cooling after pouring into the mould until the surface was effaced with glowing lines, as if 'covered with thousands of wire-worms in great activity'.[93] Even today, the phrase 'to strike while the iron is hot' derives from the smith's ability to gauge the welding heat of iron and effect a weld before the temperature fell. Heat was as much a mechanic's practical tool as a subject of philosophical research.

Further, as measuring heat depended on the visual acuity of the smith, the potter or chemist, and the latter two employed their senses of smell and taste in pursuing experiments with chemical substances, so the sense of touch was essential to accurate metalworking. Many of the tools used by smiths to work metal were manipulated not using long pieces of iron, the better to resist heavy usage, but with rods of hazel wood, carefully softened and bent to the desired shape, because a rigid iron handle would 'jar in the hand' of the blacksmith.[94] The accuracy of a metalworker's output depended on being able to maintain exact angles, and not accidentally rounding off corners. The smith had to be certain of the feel of the work when it was resting completely flat on the anvil, and ensure that the hammer fell perfectly flat when it struck to avoid making an uneven surface. He had to be able to turn the work through exactly 90 degrees, and make sure that the hammer would fall exactly centrally upon it – if a blow landed to one side, it would reduce the parallelism of the finished piece. All this depended upon 'that same degree of feeling, or intuition, which teaches the exact distances required upon the finger-board of a violin; which is defined by habit alone'.[95]

An Iron Foundery, Coalbrook Dale, 1799, print, Ackermann & Company, London. The dramatic scene is lit by the molten iron flowing from the blast furnace into moulds.

Second, making early engines depended on exercising craft skills, which in turn depended on simple hand tools made of steel as the principal available means of shaping metal. The steel tools – files and chisels, for example – may seem mundane, but without them, or with poor-quality steel, metalwork would have been slower, of lower quality and more costly. Britain would not have gained her early supremacy in making machines.[96] The humble file would prove to be mightier than the sword.

Third, just as Watt's work on the engine was driven by his moral dislike of wasting steam, so the engine's design and construction was driven by minimizing the effort used in making its component parts. Metalworking was reduced to a bare minimum: nuts for bolts had only four sides rather than six, unless they were in hard-to-get-at places. Later Watt developed his 'parallel motion' to connect the piston rod to the end of the beam, even though the former went up and down perpendicularly while the latter scribed an arc in the air. The motion was a parallelogram of metal rods, and may have appealed to Watt because it was a clever piece of geometry which he had already used on his perspective drawing machine. But, complex as it was, it required less work than the alternative of supporting the piston-rod with big vertical metal slides, which would have involved a huge amount of costly hand-chipping and filing to make. This solution only became viable in the nineteenth century with the introduction of the mechanical metal-planing machine, which reduced the cost of making a flat metal surface from twelve shillings per square foot to less than one penny.[97] And if metal wasn't essential, wood was substituted instead for lightness and ease of working; most of the engine framing and the great beam were of wood, and the sounds of hammers ringing on anvils, and files cutting away metal, were matched by those of adzes, chisels and saws applied to components made from oak or deal.

Lastly, the presence of so much woodwork is a reminder that, although the engine became the emblematic machine of the new industrial age, it was being built in advance of many of the other industrial machines which would have assisted in its production. This made its construction dependent on craft skills from an earlier age: carpentry, blacksmithing and plumbing. And it also had the effect of making the engine very functional in appearance. There was, initially at least, no decoration or ornamentation; the engine was an expression of engineering in austere terms. In a way that is Watt's character coming across in the technology he helped create.

As for steam, we leave it at an important crossroads: in time engines *would* be made in the same way as buttons, but that was a little way in the future. In the meantime Watt's engine had captured people's imagination. Watt wrote of his first Cornish engine at Wheal Bussy, Chacewater, that 'all the world is Agog to see its performance.'[98] Within six years Boulton & Watt's machine had almost entirely displaced the old atmospheric engine in Cornwall. The resources available to make engines were sparse and the machinery was imperfect compared with later models, but in Cornwall, with its dense network of mines and workings, 52 engines had been built by 1800, along with 30 constructed by other engineers.[99] By the middle of the nineteenth century more than 300 engines were at work. Here were entire landscapes overtaken and transformed by steam power, dotted with engine houses and mine workings, and busy with miners and trains of packhorses carrying the valuable metal ores away to be refined. It was a portent of things to come.

FIVE

Steam Mill Mad? 1781–95

THE CITY OF MANCHESTER divided opinion. Travelling from Stockport into the city in March 1785, a distance of about 7 miles, François de La Rochefoucauld saw 'nothing but houses. It is all one town, one continuous factory.' But he was pleased by what he saw at street level, writing that 'after the capital, Manchester is the handsomest town we've seen in England. It is well laid out; at least most of the streets are straight and the houses admirably built, of brick; the pavements are comfortably broad, the street-lighting good.'[1] Robert Southey took a contrasting view in 1807. 'In size and population' he wrote,

it is the second city of the kingdom . . . imagine this multitude crowded together in narrow streets, the houses all built of brick and blackened with smoke; frequent buildings among them as large as convents, without their antiquity, without their beauty, without their holiness; where you hear from within, as you pass along, the everlasting din of machinery; and where when the bell rings it is to call wretches to their work instead of their prayers . . . Imagine this, and you have the materials for a picture of Manchester.[2]

The differing experiences of these two visitors were occasioned by Manchester's explosive growth. In 1774, 24,386 people lived there; by 1788 the population had risen to 42,821, and then to 70,409 in 1801 – and it would double again by 1831.[3] Under population pressure the local infrastructure buckled and nearly broke. But the town buzzed with life. John Byng complained that 'Every rural sound is sunk in the clamour of cotton works . . . and the simple peasant is changed into the impudent mechanic.'[4] Richard Colt Hoare noted that there was 'less attention, less urbanity of manners; self-interest and business occupy the minds of the inhabitants and prevent that polish which the inhabitants of other towns . . . more frequently have in their manners'.[5] But others admired this; Jabez Maud Fisher was impressed that 'the Value of an enterprizing and Oeconomical Spirit seems to pervade all its inhabitants. The voice of industry is heard on every hand. Idleness is disgraceful, and a Man without Business, or some occupation, Manchester does not own.'[6]

Manchester was the city that set the benchmark for Britain's new industrial towns, and the material that formed its primary product has also become an emblem of Britain's Industrial Revolution: cotton.[7] Here we will place Boulton & Watt's engine within the context of the cotton industry, its places of manufacture and its output. This is a relationship that has long fascinated historians, who have emphasized the role of entrepreneurs and businessmen, the relative costs of steam and water power and the risks of expansion as prime factors in keeping cotton manufacturing on a small scale. As a consequence Boulton & Watt's engine, rather than being the most important power source available, was but one of a number

Peel & Williams Foundry, Manchester, 1814. The foundry yard is full of cast iron engine components, awaiting dispatch to customers.

of possibilities to drive production. Be that as it may, less attention has been paid to the input of the craftsmen commissioned to construct the mills and the machinery systems that production depended on, and which steam might drive. With their backgrounds in constructing water mills and clocks, these craftsmen also played a part in keeping industry small, but perfectly formed.

Manchester was well placed to capitalize on the cotton trade. Situated in a giant natural arena surrounded by hills, the city and its environs had plentiful streams and rivers to drive waterwheels for industry. The town also commanded the trade routes between the Pennines and the sea at Liverpool, and had grown as a market-place where goods produced in the surrounding towns, such as woollens, linens and felts, were traded. Cotton was a new trade which became, 'in the short period of thirty years, one of the most flourishing and important branches of our national industry'.[8] Josiah Tucker wrote in 1782 that 'silks, cottons and linens, combined in a thousand forms, and diversified by names without number, are now almost the universal wear.'[9] During the eighteenth century raw cotton consumption grew from 1,000,000 lb to 56,000,000 lb every year.[10] British production of printed cloth grew from 20,000,000 yards in 1796 to nearly 350,000,000 in 1830 – enough to wrap around the equator seven times.[11] Everyone, it seemed, was in thrall to Manchester's cotton.

Part of cotton's attraction was its versatility. It could be made tough enough for labourers' corduroy trousers and even the belting later used to drive machinery, or fine enough for a ball gown, shirts and desirable clothing.[12] It could be dyed and printed with bright colours and patterns, replacing the sombre 'drabs' and 'sads' of woollen cloth. This versatility made cotton a sought-after, fashion-able material. Fashion had always existed, but what characterized the fashion for cotton was the breadth and depth – one might say the intensity – of the demand for it. People bought cotton clothing, altered it, made their own or purchased it second-hand. They could buy new cotton clothes more frequently because they were cheaper. By 1800 there were fourteen women's magazines disseminating information on the latest fashions, and the demand for cotton goods led one wool merchant to complain that 'ladies think no more of

Margaret Bryan, astronomer and physicist, and her daughters, as portrayed in Bryan's book *A Compendious System of Astronomy* (1797). Fashionable cotton features strongly in their apparel.

woollens . . . than of an old almanack', and another to write that 'cotton, cotton, cotton has become the almost universal material'.[13]

The name indelibly linked with cotton manufacture is that of Richard Arkwright. Described by Thomas Carlyle as a 'plain, almost gross, bag-cheeked, pot-bellied Lancashire man', he was trained as a barber in Preston, Lancashire, and most likely became acquainted with the developing cotton industry as he travelled collecting hair to make wigs.[14] He worked in bursts of obsessive energy in days that sometimes began at 5 a.m. and finished at 9 p.m. Archibald Buchanan, who lived with him for a time, recalled that he was 'so intent on his schemes' that they 'often sat for weeks together, on opposite sides of the fire without exchanging a syllable'.[15]

Arkwright's success was based on a new type of cotton-spinning machine. Spinning relies on two processes that had always been performed by hand, one thread at a time: drafting, to tease all the cotton fibres out parallel, and then twisting, to bind them together. In 1769, the same year that Watt patented his separate condenser, Arkwright patented a machine that mechanized both of these processes: a series of pairs of rollers, each pair rotating slightly faster than the previous,

Richard Arkwright's prototype spinning machine, 1769. The drafting rollers are at the top of the machine, and the flyers at the bottom.

pulled the cotton fibres straight and parallel, before a 'flyer' rotating at high speed twisted them together into a single thread.[16] But just as important as the technical achievement of the machine itself is the way in which Arkwright sought to exploit it. Having built his first mill in at Nottingham, he constructed others in Derbyshire, most notably at Cromford, and at New Lanark near Glasgow. He also licensed other spinners to use the machines as long as they did so in units capable of spinning 1,000 threads simultaneously. This measure was intended to allow Arkwright control over who used the machines, by restricting their use to only the relatively small number of people who could afford to build a mill on such a large scale. However, this had the contrary effect of stimulating piracy of his production methods by rivals, albeit by building mills on the same scale if they were to compete effectively. The cotton industry exploded 'with a vigour and activity which has no parallel'.[17] The number of Arkwright-type mills increased nine-fold to 182 – with around one-third of them in Lancashire – between them capable of spinning 1,900,000 cotton threads simultaneously.[18] Arkwright provided the stimulus for a new factory system.

Arkwright's conceptualization of the factory certainly caught the imaginations of many of his contemporaries. Writing in 1790, John Byng was awestruck by the sight of Arkwright's mills at Cromford, Derbyshire, working 24 hours per day, 'seven stories high, and fill'd with inhabitants, [they] remind me of a first rate man of war; and when they are lighted up, on a dark night, look most luminously beautiful'.[19] Jabez Maud Fisher had earlier written of Cromford that the way 'the [water]wheel sets in motion many thousands of others; and the Sight of all this variety of motion is the most pleasing imaginable', and that it was 'the Greatest Curiosity in the Mechanical Work in Great Britain'.[20] Arkwright's scheme speaks to our traditional view of the Industrial Revolution as characterized by large-scale, powered production in a factory. However, it is telling that the power applied by Arkwright at Cromford came not from steam engines, but from a water wheel – and his cotton spinning machines were widely referred to as 'water frames' because of this. Lancashire became one of the most important markets for Boulton & Watt's steam engine, but the partners did not corner the market in engines, and engines were not necessarily the power source of choice.[21] How Boulton & Watt competed, and against whom, will be considered next.

The early 1780s were busy for Boulton & Watt. They were building steam engines to pump water from mines, and customers in Cornwall demanded their full attention. They had built three engines there by 1778, eight more by 1780, no fewer than nine in a single year in 1782 and fifteen more by 1786.[22] The engine had matured into a proven design and for Watt, the chance to consolidate this success must have been welcome. However, Boulton was already realizing what the engine's potential would be if it could not only drive reciprocating pumps, but produce a turning or 'rotative' motion to power machines in mills and factories as well. He told Watt, 'The people in London, Manchester, & Birmingham are Steam Mill Mad, & therefore let us be wise & take ye advantage.'[23]

Watt's interest in engines that would produce a turning motion – called rotary or rotative engines – was long-standing [illus. 43]. As far back as 1766 he had been working on what he called his 'steam wheel', a complex machine that used mercury as a 'liquid piston' for steam to press against.[24] Watt had great hopes for the wheel, projecting one up to 24 feet in diameter, and Boulton confidently predicted, 'If we had a hundred wheels ready made . . . we could readily dispose of them. Therefore let us make hay while the sun shines.'[25] Boulton's projections outran what was technically possible and ultimately the wheel was not marketed. However, Boulton did not forget the potential market for such a machine. With the demand for mine engines in Cornwall soon to be satisfied, he persuaded Watt that 'there is no other Cornwall to be found': the future lay in some other form of rotative engine.[26]

Watt was initially reluctant. He cautioned that the engines needed by mills and workshops would be smaller and less powerful than those needed by mines, but would be no quicker to design and build. However, the work of competitors in the field provided impetus for revisiting his earlier proposals. In 1779 Matthew Wasborough, a Bristol engineer, patented several ways of connecting an engine to a large flywheel which would produce a rotative motion and ensure the engine would continue to move as the piston changed direction at each end of its working stroke. The possibilities for such an engine

Fragments of Watt's rotary engine, 1782. These were found in a box in Watt's workshop and are the oldest surviving relics of the quest to build an engine using a pure rotary motion.

are reflected by the fact that Wasborough detailed no fewer than 29 different uses for it in his patent.[27] In December 1779 Watt was exploring the use of a crank – already widely used to drive grindstones, potter's wheels and foot lathes. A Soho pattern maker, Dick Cartwright, was asked to build a model, but Cartwright found his tongue loosened by beer in a Soho public house, declared the idea 'one of the best things Mr Watt had ever brought out' and even went so far as to chalk a plan of it on a table.[28] The plan quickly came to the attention of James Pickard, another Birmingham engineer, who patented it before Watt.

Boulton & Watt now found themselves having to find a way round the patents held by Pickard on the crank and Wasborough on the flywheel. They devised five alternative methods of creating a rotative motion. Of these the most successful of all was the brain-child of Watt's assistant William Murdoch, the 'sun and planet' gear. It comprised two gear wheels, the 'planet' gear fixed on the end of a connecting rod suspended from the engine's rocking beam, and the 'sun' gear fixed on the end of the shaft forming the axis of a flywheel. The teeth of both wheels were held together by a link, so that as the engine worked and the beam rocked up and down, the planet gear followed a circular path around the sun gear, making it rotate.

The sun and planet gear offered a credible way for Boulton & Watt to build a rotative beam engine, and they patented it in 1781. But it was just one part of a whole package of improvements to the

Model of sun and planet gear, c. 1781. This model was used by Boulton & Watt to guide the development of the full-size version for the rotative engine.

engine that they developed and attained patent protection for during the 1780s. Chief among them was the 'expansive' use of steam. Rather than steam pushing the engine's piston through its entire stroke, Watt realized that as steam has a natural propensity to expand, it would continue to push the piston even if the supply to the cylinder was shut off early.[29] The engine was also redesigned to make it 'double-acting'; that is, steam not only pushed the piston down, but up as well, combining with the effect of the sun and planet gear to provide the smooth, constant power output essential if the engine was to be used by textile mills. The final major improvement was to find a new way of attaching the piston to the beam. The old atmospheric engines only required strong wrought-iron chains for the piston to pull down upon. But with double action the piston's upward stroke would simply double up the chains. To get around this, Watt developed his 'parallel motion', a parallelogram of metal rods that provided a flexible but resisting connection between the piston rod and beam. Watt was particularly proud of its graceful motion, calling it 'one of the most ingenious, simple pieces of mechanism I have ever contrived'.[30]

The first of Boulton & Watt's rotative engines set running outside Soho was built for John Wilkinson in 1783, and by 1800, they had built 278 as opposed to 171 pumping engines. Boulton & Watt's customer list reflects the rotative engine's utility in a wide range of tasks. Customers included lead works, rope works, malt distilleries, sugar, tobacco and snuff manufactories, druggists, rolling mills, forges and foundries, glazers, bark and cork mills, even a mustard manufacturer.[31] So Boulton & Watt's engine was in considerable demand from customers spread broadly across Britain, and three-quarters of English counties had one at work.[32] There were also large concentrations of engines working in relatively small areas, and one of the greatest of these was in Lancashire, with 44 engines erected by Boulton & Watt for cotton mills, along with eleven more in other industries.

But not all was as the raw numbers suggest. Boulton & Watt's rotative beam engine was a highly effective machine, but there was not necessarily a clear-cut link between steam power and production. Potential customers' power requirements varied considerably.

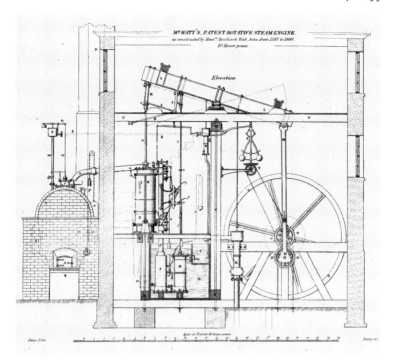

Watt's rotative engine, as built by him from 1787 until 1800; illustration from John Farey's *Treatise on the Steam Engine* (1827).

Overwhelmingly the demand for power – of any type, steam or water – was for small units. For many producers, remaining small offered distinct advantages: less risk of overcapacity in a downturn, the ability to more easily change production to suit markets. Sheer size 'guaranteed neither efficiency in good times nor viability in bad'.[33] Even where a factory was big, it was not necessarily power-hungry: Boulton's Soho Manufactory and Wedgwood's Etruria works used steam for some processes, but many of their workshops demanded no more power than could be provided by a foot treadle or a kickwheel.[34] It was common, where a large mill building was constructed, only to gradually fill it with machinery, or even sublet space to different companies, offering 'room and power' in return for rent.[35] The average Boulton & Watt engine built before 1800 developed only 15 horsepower.[36] So, potential customers for their rotative engine wanted power, if they wanted it at all, on a small scale.

Many prospective customers were also very timid in their approach to power. Although they might have had experience of production driven by waterwheels or even horses, they were less likely than miners or colliery owners to have prior experience with any sort of steam engine, meaning they needed more guidance in commissioning and operating new plant. They could be led astray by engine builders like the two Matthew Boulton described as 'drunken, idle, stupid, careless, conceited rascals [who] say, and their masters seem to believe, that it required the learning and knowledge of a University man to keep an engine in order'.[37] There was less enthusiasm for adopting an efficient but relatively unproven Watt engine if there was any chance of it being less than entirely reliable. Best to rely on a tried and tested alternative.

Often that alternative was a variant of Newcomen's atmospheric engine. This could be connected to a crank and flywheel to make a rotative motion; it might not work very evenly, due to the engine's single-acting cycle, but could sometimes be made more so by using a heavy weight on the flywheel to act as a counter to the engine's powerful downstroke.[38] Or, more simply, an atmospheric engine could be used alongside a waterwheel, recirculating water from below the wheel to a reservoir above it. If the water supply was reliable, the engine might need to be used only in the event of a summer drought. Both these schemes found favour because manufacturers accepted the atmospheric engine's higher fuel consumption as a price worth paying for simple and reliable operation. In advance of developing their sun and planet engine, even Boulton & Watt's 'Old Bess' engine was used at their Soho Manufactory to recirculate water over a wheel, and John Wilkinson had one at his ironworks, 'an engine of great magnitude which brought up the contents of the river as it were at one stroke', that 'shook the buildings and ground for a considerable distance'.[39]

Further, waterwheels remained a serious proposition for many prospective customers. They were by no means a crude alternative to steam power. The same year that Watt patented his separate condenser, 1769, John Smeaton was beginning to apply cast-iron components to a wheel at the Carron Foundry in Scotland, which was 'found to answer much better than wooden ones' and was 'constantly recommended afterwards by Mr Smeaton for other mills which he designed, and by degrees came into very general use'.[40] By substitution of cast iron, careful testing and design, Smeaton doubled the waterwheel's efficiency. And in the first quarter of the nineteenth century, Thomas Hewes did for waterwheels what Watt had done for the steam engine, particularly with the 'suspension' waterwheel, where power was transmitted to machinery not via the central axle, requiring heavy construction, but via a gear meshing with teeth around the circumference of the wheel, which only needed support from the lightest of wrought-iron spokes, like a bicycle wheel.[41] The capabilities of waterwheels are suggested by one that Jabez Fisher saw at Stockport, 40 feet in diameter but so finely poised that it was 'turned by about as much water as could go out of a Pint Mug'.[42] A waterwheel like that installed at Arkwright's Cromford mill might generate 12 horsepower but, by 1800, wheels of 80 horsepower were in use.[43] In the following decades, they reached 100, even 200 horsepower – far more than the steam engines then available.[44] These developments reduced the incentive to adopt steam power.[45]

If they wished to purchase an engine, customers need not turn just to Boulton & Watt: there were many other competing firms. Some, like Matthew Murray in Leeds, presented a major challenge, being 'the first to set an example to Boulton and Watt themselves in that superior finish to the steam-engine which has now become general'.[46] In Manchester the company of Bateman & Sherratt was acknowledged as having 'very ingenious and able' engineers who built engines that were 'of a small size, very compact, stand in a small space, work smooth and easy, and are scarcely heard in the building where erected'.[47] Others were less of a threat: an engine built by Ebenezer Smith and Co. was described by James Lawson, an engine erector for Boulton & Watt, as 'one of the worse made I ever saw'.[48] As in scientific instrument making, there was room alongside the very best for those building machines that were just sufficient for the job in hand. John Farey recorded that in the early 1790s 'great numbers' of old atmospheric engines were being constructed to drive mills on account of the cheap coal available locally: 'These engines answered the purposes for which they were applied, and were used for many years.'[49] It is telling, then, that Manchester writer John Aikin recorded that only 'some few [engines] are also erected in this neighbourhood by Messrs Bolton and Watts' [sic].[50]

So, although Matthew Boulton predicted that rotative engines presented 'a field that is boundless', this declaration did not necessarily transpose into orders for engines.[51] Boulton & Watt's engine, for all its technical prowess, was one of a number of potential options which could be provided by a range of different suppliers. Out of more than 2,000 engines built in Britain by 1800, two-thirds were of the older atmospheric type, and Boulton & Watt built only one-quarter.[52] What mattered more to their customers than the sheer scale and the type of power source used was the modernity and ingenuity of the machinery that it *drove*. This was reflected in the contrast, noted by visitors to Manchester, between the smoke and confusion outside the mills, which was in large part produced by steam engines, and the precision mechanical movements of the production machinery within.

One of visitors' abiding memories of Manchester was its 'dark black smoky atmosphere', the product of a growing number of chimneys, each connected to a boiler for raising steam.[53] In 1786 there was only a single chimney in the town but by 1801 there were more than 50 and, visiting the town in 1802, Eric Svedenstierna was moved to write how 'in order to carry away the coal-smoke, the chimneys at most of the mills are taken up high above the roofs.'[54] Together they supplied the town with a constant fug of smoke, 'an inky canopy which seemed to embrace and involve the entire place'.[55] Alongside the polluted atmosphere, Manchester at street level must have been an assault on visitors' senses; in 1835 Alexis de Tocqueville described 'the crunching wheels of machinery, the shriek of steam from boilers, the regular beat of the looms, the heavy rumble of carts' as 'the noises from which you can never escape in the sombre half-light of these streets'.[56]

If the external effects of engines were the subject of negative comment, the machinery inside, by comparison, left a very favourable impression on those who saw it. In 1782 an anonymous author wrote that 'those who are lovers of invention, and fond of mechanical improvements, must admire the ingenuity of the cotton mills and the engines lately erected in the neighbourhood of Manchester'.[57]

In 1786 Joseph Smith & Robert Peel of Manchester summed up the main advantage of the English cotton trade as arising 'from our machines both for spinning and printing; by means of these we can spin both cheaper and better, and we can print . . . cheaper and better'.[58] And from a slightly later vantage point Edward Baines attributed to cotton machines 'as great a revolution in manufactures as the art of printing effected in literature'.[59] Britain became the world's principal textile manufacturer by solving the mechanical problems of production – and that was most evident among the whirring shafts and spinning flyers inside the mills.

A question arises, then, over who the people were to best deliver this modern, mechanical world. Earlier chapters have explored the links between blacksmithing, instrument making and early machine making. Another major source of engineering skill was among millwrights. This class of men emerged to design and construct windmills and watermills, pumping machines and 'all the various kinds of rough machinery in use' into the nineteenth century.[60] A vivid description of the millwright has been provided by William Fairbairn. He characterized the millwright as a 'jack-of-all-trades, who could with equal facility work at the lathe, the anvil, or the carpenter's bench . . . he thus gained the character of an ingenious, roving, rollicking blade, able to turn his hand to anything'.

Millwrighting was originally a peripatetic job, and millwrights, 'like other wandering tribes . . . went about the country from mill to mill, with the old song of "kettles to mend" reapplied to the more important fractures of machinery'.[61] However, as the eighteenth century progressed, more millwrights were employed at a single site. Fairbairn was apprenticed to the Northumberland millwright John Robinson, who maintained all the machines working at a colliery and who, perhaps because of his wide responsibilities, had a 'rough, passionate temper' and 'indulged in . . . profane swearing, carried to such an excess that an order was scarcely once given unless accompanied by an oath'.[62] Elsewhere Fairbairn notes the existence of Millwrights' Institutes in public houses, where drink and disagreement over points of practical science led to members imparting knowledge with a fist aimed at 'the sensitive parts of the body, instead of appealing to the higher organs of intellect'.[63]

Such men, at once foul-mouthed, belligerent and highly skilled, found themselves drawn in two directions. Engines like Watt's, which required precision manufacture, needed the facilities of a dedicated works, making use of specialized equipment like cylinder-boring machines and lathes. In these places the millwright became subsumed into the machine making profession alongside engineers, turners and fitters, working alongside carpenters, wheelwrights, cabinetmakers, joiners, smiths, clockmakers and others attracted from their original trades by better wages.[64] However, a second path allowed millwrights to retain a distinct identity: the engine (or other power source) still had to be assembled on site, and its power transmitted to the production machinery that it drove. This remained the millwright's specialized domain.[65] In fact those writing in the early nineteenth century pointed to Watt's engine and Arkwright's cotton-spinning machines as leading to the advance in millwork, making the expert millwright more indispensable than ever.[66]

The millwright's particular job was to construct the shafts and wheels known as 'mill-work', needed to couple a power source to the production machinery. This entailed planning out the entire scheme, calculating the proportions and strength of the individual parts and determining the arrangement of the machinery. The mill-work was required to be strong, stiff and 'easy of repair'.[67] Fairbairn recalls rising

> with the sun in summer, and some hours before it in the winter . . . For the remainder of the day I had either to draw out the work, or to ride fifteen or sixteen miles on a hired hack to consult with proprietors, take dimensions, and arrange the principle and plan on which the work was to be constructed.[68]

Practical work was matched by skill at negotiation and draughtsmanship as well.

All was underpinned by the millwright's ability to manipulate materials. At first, they worked mainly with timber, forming 'large square shafts and wooden drums, some of them 4 feet in diameter' but this, with other associated pieces of mechanism, 'not only crowded the rooms, but seriously obstructed the light where most required, in the more delicate and refined operations of the different machines'.[69] Wood began to be replaced with metal to better withstand the higher speeds at which the machinery was required to operate; bulky millwork was shrunk, the 'ponderous masses of wood, cast iron, and their enormous bearings and couplings' giving way to 'slender rods of wrought iron and light frames or hooks for suspending them, [and] pulleys and straps of moderate diameters and dimensions'.[70]

So, the means of building the internal systems of a mill were provided by the millwright, using many of the techniques used to construct engines that we have earlier discussed. But alongside them worked a second distinct group of workmen, from the world of clockmaking.

As the eighteenth century progressed, and possession of a time-keeper became as much a mark of social standing as it was a record of timekeeping per se, horology was a growing trade.[71] It was also highly skilled, requiring 'no great strength' but 'a mechanic head, a light nice hand; and a strong sight, there being scarce any trade which requires a quicker eye or steadier hand'.[72] These factors attracted James Watt, who took an interest in clockmaking alongside his other

Thomas Allom, Swainson Birley cotton mill near Preston, Lancashire, 1834. The machinery seen in this view, used to prepare the cotton for spinning, is driven by the belts and shafts suspended from the ceiling above.

'The Watch Maker', from *The Book of Trades* (1824). Here he is using
a small watchmaker's turns, a small lathe, surrounded by a range
of clocks and watches.

projects. He and his friend William Small were exchanging notes on a new design of clock in 1771, with Small telling Watt how 'I have perfected my clock with one wheel of nine inch diameter, which is to tell hours, minutes, and seconds, and strike, and repeat, and be made for thirty shillings.'[73] And even before that, in 1758, Watt was in partnership with Joseph Black and Alexander Wilson to make clocks – his workshop contains an incomplete timepiece movement and a number of unfinished clockwheels that may date from this period.[74]

How clockmaking was organized varied across Britain. At one end of the scale were the makers based in London. The metropolis was home to a complex trade exporting finished clocks all over the world, comprising large numbers of specialized workers – Abraham Rees counted up to eighteen different trades – movement makers, spring makers, enamellers, brass founders and more.[75] The movements, springs, chains and cases were all manufactured by different tradesmen, though it was the watchmaker who 'puts his name upon the plate, and is esteemed the maker, though he ha[d] not made in his shop the smallest wheel belonging to it'.[76]

In contrast to the London trade stood those making clocks who might have been trained as blacksmiths and in associated trades, building locks or even firearms. Their biggest products would have been large 'turret' clocks intended for churches and other places from where the time was told by the wider public.[77] These clocks were accurate timepieces but, owing to their physical size, their construction owed as much to the blacksmith as to the bench-based clockmaker. For this reason, these self-contained and multi-skilled tradesmen have sometimes been called 'clocksmiths'.[78]

The nature of the clocksmith's workshop reflected their combination of skills. It would ideally admit as much natural light as possible, to illuminate intricate work such as polishing, engraving and marking out clock dials.[79] The bench would be positioned close to the window and, if very small work was carried out there regularly, might have a groove along its front and 'wings' around the sides to catch components rolling off. For very small work, wineglasses broken off at the stem were traditionally used, turned upside down, to protect delicate components placed beneath them while a mechanism was dismantled. But alongside the bench for small work, the workshop would also contain much shared with the blacksmith: 'forge, bellows, anvil, tongs, hammers, screwplate and taps, bench and hand vices, drills, and pliers'.[80] The forge might be placed in a separate, darker room, or as far away from the window as possible, the better to accurately gauge the colour and working temperature of the metalwork being heated upon it.

The presence of the forge is a reminder of the need to heat materials so that they could be shaped. Much clocksmith's work was carried out in brass, rolled into sheets or cast into columns, gear-wheels or plates. The plates would then be hammered flat using a round-faced planishing hammer to avoid leaving sharp indentations before hand-filing to a smooth finish: brass can be 'work-hardened' – that is, the more it is worked, with a hammer, file or in the lathe, the tougher it becomes. Wrought iron would be used to fabricate larger clock frames and movements, the pieces being heated and shaped using hammers and an anvil, and held together by nuts and bolts or wedges driven through holes.

The clocksmith had to carefully consider the relationship between these different materials. Components bearing onto each other, like clock-wheels and the smaller pinion wheels which connected them, were usually of different materials, brass for the former and steel for the latter. This reduced the amount of friction generated and used the stronger material where the strains imposed by the clock mechanism were largest. Although it was less easily shaped than brass, steel was cheaper: in the early eighteenth century it might cost one penny per pound compared to ten pence for brass. So clocksmiths were prepared to use steel to save money on materials, even if it took longer to work, and it was sometimes employed for parts that were hidden away inside the mechanism, unseen.[81]

Alongside tools like hammers and files, which might be found across a variety of trades, clocksmiths were early in adopting special-purpose tools. The latter were particularly useful in making the gear wheels, often referred to as 'wheel-work', that much of a clock movement consisted of. In a relatively small movement, these wheels were often stamped out of brass: material was removed to save weight, leaving spokes behind. Then teeth were cut into the circumference in two stages: a wheel-cutting engine would first produce an approximate form of the teeth, with a parallel-sided cut. Then the teeth were 'rounded up', the corners removed and a smoother profile made, using a shaped cutter, which laborious task would previously have been carried out by hand-filing. How the wheels meshed together would be carefully checked with the specialized clocksmith's depthing tool to ensure that they engaged cleanly, and then they were held in place in the clock movement, most often between two vertical plates separated the required distance apart by brass pillars, with the wheelwork positioned between them.

The complex processes of clockmaking produced, and attracted, self-sufficient and innovative craftsmen. James Watt was joined by Benjamin Huntsman, who pioneered the process of making high-quality 'crucible' steel in Sheffield in 1740 having started out as a clockmaker, his interest in steel emerging from the quest for a better material to make springs.[82] In 1741 the clockmaker Henry Hindley of York showed the engineer John Smeaton a screw-cutting lathe and a wheel-cutting machine he had constructed – both of which were later to be widely adopted in industry.[83] Later the advertisement placed in the *Manchester Guardian* newspaper by young engineer Richard Roberts in 1821, whose 'self-acting' spinning machine transformed Manchester's cotton industry, was decorated with images of what look like clock and pinion wheels.[84]

These examples show that there were extensive connections between clockmaking and larger-scale engineering, and this was widely commented upon by contemporaries. Thomas High's cotton-spinning machine of 1738 was moved 'by an aggregate of clock-maker's work and machinery most wonderful to behold'.[85] The *Manchester Mercury* newspaper in the 1780s and '90s contains a series of advertisements for clockmakers to work in cotton mills and with machine makers to 'fitt up the clock work for mules and water machines'.[86] It is surely no coincidence that Abraham Rees found himself noting that 'there are such immense numbers of each part of every machine to be made, it becomes, in the same manner as with the clock-maker, worth the machine-maker's trouble to construct complicated tools and engines to expedite the manufacture of the parts.' And in Sheffield George Gilpin was inventing a method of cutting wheels from solid cast iron 'with as much accuracy and as good a finish as brass wheels have hitherto been cut, making a very great saving in the expence of brass for a large mill, and much more durable when done'.[87] In fact, looking at machines like Arkwright's prototype, the gears driving the drafting rollers are brass clockwork scaled up for industry; John Kay, who built the machine for Arkwright, was a clockmaker by training, and the cover story for that top-secret project was that he was building a navigation device to establish longitude.[88]

So, between them, clocksmiths and millwrights were capable of building complete production systems, integrating power sources, transmission systems and production machinery. One innovation particularly encapsulates the precision that was now possible: many mills mounted a pair of clocks side by side, one turned by the mill gearing driving the machinery, the other independently regulated by a pendulum in the usual manner. Both were made with dials and hands exactly alike, but with the former having 'a title on the dial, *mill* time, and the other, *clock* time'. The motion of the mill was so regular 'that these two clocks will never vary more than two or three minutes'.[89] Rather than just the power source or steam engine, contemporaries were amazed at the possibility of constructing entire factories – modern, often small, but perfectly formed – that could operate with the precision of a timepiece.

This was achieved in large part using long-established materials. The adoption of iron was spreading but it by no means replaced wood entirely; the great working beams of Boulton & Watt's engines only began to be made from cast iron in 1800, for example.[90] Clocks might have been framed in metal, but scaling this up into production machinery able to withstand greater stresses and strains required better understanding of how to proportion iron parts to balance both lightness and strength. So the water frames at Arkwright's Cromford mill, each capable of spinning 48 threads at once, were principally built from wood, as was Samuel Crompton's 'mule', the waterframe's successor. For this reason we might describe the early industrial machines as examples of 'conservative modernity', state-of-the-art new production machines, built using old-established materials and techniques by millwrights and clocksmiths.

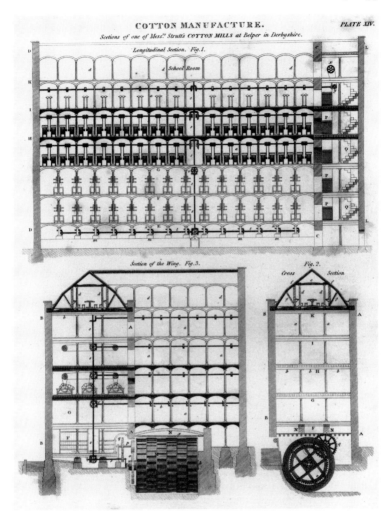

COTTON MANUFACTURE.   PLATE XIV.
Sections of one of Mess.rs Strutt's COTTON MILLS at Belper in Derbyshire.

Jedediah Strutt's 'North Mill at Belper, Derbyshire', from Abraham Rees, *Cyclopedia* (1819). The mill's internal mechanisms suggest the scale and complexity of some cotton manufacturing enterprises.

The traditional nature of the craft skills employed in devising new production machines did not reduce their imaginative influence over those who saw them. Quite the opposite: Louis Simond visited Barclay's Brewery in London, writing how the engine working there stirred 'to the very bottom the immense mass of malt in boilers 12 feet deep' and drove 'elevators which nobody touches, carry[ing] up

Improved spinning machine by Sir Richard Arkwright, 1775. Capable of spinning 8 threads at once, its timber construction was scaled up into much larger machines.

to the summit of the building 2,500 bushels of malt [about 38 tonnes] a day' – and all this while not making 'the least noise – not more than a clock; you might have heard a pin drop all over the building.'[91] And in Birmingham he saw 'enormous hammers, wielded by a steam engine . . . crushing in an instant red hot iron bars, converted into thin ribbons. Bars of iron for different purposes, several inches in thickness, presented to the sharp jaws of gigantic scissars, moved also by the steam-engine . . . clipped like paper.' Elsewhere, engines turned millstones for polishing metal 'with so great a velocity as to come to pieces by the mere centrifugal force', and copper 'spread into sheets for sheathing vessels under rollers . . . like paste under the stick of the pastry-cook'.[92]

Boulton & Watt capitalized on the imaginative attraction of machines by establishing a series of showcase engine installations. The mine pumping engine at Ting Tang in Cornwall was joined by rotative engines at the Whitbread Brewery and Albion Mill in London, showing what was possible in brewing and corn milling respectively. A renowned visitor to the Whitbread engine, in May 1787, was George III. Watt met him, noting how he was 'most graciously received by the King, who expressed himself most highly pleased with everything he has seen'.[93] The royal visitor would have been equally impressed by the Albion Mill, with a pair of sun and planet engines driving up to ten sets of millstones each. It was the largest corn mill built up to that time and the first establishment to use cast iron for all its machinery.[94] Showcases like this helped consolidate the company's reputation for the future.

To fully secure the company's future prosperity, one last, major matter remained to be resolved. In Cornwall mine owners depended on Boulton & Watt's engine to keep their mines free of floodwater economically, but bitterly resented paying a royalty for the privilege. Watt wrote of their complaints, 'They say it is inconvenient for the mining interest to be burdened with the payment of engine dues, just as it is inconvenient for the person who wishes to get at my purse that I should keep my breeches-pocket buttoned.'[95] In the late 1780s, as Boulton and Watt turned their attention to the rotative engine, two competitors, Jonathan Hornblower and Edward Bull, designed and constructed pumping engines that could compete with theirs on an equal footing – and they had a ready market among the recalcitrant Cornish miners. Watt contended that both Bull and Hornblower infringed his patent on the separate condenser and in 1792 began a legal battle against them that took seven years to resolve.[96] The initial proceedings were indecisive, raising hopes among Watt's competitors – and, indeed, the many other pirates of his engine design who stood behind Bull and Hornblower – that his patent might be declared void. Pirates were at work closer to home than Boulton & Watt realized: without their permission, John Wilkinson, upon whom they depended for engine cylinders, built and sold no fewer than 34 engines based on their designs, and this indicates the high financial stakes for all concerned in the form of unpaid engine royalties.[97]

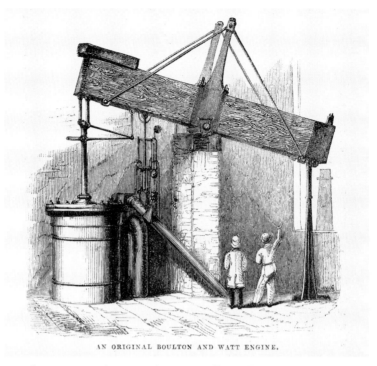

AN ORIGINAL BOULTON AND WATT ENGINE.

A Boulton & Watt engine at Fazeley Street Rolling Mills, Birmingham, 1790–1800, as illustrated in Tomlinson's *The Useful Arts and Manufactures of Great Britain* (1861).

Hornblower held out to the very end: the validity of Watt's patent was only finally upheld in 1799, upon which he and Boulton immediately sued for payment from all the engineers copying their separate condenser, and Cornish miners who had withheld payment for using the engine pending a legal decision. In total they stood to gain £162,000 (more than £10 million at today's prices) – the amount they actually received was less, but still enough for Watt to retire from the business on a comfortable income.[98] Thus was passed a major milestone in handing over to the company to Boulton & Watt's successors – their sons.

The legacy of Boulton & Watt as their partnership ended in 1800 has proved controversial. They had established an 'industry standard' for the steam engine – a basic pattern of a useful, efficient, and reliable machine – and produced ten times more engines than their next biggest competitor.[99] Even top-quality competitors like Matthew Murray in Leeds 'attempted to improve the construction of Mr Watt's engines', but after some years were 'obliged to follow the models of the engines made at Soho'.[100] Some historians have argued that the authority Boulton & Watt wielded was 'sufficient to clog engineering enterprise for a generation'.[101] There is a broad consensus that the extension of Watt's patent right up to 1800, matching the length of his intended partnership with Boulton, did act as a brake on the wider development of the engine. However, up to 1800 and even beyond, the small scale of industrial enterprise, even in textiles, where powered machines 'achieved their most famous triumphs', limited the demand for radical transformation in engineering technique.[102] What was needed, as this chapter has explored, could be met by adapting and scaling up existing, long-established craft skills. Despite the patents on their engine, Boulton and Watt by no means monopolized those skills. And after 1800 the construction of machines *by* machines would remain exceptional for several decades. William Fairbairn wrote that, as late as 1817, 'even Manchester did not boast of many lathes or tools, except small ones in the machine shops', and that even when assembling complete cotton mills, 'Our means were but small; we were without a steam-engine, or any other power, except Murphy [an Irish labourer] and three more assistants who turned the lathes.'[103] The time when Sir George Head would see 'the beam of an engine, weighing three tons' being worked on in a lathe and 'not withstanding its vast weight, revolving on a point which entered only three quarters of an inch, with as much ease as if it had been a peg top' was some time in the future.[104] So a range of new opportunities, including innovation in machine tools, remained open for machine making men to explore in the nineteenth century. Boulton & Watt's engineering achievements were not the *ne plus ultra* of engineering but a symbol of what *could* be done. Next we will explore how the imaginative possibilities of the engine covered here were exploited by the new generation of engineers and expressed in the products that they built.

SIX

Inventive, Creative Genius,
1795–1819

The road from the centre of Birmingham to Handsworth, on the city's outskirts, was pleasant and much frequented by James Watt, his family and their visitors. The locality was becoming increasingly populous, and the 'many respectable residences' were commented on by local historian George Yates, who described 'a barren heath . . . [now] covered with plenty and population'.[1] And as travellers approached Boulton and Watt's Soho Manufactory, Yates also noted how they passed 'gardens, groves, and pleasure grounds' that rendered Soho 'a much-admired scene of picturesque beauty, where the sweets of solitude and retirement are to be enjoyed, as if far distant from the busy hum of men'.[2] It was to this place that the Swiss steel-maker Johann Conrad Fischer came in August 1814 to explore, concealed amid the trees and gardens, an amazing new engine works.

Fischer's first port of call was the engine yard at the Soho Manufactory, and he was 'dumbfounded' at what he saw: 'No description could do justice to the building in which these works are housed. I was amazed at both the great masses of iron and at the skill which the workmen had devoted to the construction of the building.'[3] He then visited the turners' and smiths' workshops, where he 'admired the wonderful craftsmanship of the smiths' and a workshop containing 'a large number of copying machines and here again I could not help admiring the characteristically high standard of craftsmanship of the workers'.[4] The following day Fischer was admitted to the latest buildings where engines were constructed – a highly unusual event, since what happened within was usually kept carefully hidden from the outside world. He wrote that

The works are completely enclosed by a high wall and consist of several separate buildings, each of which is many hundreds of feet in length. The most important are the foundry, the pattern shop, and the new workshop. Four furnaces produce enough molten iron to enable castings to be made up to a weight of 200 hundredweight.

In all these buildings steam engines were at work, performing their tasks 'quietly, regularly and efficiently – a tribute to all that human ingenuity has contributed to their construction'.[5]

What is most notable about Fischer's account is who was responsible for what he saw in the works. From the workshop making copying presses, to the design of the foundry, was not the work of James Watt and Matthew Boulton but of their sons, James Watt Junior and Matthew Robinson Boulton. We have seen how their fathers developed steam engines, first for pumping water and then, from the 1780s, for producing a rotative motion. We have also recounted briefly the legal measures taken to secure Watt's patent of 1769 and underpin the prosperity of the company before 1800. This chapter will explore the means by which the business was continued in the hands of the next generation after 1800: how the men who drove the business forward were trained, the nature of the challenges that they faced and how they responded to them. There took place what we will call an 'affective revolution' in engineering, which turned the engine from just a machine into a product of which its creators' antique forebears might have been proud.

Two major technical issues affected the firm in the late 1790s. First, and most importantly, established suppliers could no longer be relied upon. The ironmaster John Wilkinson had made the majority of Boulton & Watt's engine cylinders, but a bitter feud with his brother, and the revelation of his piracy of Boulton & Watt's engine designs, brought the association to a close. The capacity for Boulton & Watt to accurately make cylinders – the heart of each engine – had to be acquired as a matter of some urgency. Second, work was being put in hand to standardize the design and manufacture of engines at Soho. Matthew Boulton had suggested a 'pattern card' of engines in standard sizes in 1782, and four years later, Watt proposed to 'methodize the rotative engines so as to get on with them at a great pace'.[6] Some aspects of the move towards standardization are still with us today: for example, Watt defined 'horsepower' as a unit of measurement for the first time, as a way to compare the power output of different engines, and to help establish how much machinery engines with different power outputs could drive. This new and enduring definition represents a major rethink of how the company worked. Whereas production had previously evolved in an organic way, a new scheme was now in prospect: the Soho Foundry, the secretive works visited by Fischer in 1814.

The Soho Foundry was designed from the start along rational, pre-planned lines. Entirely separate from the old Soho Manufactory, the Foundry began work in the spring of 1796, and was intended to construct a standardized range of engines, from an 8-horsepower engine costing £525 (or about £20,000 at today's prices), progressing in increments up to a 50 horsepower engine costing £2,109. To construct this range, particular care was taken in arranging how the Foundry operated. As one account has styled them, the senior Boulton and Watt were builders, but their sons were organizers.[7] This new project brought the organizational talents of the junior Boulton and Watt to the fore. Of the two, James Junior was the foremost, with the younger Boulton concentrating more on the other output of the Soho Manufactory and new ventures in minting coinage.

The Foundry was built around nine workshops, each dedicated to a particular process: for example, cylinder boring, turning, fitting, smithing and pattern making. The shops were positioned so that the movement of heavy iron components was minimized, or made as easy as possible, and men were appointed to particular work specialisms. For example, 'Wells and two assistant men, one lad' were 'employed constantly' in fitting engine nozzles, controlling the flow of steam in and out of each engine's cylinder. William Buxton and John Mincham were dedicated to 'turning, draw filing and finishing piston and air pump rods'. 'Foreman and three assistants, with lad to grind chisels' were assigned to 'sundry chipping' of iron surfaces. And increasing use was being made, not just of hand skills, but of purpose-made machine tools: special lathes for pistons and shafts, vertical drills in the fitting shop and other lathes devoted to woodturning and making engines' parallel motion, all with 'connecting machinery', the shafts and gears allowing them to be driven by steam. But what really stands out is how all these elements – workplace, workman, process, and tools – were carefully specified, one might even say choreographed, in sequence for each engine, from the first step of making the cylinder lid, to the final one of packing everything up ready for dispatch to the customer. Even the speed of the individual machine tools was defined. Not for nothing did Eric Roll, whose researches unearthed the details of production at Soho outlined here, claim that 'neither [Frederick] Taylor, [Henry] Ford, nor other experts devise anything . . . that cannot be discovered at Soho before 1805.'[8]

The Soho Foundry was vital to the continued success of Boulton & Watt, and it came alongside a business strategy that was markedly different from that previously adopted, and which contributed to the company's success into the nineteenth century. This strategy was based on innovation both in products and in the markets where they were sold.

As well as building beam engines, the company recognized the increasing demand for smaller, more compact and self-contained engine designs. One of the most prominent of these products was the 'bellcrank' engine, which replaced the rocking beam with a pair of triangular levers, or bellcranks, pivoting on the engine's sides. The large, cast-iron bellcranks were liable to break after a time, but the design remained in production until 1814, when self-contained beam engines were introduced as an alternative.[9] Equally important were marine engines to power ships at sea, and in this respect Boulton, Watt & Co. worked on a number of landmark projects: the engine used by the American engineer Robert Fulton in his ship the *Clermont*, which heralded the opening up of North America's great rivers by steam; the first steamship used by the Royal Navy, HMS *Comet*; and finally the screw propeller engines for Isambard Kingdom Brunel's mighty *Great Eastern* in 1854.[10] Over the period from 1804 to 1847 the firm built 286 marine engines – as a rough guide, about one every two months.[11]

As well as new products the company also more actively sought new markets. An office was opened in London, primarily to obtain orders for marine engines from prestigious customers like the Royal Navy and, later, the Post Office, which was developing a fleet of steam-powered mail ships. Caribbean sugar plantations demanded engines to drive cane-crushing mills, and the company found itself working in Demerara, Trinidad and the West Indies as well as Manchester or Oldham. A steady overseas engine trade was developed: Boulton & Watt built just twelve engines for foreign customers between 1786 and 1795. However, between 1795 and 1825, they built 102 – the majority after the end of the Napoleonic Wars in 1815 – and they proved to be highly profitable.[12]

The Soho Foundry was a major landmark in the history of machine making: it was the first purpose-built factory dedicated to constructing machines. Such was the demand for its output that, even supplemented by the older engine workshops at the Soho Manufactory, there was still a waiting time of from eight to ten months between ordering an engine and taking delivery of it.[13] Consequently, the Foundry received a series of extensions to provide additional workshop space in the first eight years of its existence.[14] By 1804 the total construction cost amounted to more than £27,000, over £850,000 at today's prices, but the whole debt had been repaid out of profits by 1812.[15] If the Foundry's success was as much a feat of organization as it was of engineering, what sort of education produced organizers like this?

The young James had been intended to have a similar grounding to his father: conventional training in carpentry along with bookkeeping, mathematics and the rudiments of running a business, with a view to becoming an engineer or a manufacturer. Starting in May 1784, he was dispatched for a year to John Wilkinson's ironworks. But then, just four months into his placement, he was uprooted again to be educated in Geneva in natural philosophy, mathematics and drawing. In the summer of 1786 he again moved on, to Eisenach and then Freiberg, to learn German, mathematics, chemistry and mining. By the middle of 1787 he was travelling the Continent, finally arriving home again in October.

If Watt Junior had received a thorough and comprehensive education, however, his efforts very often were seen in a dim light by his father. Through his letters Watt Senior applied constant pressure

Model bellcrank engine, possibly by William Murdoch, c. 1799. The bellcrank engine was the first compact, self-contained engine available commercially.

to work harder and achieve more. He sent mathematical problems to test him, and exhorted him regularly to refrain from swearing, to be frugal and not to drink (or talk) too much, not to play cards, or indulge in theatre, music nor, it would appear, any other form of leisure. Indeed, he was to be awake early enough to begin his studies by six every morning.[16] Watt Junior wrote to Matthew Boulton, complaining that his father did not understand him, 'never having been a young man himself'.[17] And his return to Britain saw little

James Watt Junior portrayed by an unknown artist, c. 1800.

improvement in relations – in fact they deteriorated, and he finally quit his home, having discovered that his father did not consider him up to the job of running the engine business. Cast adrift, young Watt's education took on a more rebellious nature.

In 1791 he relocated to Manchester as apprentice with Taylor & Maxwell, a company of cotton dyers and printers, and came under the influence of Thomas Walker, an ardent republican whose views must have appealed to his latent sense of rebellion, and Watt

Junior found himself taking a leading role in the city's Literary and Philosophical Society celebrating the Revolution in France.[18] By the spring of 1792 he was travelling to France, even addressing the Jacobin Club of Paris – and his activities were soon denounced in the House of Commons in London. Yet even as the younger and elder Watt traded letters arguing furiously the case for and against the French revolutionary cause, Watt Junior realized that he was in a dangerous predicament. As the country descended further into political turmoil, he found himself a witness to bitter retribution and bloodshed; although the story that he only narrowly escaped arrest during the Terror is not quite true, he was lucky to escape when many others (including the scientist Antoine-Laurent Lavoisier) lost their heads. In England the reactionary government was suppressing dissent, and young Watt potentially faced charges of sedition. But Watt now offered his son a lifeline: credit so that he could remain in France until circumstances were right to travel back, and gentle encouragement that he would not lose face by returning, in letters which exuded 'a warmth of affection I never before experienced from him', confided young James.[19] By the autumn of 1792 he had quietly slipped back into Britain after a separation from his family and home of some five years.

If James Watt Junior's revolutionary education came to a premature end, he still benefited from a further education of an affective nature. Some historians have suggested that in the period after the French Revolution there can be detected among young people like James not just a desire to challenge authority in personal relationships and political life, but a heightened desire to experiment with 'outrageous forms of expression or even with their own bodies'.[20] This, it is argued, amounted to an 'affective revolution' in which people for the first time expected their emotions to have some kind of tangible expression. Letters from young Gregory Watt to William Creighton, one of Boulton & Watt's engineers, went beyond references to 'filth, farting and explosions' to include erotic imagery that went far beyond the usual young men's humour.[21] Watt and his associates even sniffed nitrous oxide gas in Humphry Davy's scientific laboratory. In December 1799 Davy sealed himself in an airtight box filled with 20 quarts of nitrous oxide, resulting in sensations 'superior to any I ever experienced. Inconceivably pleasurable. Ideas were more vivid & associated together much more rapidly & so associated with words as to produce, perceptions perfectly novel. Theories passed rapidly thro the mind believed I may say intensely.'[22] This wasn't just a one-man project: Watt Senior designed and built the gas-making apparatus. The poets Samuel Coleridge and William Wordsworth were involved as well, mainly in an imbibing role.

This is not to suggest that early engineers and machine makers were all nitrous oxide fiends and libertines, although Joshua Field recalled the 1820s ironmaster John Tickle as 'an extraordinary character – a kind of excentric genious a Chymist & a Poet', which sounds close.[23] But those making machines in the decades around 1800 had an affective revolution of their own; it was not always catalysed by revolutionary politics, but was more likely to have its origins in the world of antiquity.

Classical influences pervaded the education that a young man like Watt Junior might receive in the late eighteenth century. The historian Viccy Coltman writes that 'education at public school amounted to a prolonged and thorough exposure in, first, the languages of the ancient Romans and the ancient Greeks, and subsequently, to a selection of their literary works.' A student at Eton, for example, would attend 27 hours of teaching every week. Of those, three hours were intended for mathematics and writing, three were taken up by religious study, and all of the remaining 21 hours – three-quarters of their time – were filled with antiquity, a diet that sustained them for six years.[24]

The influence of the antique is suggested by the schoolbooks, notebooks and reading undertaken by James Junior's half-brother, Gregory, totalling approximately 120 items, which are contained in a hair chest stored inside Watt's workshop. Gregory died of tuberculosis in 1804, aged only 27, and it would appear that his father was greatly affected by his death, because he had his belongings placed in the workshop where his eye could on occasion rest upon them. Among the chest's contents are a *Compendious Treatise of Astronomy* from 1762, chemistry notebooks, lists of books and tracts to be bound, notebooks and textbooks on maths, geography, navigation, astronomy and algebra. There are even 49 accomplished paintings and drawings, from anatomical sketches to images of Powis and Caernarfon castles in Wales and views of the Lake District and Clyde valley. But very prominent are no fewer than 23 books relating to the classics, including *A New English–Latin Dictionary* by John Entick and Thomas Ruddiman's *The Rudiments of the Latin Tongue; Or, a Plain and Easy Introduction to Latin Grammar* of 1782. Here is a young man's grounding in antiquity captured in paper form.

So, in advance of the emergence of a formal curriculum for training young engineers, their education might be both wide-ranging and disparate. This broad education encouraged Watt Junior to take a different approach to building engines from his father. He was conscious not just of the technicalities of realizing new mechanical ideas, but of having to sell a *product*, a thing not just efficient and mechanically effective but packaged and marketed. The next big challenge, which he faced alongside the wider machine making industry, was to go from building the steam engine per se to the steam engine as status symbol. This meant it had to change from being a purely functional machine to one which was also in large part an aesthetic one. And in this respect the world of the antique that Watt Junior experienced as part of his education comes to the forefront of the discussion: antiquity had considerable influence over the making of many types of products.

Boulton & Watt's work on the engine happened in parallel with tremendous popular appetite for the antique – the culture, architecture and artefacts of ancient Greece and Rome.[25] Discoveries made during archaeological excavations at Herculaneum in 1738, Pompeii in 1748 and at Paestum in Southern Italy were widely broadcast in a series of books. Isaac Ware translated the works of Italian Renaissance architect Andrea Palladio into English in 1738 and followed it up with *A Complete Body of Architecture* in 1756, which was intended to 'serve as a library . . . to the gentleman and the builder' and to 'instruct rather than amuse . . . nothing will be omitted that is elegant or great, but the principal regard will be shewn to what is necessary and useful.'[26] Ware was followed by James Stuart and Nicholas Revett, who published *The Antiquities of Athens* in 1762, and Johann Joachim Winckelmann, with his *Reflections on the Painting and Sculpture of the Greeks* in 1765. And between 1746

Gregory Watt's trunk, inside James Watt's workshop.

and 1778 Giovanni Piranesi produced over 100 large, immaculately detailed and popular views of Rome. Rather than appealing just to scholars and antiquaries, these books' descriptions and illustrations also became widely used source material for architects and designers, too.

They also got into the hands of Watt's associates. Matthew Boulton had all seven volumes of the French Comte de Caylus' *Recueil d'antiquités égyptiennes, étrusques, grecques, romaines et gauloises*, published in 1752–7.[27] Josiah Wedgwood took inspiration from Sir William Hamilton's *Antiquités étrusques, grecques et romaines* of 1766–7, which he referred to as 'Hamilton's Antiquitys'.[28] The architect James Wyatt built the main building of the Soho Manufactory, with its imposing frontage, in 1765–7, described by historian Jennifer Tann as 'a classic piece of English Palladianism'.[29] He also designed Boulton & Watt's huge Albion Mill in London and refashioned Matthew Boulton's Soho House in the Palladian style.[30] Antiquity permeated the environment in which they lived.

There is a question over how far into the ranks of Britain's machine makers antique influences pervaded. Not everyone had access to a classical education. But Wedgwood commented how many customers had a discerning eye for the antique, noting how some likened a particular vase design to 'the things on the tops of Clock cases, or Beds heads. They are certainly not Antique, and that is fault enough to Damn them for with most of our customers.'[31] And even without a formal introduction to the classical world, the workmen in a town like Birmingham would have had an eye for what looked right. Writing to Watt in 1775 regarding the design for a barometer, Gilbert Hamilton wished he could

get some neat contrivance in order to make them in the form of a Corinthian pillar, the Base to open for adjusting them & on the top of the Pillar . . . to have a neat brass or bronze figure holding the scale. *As the workmen with you are more in the way of fancy things they could hit if off better there* than could be done here.[32]

With particular reference to those making machines, there survives a sketchbook that belonged to William Creighton, who rose from erecting engines for Boulton & Watt to become head of their drawing office in 1815, and was a highly active contributor to James Watt Junior's affective education.[33] The sketchbook is a weighty tome, the size of two modern telephone directories, and among well-drawn maps and astronomical charts there is an entire section titled 'Architectural Scraps'. This is packed with drawings, not just of bridges, factory chimneys, and one or two mills, but principally of 56 British cathedrals in intricate detail, complete with measurements, antique temples, and over 100 Ionic, Doric and Corinthian columns, all carefully drawn, proportioned and dimensioned.[34] Creighton noted the source that inspired each drawing, and from this information we can see that he used Ware's *Complete Body of Architecture*, the *Antiquities of Athens* and Chambers' *Treatise on the Decorative part of Civil Architecture* (first published in 1759), as well as referring to Piranesi. These, then, suggest that others beyond Boulton & Watt took inspiration from the antique.

It may be that producing work inspired by antiquity was a more accessible occupation than it might initially appear. Piranesi declared in 1769 that 'An artist, who would do himself honour, and acquire a name, must not content himself with copying faithfully the ancients, but studying their works he ought to show himself of an inventive . . . and of a creating genius.'[35] Rather than rigidly copying antique forms, with all the study and scholarship of the literature that would entail, Piranesi suggests progressing beyond those forms, using them as a platform for exploration and invention.[36] The springboard for this leap was already being assembled in the world of manufacturing and consumption as Boulton & Watt developed the steam engine.

Antiquity inspired much of the output of Matthew Boulton's Soho Manufactory. In 1767 the Duke of Cumberland commissioned Boulton & Fothergill to make 'three Great Solomonean Candlesticks', each almost a metre tall, comprising fluted Corinthian columns on decorative plinths surmounted by the candleholders, themselves formed of decorative tripods.[37] Slender wine jugs and flagons were made with vase-like bodies, tall 'loop' handles and surfaces decorated with Vitruvian scrollwork.[38] Candle vases and other exquisite objects were embellished with goat's or lion's head motifs, satyrs,

Sphinxes, gold decoration, acanthus leaves, engravings of classical scenes and even beautifully detailed sculptural figures wearing robes. Boulton pushed his workmen to the limit when producing such items: Josiah Wedgwood wrote that

Mr Boulton was making an immense large Tripod . . . to finish the top of Demosthenes Lanthorn building . . . from Mr Stewarts design.[39] The legs were cast and weighed about 5 cwt. But they (the workmen) stagger'd at the bowl, & did not know which way to set about it. A council of the workmen was call'd & every method of performing this wonderfull work canvass'd over. They concluded by shaking their heads, & ended where they begun.

Wedgwood obtained the work for himself by cunningly suggesting they should 'call in some able Potter to their assistance . . . Would you think it? they took me at my word & I have got a fine jobb upon my hands in consequence of a little harmless boasting'.[40]

Although the most attention was devoted to these very expensive objects, made in relatively small quantities, antiquity also found its way into the output of Boulton's toymakers. Chatelaines for holding keys, scissors and other useful items incorporated intricate outlines of acanthus leaves with classical imagery, flowers and putti – tiny winged people – stamped into them, and buttons used polished steel frames around tiny Wedgwood jasperware medallions representing figures from Greek mythology or the signs of the zodiac.[41] Boulton employed at Soho one P. J. Wendler, who wrote from Naples that he had obtained a copy of Hamilton's *Antiquities*, comprising 'about 456 prints in folio divided into 4 volumes [comprising] handsome Designs & patterns for the Birmingham Manufactorys . . . I am certain, that . . . all our chief manufacturers . . . would be very glad to have those Prints, for they may be very usefull for Birmingham.'[42] This would suggest a wider utility for such source material beyond Boulton's works.

So, antiquity pervaded the environment in which machinemakers and manufacturers like Boulton & Watt operated. If they were successful enough (as the elder Boulton and Watt were) to commission portrait busts of themselves, they were often portrayed as antique figures: the eighteenth-century industrialist recast as a Roman clad in a toga.[43] Even their hair might be cut in the 'Brutus' style, cropped short and brushed forward, replacing a formal wig. Boulton and Watt were too old for this new fashion but their sons were not.[44] The men who worked for them, while not necessarily possessing the same detailed command of the literature explaining ancient worlds, might nonetheless have buttons, pieces of Wedgwood or other possessions referencing Greece and Rome. As far as engine making at Birmingham went, with components being designed and in part constructed in a complex of buildings designed in the antique style, in proximity to objects designed after the antique, it was almost inevitable that at some point those components would begin to look antique too! The next step for engine builders was to take up Piranesi's challenge and use their inventing, creative genius to apply the antique to new forms – the steam engine.

William Chambers's *Treatise on the Decorative Part of Civil Architecture* provides a springboard for exploring how they did so. First published in 1759, Chambers's work was republished in 1825 by the English architect Joseph Gwilt. Gwilt's analysis from his introductory essay on architecture's 'elements of beauty' can be transposed to the new world of machines. He outlines his belief

Hand-coloured etching by Peter Fabris showing the Temple of Isis at Pompeii being unearthed, published in William Hamilton's book *Campi Phlegraei* (1776). The unearthing of the temple is suggestive of engineers' mining of antiquity for inspiration.

that artists should 'study the effects that flow' from those works of art 'which by the common consent of ages are esteemed beautiful'. By doing so, they would understand those works' qualities 'which act on the understanding and excite our affections by means of the beautiful result they exhibit'.[45] Gwilt believed that we construct meaning about a piece of architecture by looking at it, by striving to understand it and by devising an emotional response to it, and we can frame an analysis of machine making and engine making in these terms. As we saw in the previous chapter, the new technologies of the 1780s had made their mark in terms of visual impact. The steam engine in particular had amply conveyed what Gwilt would call its 'magnitude and strength', not least through the approach pioneered by Boulton & Watt. The two areas where progress was more constrained – or, perhaps it is more accurate to say, where greater codification of practical machine-builders' tacit knowledge would be most advantageous – were in achieving a more widely held understanding of the engine's internal operations, and in establishing how it could further appeal to the emotions of those who saw it. The former could be addressed by greater experiment and theoretical work on the proportioning of parts, and how they formed together into an integrated machine – what Gwilt might have called the engine's 'order and harmony'. The latter could be addressed by placing greater emphasis on the engine's aesthetic design, the qualities Gwilt described as 'richness and simplicity', which were strongly influenced by prevailing fashions and taste, and its overall 'design or disposition', or how it was decorated.

Regarding how the engine worked, Boulton & Watt had taken great care with their standardized range of machines to define the physical characteristics of each – so much so that John Farey devoted an entire chapter of his magisterial *Treatise on the Steam Engine* (1827) to discussing them. The engines were constructed in 23 different sizes, ranging from 4 to 100 horsepower. For each size, the diameter of the steam cylinder, the length of stroke and number of strokes per minute of the piston, even the volume of steam expected to be consumed per minute, were all carefully defined.[46] Farey expended a huge amount of effort studying individual engines in the flesh and added even greater detail, all of which was rendered into simple rules of thumb, 'stated in the most concise terms which could be chosen' for '*practical* engineers'. For example, 'the length of the great lever should be rather more than three times the length of the stroke of the piston', and 'the diameter of the aperture opened by each valve' had to be 'one-fifth of the diameter of the cylinder'.[47]

The same year that Farey's book was published, Thomas Tredgold produced his own book, *The Steam Engine*. Reading both tomes together, Tredgold's is much more theoretical – as Tredgold described it himself, it is about 'the application of science to art', and descriptions, drawings and rules of thumb are matched by complex equations and algebra.[48] As historian Tony Woolrich has described him, Tredgold was 'a compiler of formulae and rules and not a practical mechanical engineer'.[49] But together, the books represent an immense quantity of knowledge about steam, codified and made available to readers. And in this respect they exemplify an explosion in the number of books about the engine written in the 1820s.[50]

However, the sudden expansion of publishing about steam raises an important question: Boulton & Watt's partnership had ended in 1800 and since then, two decades had elapsed with no clearly formulated guides on how to make those engines beyond those materials already written by the firm of Boulton & Watt. Tredgold claimed in 1827 that 'the effects that may be obtained by engines of different species, have now been reduced for the first time, to definite measures, and their proportions referred to scientific principles'. John Farey had produced an authoritative article in Abraham Rees's *Cyclopedia* of 1816, but that was too short to provide the detailed technical guidelines that many engine builders would have wanted.[51] So the question is: what was the received wisdom underpinning engine building in the critical two decades after 1800?

As a first step, we return to the influence of antiquity. After all, just as Farey considered the proportions of engine components, and the millwright Andrew Gray was declaring that 'proportion is the foundation of all good mechanism' as early as 1806, so proportions were long prescribed in the classical orders of architecture, from the 'plain and robust' Tuscan, to the Doric, Ionic and the 'virginal slenderness' of the Corinthian.[52] The component parts of each were described in immense detail: a column divided into a pedestal, the shaft itself and the entablature resting on top. In turn the pedestal comprised the base, trunk and corniche; the column consisted of the base, shaft and capital; and the entablature was formed of the architrave, frieze and a final corniche surmounting all. Each of these components in turn resolved into tiny details: ovolos, astragals, fillets, larmiers, ogees, reglets and annulets, each contributing its mite to the appearance of the whole. And the relative size of all these was expressed in 'modules', one of which usually equalled the diameter of the column; an ideal Doric pedestal was two and a half modules in height, the column eight modules and the entablature two.

It is tempting to suggest that here was a system ready-made to be appropriated when designing engines. Certainly the classical column quickly found its way into mechanical designs: Boulton & Watt were designing a 52-horsepower engine for the cotton spinner James Kennedy of Manchester in 1806 for which the valve gear controlling the flow of steam to the cylinder was in the shape of a pair of fluted columns, topped by a finely detailed entablature.[53] Tellingly the pair were in exactly the proportions required by the Tuscan order. And some of the columns employed in another engine, built for Samuel Bridge of Manchester, match the Doric order exactly.[54] However, these are just two examples out of hundreds where there was no precise association with the classical orders. Even the slender columns supporting the engine beams (which became a signature feature for Boulton & Watt and were widely copied by other engine makers) are generally designed in a ratio of height to diameter of about 18:1 – which has no equivalent in the world of antiquity.

We must not forget that as understanding of its internal workings grew, the engine was increasingly perceived not as a static structure, but as one subject to dynamic stresses and strains, which would change continuously as it worked. John Bourne carefully differentiated between 'the dimensions proper to be given to the various apertures, pumps, and vessels in connection with the engine, to ensure the maximum amount of efficiency' and 'the necessary sizes to ensure strength which should be given to the fixed and working parts'.[55] The former, necessary to safely and economically ease the flow of steam around the engine, was not an issue that

Boulton & Watt's forebears in antiquity had to consider, but it played a decisive role in engine design alongside the latter.

This is not to entirely discount the influence of antiquity on engineering design. Flashes of it occasionally illuminate engineers' letters. John Southern, head of Boulton & Watt's drawing office until 1815, once wrote, with a dry sense of humour,

> We have rummaged all the ancients and moderns from Palladio to that great aristocrat and Knight Sir William Chambers in quest of tables and propriety and having altered and altered and altered again and again various ingenious and highly meritorious designs have at last concentrated the essence of our 'labours' in one which for taste, beauty, magnificence, and utility will vie with the most renowned products of any genius of any age or nation before the conquest of Egypt.[56]

The maker of this small beam engine, *c.* 1840, is unknown, but its excellent design includes many classical design motifs, including finely detailed columns.

Later James Nasmyth wrote that 'viewing abstractedly the forms of the various details of which every machine is composed, we shall find that they consist of certain combinations of six geometrical figures, namely, the line, the plane, the circle, the cylinder, the cone, and the sphere.'[57] Nasmyth's comment mirrors Plato's view of the beauty of 'abstract geometrical' shapes which, he explained, did not refer to 'living things or pictures', but to 'straight lines and circles, and shapes, plane or solid, made from them by lathe, ruler, and square'.[58] But if the precise nature of antiquity's influence is hard to quantify, what other factors influenced engineering's evolution after 1800?

First and foremost, Boulton and Watt continued to wield considerable moral influence, even though they were personally no longer involved in building engines. John Farey wrote that 'all those essential forms and proportions which affect the performance of the machine were so ascertained by the first inventor, that no improvement has since been made in them', and that 'the engines made at the Soho Manufactory, for some years after Mr Watt retired from the business, continued to be proportioned by his scale.'[59] Even Thomas Tredgold, one of Watt's critics, wrote:

An almost innumerable quantity of schemes for improvements on the steam engine have been crowded on the public eye within the last ten years, but except a few for improvements in construction, of small importance, there has been nothing done that is worthy of detaining the reader to notice.[60]

As late as 1868, John Bourne was still publishing Watt's rules of thumb for engine making – for determining the thickness of the connecting rod, the diameters of shafts and the size of beams, for instance – alongside more recent theories.[61]

How far engineers actually stuck to Boulton and Watt's plans is questionable. Tredgold noted that there was

no indication of a settled rule for the proportions of the cylinder, when the length of the stroke is unlimited by convenience. The proportions followed at different times by the firm of Boulton

& Watt, in cases where the stroke was not limited, vary from 1 3/4 to nearly three to one [that is, length of stroke to diameter], the most common about 2.7 to one, the changes having no regularity . . . Equally irregular are Maudslay's proportions but approaching to 2 to 1; Fenton, Murray, and Wood's about as 2 1/2 is to 1.[62]

The occasional effects of these disparate approaches were seen by William Creighton in Glasgow, where he wrote in April 1803 of having 'visited several of the engines here . . . they are as usual dirty and from the insufficiency of thin framing & construction of the frames are all distorted'.[63] Even John Farey, with his very wide practical knowledge of who was building what, lamented that 'owing to defective workmanship, and want of knowledge of the true proportions, it was generally found that the engines first executed by these new makers, fell very short of the performance of the pattern engines.'[64] This last quote gives us a way out of this impasse: Boulton & Watt set the benchmark for how the engine *performed*. The challenge to other engineers was how to fully realize what John Farey called 'the *permanence* of the machinery', its practical embodiment.[65] This was the subject of widespread and creative experimentation in machine making.

Not all engineers were single-minded, deadly rational beings like Watt. As may be surmised from the preceding debate, there was a tremendous range of opinion on the nature of engine making. As John Farey declared that 'every departure from [Watt's] forms and proportions has impaired the performance, to a greater or lesser extent', so Thomas Donaldson argued that 'old machines, when they were originally invented, had not any beauty of form: they were of large proportions', and they had to be relieved 'from cumbrous proportions'.[66] Even a hardened theoretician like Tredgold could note with approval that 'appropriate forms, good proportions, and excellent workmanship should be attended to in all machinery; and in many instances it is desirable that they should be beautiful.'[67] The historian Lewis Mumford, in *Technics and Civilisation*, calls Britain's machine makers at the turn of the nineteenth century 'a new race of artists'.[68] It is as artists that we should review their products. For the first time, after all, they were as much concerned with the outward appearance of the engine as with its internal workings. Here is Gwilt's richness and simplicity, design and disposition, applied to making machines.

As we left the engine, being built on a new standardized scheme at the Soho Foundry, it was very much a functional machine, accurately built but with little conscious thought given to its outward appearance. Matthew Boulton stated his preference for 'a simple, clean, orderly, convenient, modest building with good machinery' compared to 'that which is magnificently bad'.[69] Form followed function, and the engine's function was to facilitate the manufacture of other products, from spun cotton to beer. But the engine was becoming thought of more as a desirable product in itself. Engines built by Henry Harvey at Hayle, for example, were 'more like ornaments for a show-room than machines for draining a mine'.[70] Rather than the traditional division between process and product, what we have here is the process *as* product.

From the 1790s cast iron was being employed in greater quantities, and the means of shaping it offered new aesthetic possibilities. Beyond the cylinder, one of the earliest, and largest, of the component parts of the engine to employ cast iron was its working beam. This was no mean feat, given the huge stresses that it was subject to, and the early cast beams by Boulton & Watt were monolithic, not dissimilar to the baulks of seasoned timber that they replaced. But gradually, with the realization that the greatest strains were at the centre, the beam was transformed into an ellipse, deepest at its centre, where more strength was needed, and tapering towards each end. This was a defining moment in the engine's transformation, giving it 'a grace of motion not hitherto perceived'.[71] The properties of cast iron afforded gradual change to other components: the connecting rod linking the beam to the crank, and from there the flywheel, gradually took on a cruciform section, principally because it was the shape that let the cast iron cool at the most uniform rate, maximizing its strength.[72] Returning to the beam, experiments showed that the greatest extending and compressing strains were withstood by the upper and lower edges. These could be increased in breadth by half at the expense of the inside of the beam, which

Boulton & Watt's 'Lap' beam engine, 1788. This is the oldest essentially unaltered rotative engine in the world, and incorporates all Watt's design improvements into a highly functional design.

could be made 'open' using a carefully designed latticework in place of solid material, for example.[73]

All this work depended on improved pattern making and foundry work. The pattern maker required 'all the methods, care, and skill, of good joinery or cabinet-making' and a detailed appreciation of the characteristics of cast iron down to making an allowance 'of about one-eighth of an inch per foot . . . for the contraction of the metal in cooling' and a bevel of 'about one-sixteenth of an inch in six inches' to allow the pattern to be easily removed from the sand mould prior to the molten metal being poured in.[74] The foundryman had to avoid air bubbles in castings and sought to ensure toughness by carefully cooling the finished product over a long period.[75] This degree of care and precision beyond what had been done before made possible Samuel Clegg's contention that with cast-iron construction, 'It does not cost one farthing more to construct an elegant figure, than it does to create a deformity.'[76]

The potential of cast iron for multiplying decorative details in machinery was not lost on contemporary engineers, who wrestled with the question of what an aesthetic reflecting the steam engine's importance, status and power should consist of. Engineer and historian Greville Bathé described the period from 1840 until 1860 as a 'somewhat glamorous period in engineering progress'.[77] Similarly Julie Wosk believed that 'after 1830 . . . designers confronted the need to create engine frames that embodied the century's pride in technology'.[78] However, both these authors place the emphasis too late: there was considerable work on a new aesthetic for the engine much earlier than 1830. And rather than a series of phases that machine design went through, it is more useful to identify a number of parallel strands in machine design.

First among these was the application of antiquity. Even if a formal relationship between the classical orders and engineering is difficult to identify, antique details were widely adopted and enduring. As beam engines evolved into self-contained structures from being built into a masonry engine house, columns proliferated, often fluted, with plain Doric and more ornate Ionic and Corinthian capitals, and supporting entablatures that included delicate moulded detail.[79] The frames of marine engines followed suit on a larger scale, frequently incorporating arches with a decorative keystone cast into the metal above.[80] Later the number of columns was reduced, the entablature done away with and the rocking beam supported on a single, much more robust column.[81] Alternatively the beam could be supported by an A-frame, which might comprise columns set at an angle (which type was favoured by Boulton & Watt's archrival Matthew Murray of Leeds), or a cast plate frame with carefully rounded cut-outs to reduce the amount of metal needed, with indented panels and decorative roundels.[82]

The aesthetic transformation of the engine was noted by contemporaries. Visiting the Soho Foundry in 1814, Swiss engineer Johann Conrad Fischer was amazed that 'What might have seemed impossible has now been achieved. What was once a confused pile of piping and cylinders has become an elegant iron building of Doric and Corinthian pillars.'[83] Yet at the same time, since Boulton & Watt's patents were no longer valid, they had no claims to a monopoly on decorating their engines – in fact they may even have lagged behind. James Watt Junior wrote in September 1823 that an acquaintance had visited the works of London engineer Henry Maudslay and spoke of 'the workmanship and appearance of the engines he has completed for the Navy: Wonder we cannot adopt the same beautiful Gothic in our framing and the same neatness of finish?'[84]

This quotation leads us beyond the purely antique forms towards other influences that came to bear for relatively short but intense periods. The nineteenth century saw a revival of medieval Gothic architecture in Britain, from Horace Walpole's house at Strawberry Hill in southwest London, begun in 1749, to the new Houses of Parliament at Westminster, rebuilt by Augustus Pugin and Charles Barry after being devastated by fire in 1834. Similar influences quickly spread into engineering: John Braithwaite of London built a water pump for Lord Brownlow's country house in 1817 which had its cylinders, air vessels and pipes encased by pointed-arch framing.[85] The 1830s saw a range of similar designs: William Joyce of Greenwich built 'Pendulous' steam engines with Gothic frames in 1834 and W. Pope of London built an even larger version which was 'clothed with iron Gothic tracery'.[86] Gothic influences endured particularly in the u.s.: the Henry Ford Museum has an outstanding engine by New York's Novelty Ironworks dated from 1855, which would not look out of place working in a cathedral.[87]

Gothic forms were supplemented by an Egyptian revival in mechanical form. In 1840 John Marshall, flax spinner of Leeds, commissioned a new building in the Holbeck area of the city from the architect Ignatius Bonomi.[88] It was partly inspired by the temple at Edfu on the River Nile in Egypt, after which it took its name of 'Temple Mill', and its immense internal area had a frontage comprising stout columns with papyrus-headed capitals support-ing an entablature decorated with other Egyptian motifs.[89] Inside Benjamin Hick of Bolton constructed a powerful twin beam engine which repeated many of the Egyptian details from outside, down to the 'chronometric' governor, a name evoking the capabilities of its builders, in the form of a winged scarab beetle.[90]

If these startling reinventions of long-established designs suggest discontinuity, they are balanced by strong elements of stabi-lity and continuum. By adopting classical, Gothic or (to a lesser extent) Egyptian stylings, engineers were experimenting on the basis

Pumping set with framing in the Gothic style, by John Braithwaite of London, 1817.

of their prior knowledge, which was as much cultural as technical. But alongside these projects, working out the best balance between functional utility and decorative appearance, evolved a new aesthetic informed not so much by the past, as by formal knowledge of materials, assessment of how they could be worked, and understanding of the effects that could be achieved.

This approach is best conveyed, not by Boulton & Watt in Birmingham, or even Murray in Leeds, but by the engineers of London and, particularly, Henry Maudslay. Maudslay's works, just off Westminster Bridge Road and across the river from Whitehall, have been alluded to already: they were founded in 1798 and became a hothouse for engineering talent. Many engineers, including James Nasmyth and Joseph Whitworth, worked there before founding their own companies.[91] Nasmyth recalled Maudslay's maxims for machine design: 'First, get a clear notion of what you desire to accomplish', 'keep a sharp lookout upon your materials; get rid of every pound

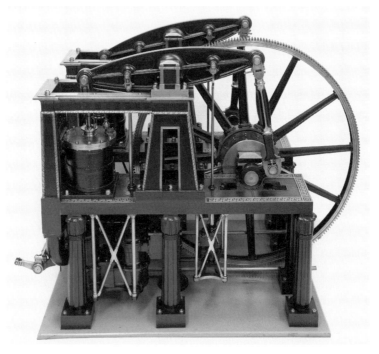

Model Hick double beam engine in the Egyptian style, 1840, and displayed at the Great Exhibition of 1851.

of material you can do without', 'avoid complexities, and make everything as simple as possible' – or, as the historian James Hamilton has put it, understanding, economy, simplicity.[92] Maudslay had given physical form to these concepts as early as 1802, when he secured the contract to construct a suite of machines to make pulley-blocks at the Royal Navy's Portsmouth Dockyard. The demand was so prodigious – over 100,000 blocks per year, in a range of sizes – that he constructed 45 machines that together formed a production line, the first set of single-purpose, entirely metal-constructed machines anywhere in the world. The machines paid 'the most scrupulous attention to accuracy and durability . . . presenting an elegant proportion in their form, which is very agreeable to the eye', and set new standards in metal construction: economy in the use of metal, the replacement of solid forms with carefully formed bracing and restrained use of decorative details like plain columns and finials.[93] This approach was carried through to the machine tools Maudslay built for his London works, and in turn influenced those who trained there.[94]

Here, then, was the start of a new machine aesthetic which had its own character. Just as Augustus Pugin complained that architects constructed ornaments instead of ornamenting construction, so the new aesthetic was informed by the basic form of the mechanism itself. With 'strength in the proper place, stability without unnecessary weight, and simplicity of form without meanness', further ornament was unnecessary, 'because their own proportions [would] constitute their greatest'.[95]

After 1800, two competing pressures shaped how this new approach evolved. On the one hand, as machines became larger and more self-contained, the aesthetic opportunities increased. Marine engines were some of the largest engines built at the time and offered some of the greatest opportunities for decoration.[96] On the other, engineers sought to reduce weight and lower the centre of gravity, doing away with as much framing as possible and making engines 'direct-acting' to remove the need for the great rocking beam. As they did so, these engineers were 'exhilarated and enthused about the beauty of their own creations, about whose formal qualities and the newness of these qualities they were quite clear in their minds.'[97]

Remnants of old forms began to disappear, and the new approach, 'equally remarkable for elegance of appearance and compactness of arrangement', gained ground.[98]

This is not to characterize the new way of designing machines as a complete break with the past: in its details, it was not. As Michael Wright has written of the Portsmouth machines, icons of modernity that became 'must-see' tourist destinations on a par with the Soho Manufactory or Etruria, 'there are features that seem to be borrowed from woodwork and others from the smithy: cross-bracing certainly looks like carpentry' and other details 'are reminiscent of the way that the parts of wagons and carriages are lightened; while the use of latticework . . . imitates wrought ironwork'.[99] This most likely reflects Maudslay's training as a carpenter and blacksmith. In fact, Maudslay's 'table' steam engine, a compact machine patented in 1807, was criticized as being 'a little too complex . . . its frame reminds one of an antiquated style of cabinet work'.[100] As for Maudslay's famous maxims, Jean-Antoine Knollet (1700–1770) a prominent lecturer in natural philosophy, constructed his own scientific instruments and, in doing so, had developed four guiding principles: that they should be precisely made; with no superfluous decoration; of the simplest and strongest construction; and capable of performing several tasks.[101] Maudslay was early in scaling up these principles onto an industrial scale, and particularly in applying them to cast iron, but the principles per se had existed for some time. And the delineation between scientific and industrial scales could be hazy: the mural quadrant made for Kew observatory in 1770 by Sisson of London needed a robust latticework of struts for rigidity across its great 8-foot radius, for example, and the instrument maker Edward Troughton had large items cast and machined by Maudslay's engineering competitor Bryan Donkin at Bermondsey.[102]

Although we have described distinct 'design styles' – classical, Gothic, a new 'machine aesthetic' – surviving artefacts also point to the parallel existence of an active vernacular school of engineering design. A Lancashire clockmaker needed a small full-size engine to drive his tools and commissioned it from a local blacksmith. It was relatively unadorned when compared to the polished products from a works like Maudslay's, but entirely appropriate for the job

Mortising machine from the Portsmouth blockmills, 1803. The machine cut a slot through a thick block of wood to accommodate a pulley-wheel, around which ropes could pass. Its design combines strength with elegance.

it was required to do, and its simple, robust design spoke of the smith's versatility and sense of authorship, down to the incorporation of a small brass heart inlaid into the base.[103] An individual named Blankly built an exquisite gilt-brass beam engine model, decorating the cylinder with an engraved masonic badge including the eye of God, a sun and moon, a compass and a square.[104] Other models became *objets d'art*, with the balance between function and decoration tipped firmly to the latter: decorative 'bun' feet, spiral knurled columns, condenser cisterns or boiler casings surrounded by brass sheet decorated with patterns, flowers or leaves, even construction in silver.[105] Still more are fine examples of engineering skill, but follow a design entirely unique to the builder, with suggestions of classical columns and free-style decoration, all brought to a bright, finely polished finish.[106] This vernacular style emphasized engineers' personal motivations and interests, not formal design protocols.

Some nineteenth-century commentators would take a dim view of this approach. Samuel Clegg wrote his *Architecture of Machinery* to 'inquire into the reasons of error, and to endeavour to point out certain rules for design, by attention to which the many irregularities in *construction* and *form* so constantly met with in machinery are to be avoided; and to explain the correct principles of "taste".'[107] Clegg's father had been apprenticed to Boulton & Watt, so he may have inherited some sense of the proper (or one might say austere) in his approach to machines.[108] But Clegg in his turn had critics: some of his examples of tasteful engineering design were dismissed by the editor of the *Civil Engineer and Architect's Journal* as 'architectural monstrosities' that were 'vapid and quakerlike'.[109]

In treating the output of the early nineteenth-century engineers as art, then, we can see that its substance, and its virtues or defects, were both varied and contested. In an age before standardization engineers were free to pursue their own paths within the parameters set by the need to stay afloat commercially, and they did so with diverse results. The antique continued to hold sway into the 1840s but, in the United Kingdom at least, it was increasingly surpassed by the new functional approach.

Regardless of how it was attained, however, the period until the 1840s was unrivalled in its pursuit of beauty in engineering. Thomas Tredgold might have criticized Maudslay's table engine, but he still believed 'the beauty of the workmanship is unequalled'.[110] Maudslay's epitaph, fittingly cast into an iron tombstone, remarked on his combination of 'mathematical accuracy and *beauty of construction*' (my emphasis). Engineers found beauty even in simple aspects of their work. John Robison noted that a slide valve's 'sliding plate performs the office of four cocks in a very beautiful and simple manner'.[111] When Hans Casper Escher visited Manchester in 1814, he wrote that 'One must admire the steam engines here. In beauty and efficiency they bear the same relationship to French steam engines as English spinning engines bear to those of Saxony.'[112]

The engine in all its forms exerted a continued imaginative effect on those who saw it at work. Sir George Head wrote of the engine supplying air blast to iron furnaces at the Low Moor Iron Works, 'I have listened to a storm on the Atlantic, I have stood on the Table Rock at Niagara, yet never did I hear a sound in nature equal to this – so terrific, or of so stunning a din.'[113] Summarizing the effect of steam in a Leeds cotton mill, Sir George was convinced that

> the movements of the engine altogether were so perfect and free from friction, the brilliancy of polish bestowed on many of its parts so lustrous and the care and attention paid to the whole so apparent that imagination might readily have trans-ferred the edifice to a temple, dedicated by man, grateful for the stupendous power that moved within, to Him who built the universe.[114]

The emergence of the engine as a carefully styled object reflects its role as symbol of the new industrial age, signalling dignity, prosperity and status as much as technical mastery.

This approach was entirely congruent with how the antique was appropriated and imitated in other industries, comprising 'an evocation of objects in other forms, and indeed the new form might well surpass the original in inventiveness'.[115] Before the emergence of a formal engineering profession, engineers built an entire generation of machines that amplified ancient designs into new, confident and imaginative forms. This process was not just explored at the Soho Foundry or in Birmingham. As Boulton & Watt left the scene, they handed over to engineers spread across Britain: in London, Manchester, Lancashire and Tyneside. But what, so to speak, of James Watt and his son? The younger Watt settled down to become, in the words of historian Eric Robinson, 'a pillar of society as well as something of a dandy', while Peter Jones has him living 'a solitary, bachelor existence with just a cat, a dog, and a Sicilian manservant for company'.[116] With the future of the engine-building company in safe hands, his father was about to embark on one last, big project: sculpture copying.

SEVEN

Life after Death, 1800–1924

THE STAIRCASE UP TO the second floor of James Watt's house, Heathfield, was steep and dark. Going up from the first-floor bedrooms to the two servant's rooms and a cistern cupboard above, visitors reached a landing with an insubstantial wooden banister. At the far end was a broad wooden door, to the left of which was a demi-circular shelf ready to receive plates of food if the occupant of the room beyond was too busy to be disturbed. From beyond the door would come a rhythmic whirring and grinding. Lifting the latch and peering in, the visitors would see James Watt, clad in a leather apron, head down and brow furrowed in concentration as he worked the treadle of a giant machine reaching almost to the ceiling. Part of the machine's framing would be covered with a piece of cotton waste secured with string, so that Watt wouldn't strike his head on it, and the cutting tool sent out showers of dust as it bit into a piece of plaster of Paris. Around the workshop plaster moulds lay half-assembled with string, containers held plaster mixtures and on the shelves rested figurines styled after the antique. This was James Watt's workshop.[1]

The workshop was in the attic of Heathfield, commissioned by Watt from the architect James Wyatt in 1789 for a site on Handsworth Heath, a mile and a half northwest from the centre of Birmingham. Watt and his family moved in during September 1790. The following year, they took the opportunity to buy more of the surrounding heathland, and amassed 40 acres of grounds, gardens and woodland to form a 'large and charming park'.[2] Heathfield would be Watt's home as he withdrew from the steam-engine business, and for the

Watt's workshop, as illustrated in Samuel Smiles's *Lives of the Engineers Boulton and Watt* (1865). This is the earliest known image of the workshop.

rest of his life. It was a fine house, in a marked Neoclassical style, of which Mrs Watt was both proud and protective: having indoctrinated the servants with 'the thrifty and far-seeing habits of the most enlightened Scotch housewifery', she taught the family's two pugs to wipe their feet before entering the house and, being 'not so amiable in her household as she might have been', was alleged to have had a window 'placed in the wall which separated her sitting room from the kitchen, so that she had the servants continually under her eye'.[3] Watt may have been a 'potent commander of the elements', an 'abridger of time and space' whose 'cloudy machinery' had changed the world, but at Heathfield Mrs Watt held sway.[4] Watt, with his penchant for chemical experiments and instrument making, retired to the attic.

The room that Watt chose to be his workshop was at first simply a place to stow away belongings; in 1801 he sent for a quantity of possessions from Glasgow, and these duly arrived.[5] Then the room was transformed from being a storeroom into a fully equipped workplace. It was rather gloomy: the ceiling sloped down on three sides under the roof eaves, and it was lit by a single east-facing window that overlooked a kitchen yard and outbuildings. But the room's solitariness was an advantage for Watt's purposes: here he could pursue projects and experiments undisturbed.[6]

The garret workshop had a dual purpose. First, it was an active workplace where Watt could pursue the manufacture of sculptures on his copying machines, one of which was alluded to above, its frame partly padded with cotton waste and spitting plaster dust. Watt devoted considerable effort to the machines, and they are emblematic of a new world of mechanical sculpture, even a new world of mechanization as more broadly defined, that flourished in the early nineteenth century. Here we will explore the crossovers between copying sculpture, Watt's last big project, and the second purpose for the workshop: it was a personal museum for Watt, containing objects from his entire working life, and after his death in 1819 it assumed a role as a place that memorialized and commemorated Watt for others, too. These aspects of the workshop are interlinked: Watt's interest in sculpture was of long standing, and as he began to multiply his own image on the copying machines, he was carrying out a process multiplied on a much greater scale after his death, when he became the personal embodiment of a new mechanical age and his image was appropriated and reappropriated by successive interested parties. What the workshop was, and what it stood for, together ensured that Watt remained a commanding presence long after his death.

Watt's sculpture project was not confined to his workshop but sprawled over several different parts of Heathfield. His will records that he had things stored in his study and 'the two rooms in the South East corner of my house and . . . my laboratory or elsewhere'.[7] The children of the Pemberton family, tenants living at Heathfield in the 1860s, recalled 'wonderful discoveries of out-of-the-way things . . . discarded clay crucibles of all sorts and sizes; worn-out and queerly-shaped earthenware retorts; empty phials of all shapes and dimensions, with strange inscriptions on their labels . . . in an out-building we came across two huge blocks of roughly-hewn white marble'.[8] The wide-ranging nature of these discoveries reflects, among other things, the complexity of Watt's sculpture projects.

The two sculpture-copying machines embody Watt's continuing fascination with precision manufacture. The first was designed to make reduced-size copies of an original, while the second was intended to make equal-size copies, a more difficult technical proposition. Both used the same basic principle: an item to be copied and material to make the copy from, usually a block of plaster of Paris, were positioned on the machines side-by-side. A feeler and a rotating cutting tool were also positioned side-by-side, and mounted so that as the feeler was carefully traced across the surface of the original, the cutter followed and repeated exactly the same movement. As the tool was rotated at high speed by a treadle, so plaster was removed and the copy formed. A portfolio in the workshop contains drawings of the reducing machine in an early form, dated 1804. Watt had visited Paris in 1802, seeing a machine called a *tour à medaille* for tracing and multiplying the dies for medal making, and this may have inspired him to undertake the project.[9] Watt must quite quickly have realized the constraints of the reducing machine: it was most capable of making small objects like medallions in low relief, so in about 1809, he began on the second, equal-size machine, which was also more capable of producing three-dimensional objects with a greater degree of surface relief.[10]

Development of the machines presented Watt with several challenges. The workshop was a far from ideal workplace. He wrote in July 1811, 'I am not able to work any with my machine at this season my Garret being too hot to be tenable.'[11] Conversely winter also limited the progress achieved, with Watt complaining of 'the place having been too cold for me'.[12] Watt experimented working with marble, developing new cutting tools and a more robust frame for the equal-size machine to cope with the harder material, but the results seem to have been indifferent. Watt gave the steam engineer John Farey a small piece made on the machines in 1814, and Farey noted Watt was 'striving to . . . carve marble and hard materials, and he showed me some first trials in stone, but they were not perfect'.[13] Nonetheless, Watt made the equal-size machine capable of cutting more than one copy at a time, and by 1814 he was drafting drawings and a specification for a patent.[14]

The machines built on a broader interest in sculpture, and connections to the sculpture trade, that reached back into the 1790s. For example, Watt corresponded with the mouldmaker John Pierotti.

Watt's reducing machine, re-erected in his workshop at the Science Museum, London.

Pierotti came from Lucca in northwest Italy and had arrived in England at Dover in 1770 before living in Birmingham and then Edinburgh, where he was entered on the Register of Aliens on 2 December 1803.[15] Nothing is known about him beyond this, but we do know that considerable numbers of mould makers or *formatori* came from Lucca, itinerant makers and vendors of plaster casts.[16] And we know about Pierotti's work from a 'Catalogue of Figures of Plaister of Paris' which survives in Watt's workshop.[17] The catalogue includes the prices of the figures in different sizes, and the range of subjects is broad: antique figures like the Apollo Belvedere, Antinos and small copies of a renowned statue of Hercules from the Palazzo Farnese in Rome. Other figures were evidently named for their moral connotations: Virginity, Innocence, Prudence and Fortitude. Pierotti also made anatomical figures after 'Bugiardon', 'Mr Hudon' and 'Michel-Angelo', and busts 'large as life' of Clytie, Atalanta, Sappho and the composer Handel. Other subjects included Shakespeare, Joseph Priestley and, in a nod to then-current fashions, 'Three deferent [sic] Vases at 3s. each'.

Watt evidently purchased some items from Pierotti while the latter was based in Birmingham because, alongside his catalogue, there survives in Watt's workshop a bill 'for making moulds of Plaster of Paris', marked 'Birmingham October the 8th 1792'.[18] It is a receipt for mouls [sic] of Plaisters of Paris for Mr Watt', with details of the moulds: for a figure of Antinos, Venus, Atlas (misspelled as 'Atals'), as well as 'tow [two] bass relivos'. And among the items in Pierotti's catalogue is an entry for 'Small heads – Proserpina'. This traces back to an original, *The Rape of Proserpina*, dated 1621–2, by the Italian sculptor Gian Lorenzo Bernini in the Galleria Borghese in Rome. In turn, this matches a plaster copy in Watt's collection of sculpture figures.[19]

As well as finished casts, Watt was also an avid collector of moulds for antique figures. Indeed, Pierotti's catalogue includes prices for these moulds alongside casts made with them, allowing purchasers to make their own reproductions. Watt's workshop contains 23 plaster of Paris moulds. Some were used, and can be associated with particular figures. For instance, a small three-part mould for a vase matches a vase elsewhere in the workshop, and there also survives

The bust of Proserpina in James Watt's sculpture collection, purchased by him from John Pierotti.

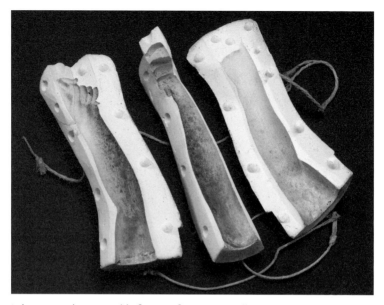

A three-part plaster mould of an arm from Watt's collection inside his workshop.

a figure of Atlas, complete with a globe to rest on his shoulders, which I suggest is a match for the figure of 'Atals' ordered from John Pierotti in October 1792.[20] Others of the moulds appear to be unused. Many are highly complex, consisting of numerous parts locating tightly together using hemispherical projections (fitting into corresponding indentations), and with detailed internal parts to reproduce the complexities of the human form. Watt's interest in casting his own sculpture is reflected in another document in his workshop, entitled 'List of Pots', detailing, for instance, '5 – Glover's plaister burnt' and '12 – very fine faceing [plaster] for moulds', which appear to match some of the jars bearing those numbers on the workshop shelves.[21] Elsewhere large boxes and jars contain plaster of Paris awaiting use.

Watt's copying machines were, then, the culmination of a sustained interest in the world of sculpture that extended to purchasing moulds and taking his own copies from them. That Watt might seek to mechanize that world suggests how the market for sculpture was changing quickly. Traditionally sculpture had been a fascination of the wealthy and educated. Thomas Howard attempted to 'transplant old Greece into *England*' through his extended pursuit of statuary. Likewise Charles I's 'liking of ancient statues' had caused 'a whole army of Old forraine Emperours, Captaines, and Senators all at once to land on his coasts, to come and do him homage, and attend him in his palaces of Saint James, and Sommerset house'.[22] There emerged in the eighteenth century a trade in marble copies of originals in Rome, for example, which were hugely costly on account of the time they took to make: one Italian maker had spent fourteen months on a copy, with another five months expected to finish it off.[23] There was also a trade in plaster copies, full-size and prestigious, for the homes of wealthy gentlemen and aristocrats. So, sculpture was appropriated by Britain's upper classes using a range of materials, and specially commissioned as part of design schemes for both domestic and architectural spaces.[24]

Further demand for sculpture was driven by the Grand Tour, as the well-to-do and classically educated set out from Britain to see the antique sights of Italy, visiting Rome, Pompeii, Herculaneum and Venice, among other places. For the first time they confronted the reality of what they had so often learned so much about in the course of their education: As John Northall wrote in his *Travels through Italy* of 1766, seeing statues of

emperors, consuls, generals, orators, philosophers, poets and other great men . . . gives a man a cast of almost 2,000 years backwards, and mixes the past ages with the present . . . Besides the countenance, we see in the statues the habits of those times which give a complete idea of the whole person, and in that respect make every portrait a history piece.[25]

Returning from that experience, they sought small, portable pieces of sculpture that could be displayed in their homes as symbols of wealth, knowledge and connoisseurship. If the statuary could not be obtained, substitutes were available: many great English houses had 'niches filled with famous antique statues . . . painted in grisaille' – monochrome two-dimensional paintings imitating three-dimensional sculpture.[26] Gilbert White took this one step further at his house in Selborne, Hampshire. Unable to afford a statue for his grounds, he mounted a carefully painted wooden outline of a sculptural figure on an appropriate plinth; from a distance it could not be distinguished from a three-dimensional statue.[27]

By the mid-eighteenth century, then, a professional trade had emerged in England, to satisfy the demand for sculpture. The more expensive traders were based around London's Hyde Park, West-minster Abbey, Covent Garden and Marylebone.[28] One historian has claimed that these shops became 'well-known places of public resort, operating partly as forms of commercial galleries . . . every fashion-able person in London came to know what the Cheere brothers' lead and plaster cast shop on Hyde Park Corner looked like from within'.[29] But another, unique trade in cheaper statuary and statuettes, most often made in plaster, evolved in early nineteenth-century England. Rather than pieces of 'art', the output of this trade was regarded as a commodity to be bought and sold.[30] As Watt worked on his sculp-ture machines, so this trade also bridged the gap between the fine and manufacturing arts, supplying three-dimensional images for 'architects, cabinet-makers, clock-makers, goldsmiths, cast iron and brass foundries, jewellers, toy-makers, potters and porcelain manu-facturers', and it is a possibility that Watt had first come into contact with plaster copy makers during his association with the Soho Manufactory in Birmingham.[31] A range of workshops, itinerant tradesmen and even vendors trading plaster figures from trays bal-anced on their heads met a fervour of demand for statuettes in the nineteenth century.

How the plaster copy trade generated reproductions was a tortuous process. To make a cast, the statue was divided into layers, one above the other, and each surrounded by a hollow box. This process would be complicated by the presence of any 'undercut' detail, protuberances that the liquid plaster could get behind and then harden so that the mould could not be released without being broken. A wet plaster mixture was poured in to fill the space between the box and the original, with a suitable substance painted onto the original to ensure the plaster did not adhere as it dried. When the plaster had solidified, the mould for each layer was carefully removed, and then all were pieced back together so that, with plaster poured in, the replica was formed.[32] The multiplication of copies of copies meant that slight imperfections were magnified. While some sculpture makers prided themselves on working from the best copies available, or even the originals, others sold copies from 'broken casts so that bits of the god's hair were missing and his neck was thick because of the expansion of the plaster each time a cast was made'.[33] The precision obtained, then, was highly variable.

This background helps contextualize Watt's copying machines: he had an interest in sculpture of some long standing, there was a widely held appetite for sculpture in materials ranging from marble to plaster, and low-quality copies offered the potential for improvement. Also there was a chance that the trade might prove lucrative: when Joseph Nollekens carved a statue of the statesman William Pitt in 1808, the original, with its associated pedestal, earned him £4,000. However, 74 marble copies of the bust each earned him 120 guineas, and he also sold 600 plaster casts for six guineas each – the entire project earned him £17,000 (or more than £500,000 at today's prices), of which three-quarters came from manufacturing the copies.[34] The technical challenge and financial rewards of making high-quality copies of sculpture was one that Watt, and others like him, could not resist. He was early in a wave of engineers and inventors motivated by the financial returns arising from an efficient way of mechanically copying sculpture.[35] Five different machines were patented in France alone between 1835 and 1840. In England Angus Robertson of London patented 'machinery for sculpturing and working marble, stone, alabaster, and other substances, and for taking copies' in 1837, Thomas Jordan patented a machine in 1845 that was used to produce much of the carving in the newly rebuilt Houses of Parliament, and Benjamin Cheverton perfected a capable and particularly well-regarded machine in the course of 1826 capable of making copies of busts by famous sculptors like Sir Francis Chantrey, Joseph Nollekens and L.-F. Roubiliac in ivory, incorporating highly intricate detail.

What is notable about all these machines is the length of time after Watt's that they were made. But there is, in Cheverton's machine, a link back to Watt. Cheverton developed his machine in partnership with an inventor named John Isaac Hawkins. Hawkins (1772–1855) was a multifaceted man, a civil engineer, inventor and sometime

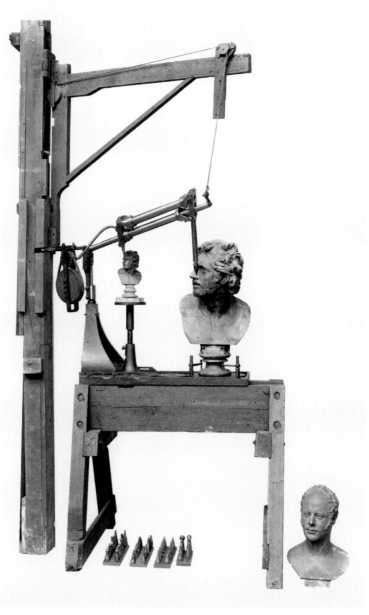

Benjamin Cheverton's machine for reproducing sculpture, 1826. The mechanism was driven by an ingenious flexible drive and could pivot around a ball joint, creating a larger range of movement compared to Watt's machines.

composer, poet, preacher and phrenologist whose father had been a clockmaker.[36] He had emigrated to the United States in 1800 and while there had produced two machines, a 'physiognotrace' and a 'polygraph'. The former allowed a sitter to draw a silhouette profile of themselves and the latter, rather than being the lie detector the word denotes today, used an ingenious mechanism so that a writer could draft a letter and the machine simultaneously wrote a copy. Thomas Jefferson purchased two to keep up his voluminous correspondence and declared it 'one of the greatest inventions of this age'.[37]

With his experience of turning either a three-dimensional shape or a two-dimensional letter into a two-dimensional image (as with his physiognotrace and polygraph respectively), it was a logical next step for Hawkins to experiment with turning a three-dimensional original into a three-dimensional copy – as in sculpture copying – and that is exactly what he did. Hawkins returned to Britain in 1803, and what happened next was explained in the *North British Review* of 1855:

We had an opportunity when at Heathfield in 1818, of seeing some specimens of the work which Mr Watt had executed [with his sculpture machines], and then he told us that a neighbour of his who could have had no knowledge of his invention, had made considerable progress in the construction of a similar machine. This gentleman offered to take out a joint patent with Mr Watt; but he had suffered so much from former patents, that he was unwilling to embark in any new concern.[38]

That neighbour was Hawkins. There are no letters between Hawkins and Watt in the latter's correspondence, and the details of any meeting are lost. We can only arrive at any idea of how the machine he developed worked at one step removed, by considering a description of how it was later developed for Cheverton: to avoid giving the latter's secrets away, it was only ever described in very general terms, as 'a lever turning on a fulcrum at one end . . . furnished with a tracing point at the other end, and between the tracing point and the fulcrum there is a drill in rapid motion; as the tracing point is carried over the model, the drill travels over and carves the ivory'.[39] This description fits exactly Watt's reducing machine, too. This is to be expected to some extent: the geometrical principles of the machine were widely known. Less well known was how to apply them, not just to semi-relief pieces like medallions, but to 'round figures' as well – which Hawkins could, but Watt could not – or not immediately.[40] Watt, getting old, and confronted by the young, energetic Hawkins, may have felt discouraged. He left off pursuing the machine as a commercially viable project and contented himself with the technical curiosity that it offered.

Whatever happened, Watt's sculpture-copying machines were the first of a new generation of machines constructed to the same end. A reviewer for *L'Artiste* in 1839 noted how that built by Achille Collas in 1837 could reproduce with ease 'individual bas-reliefs of the Parthenon, twelve inches in height . . . with scrupulous exactitude to the minutest details of the plaster' and 'a cut ivory cup of Benvenuto Cellini, the size of a coin'. Some months later Jules Janin wrote that this type of work 'was made in six hours by a man turning a foot crank, while reading a new novel', and its implications were that 'the Louvre Museum is no longer in the Louvre . . . the masterpieces of statuary are reproduced everywhere.'[41] The Cheverton/Hawkins machine used some cutters 'as small as a pin's head', and in many parts of the machinery 'an error of 1000th part of an inch would be destructive'.[42] As may be surmised, the great advantage of the sculpture-copying machines was their tremendous accuracy. Providing this accuracy was part of the machines' appeal to Watt.

However, precision did not necessarily trump cheapness in the world of sculpture copying for the masses; it is telling that both John Hawkins and, to a slightly lesser extent, Benjamin Cheverton died in reduced circumstances. For all the ingenuity of their machines, mechanical sculpture copying was time-consuming, and that made it costly. A prime demonstration of this is provided by Watt, who conscientiously noted the time taken for each of the processes needed to make a single bust of Sappho in January 1811: a total of 39 hours.[43] Assuming a mechanical carver could produce two busts in a long, 80-hour week, perhaps three with practice, this was still far behind the output for producing plaster casts. Making portrait busts after the antique, the drapery of robes around the shoulders and breast, with complex folds and layers, was very expensive to produce by hand, whereas in cast form it could be executed quickly and cheaply.[44] And Achille Collas, manufacturing sculpture by machine in France, found that pirates immediately cast copies of his copies and sold them much cheaper than he could.[45] Francis Chantrey's bust of Sir Walter Scott was considered to be one of his finest works, and Chantrey himself made 40 copies to give to Scott's admirers – but thousands of poor-quality copies were also quickly made by Italian craftsmen based in London.[46] Watt's decision to leave the exploitation of the sculpture machines to others, like Hawkins, was a prudent one.

Watt's sculpture-copying machines are enigmatic, then. They show Watt's instinct for latching on to a new area of work and coming up with a solution. However, whether that solution would ever have found a viable purpose outside the workshop is questionable. Late in life Watt turned away from a commercial application for the machines to making sculpture simply for the stimulation and challenge of creating something new. And create he did, in vast quantities: Watt's complete sculpture collection, which remains largely hidden in the Science Museum's stores, contains approximately 400 casts, originals, copies, busts, cameos, medallions and more, from figures in the Egyptian style to busts of Niobe, Homer and Aristotle.[47] Friends and associates from Joseph Black to the astronomer William Herschel found their image multiplied on the machines. Watt even obtained a death mask of Matthew Boulton following his death in 1809, and this was copied six times in reduced form.

What became more significant than the commercial aspects of sculpture for Watt were the practicalities of multiplying his own image. And among his friends and colleagues, Watt found time to manufacture self-portraits in considerable numbers. Twenty small medallion-size portraits survive in his sculpture collection, and so do a number of large portrait busts: two by Sir Francis Chantrey and three by Peter Turnerelli. The Turnerelli bust, executed in 1807, is rather unflattering, but Chantrey's, commissioned by Watt in 1814, was strikingly successful; Watt himself copied it to send to his friends 'as the productions of a young artist just entering on

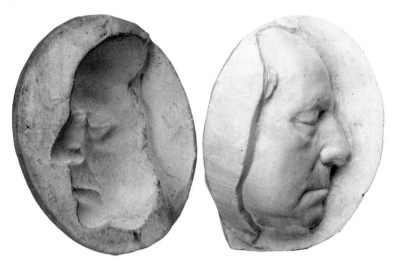

A reduced-size plaster mould and cast from the death mask of Matthew Boulton, James Watt's business partner and friend, made 1809–19.

his eighty-third year', reduced in size as he did not think himself 'of importance enough to fill up so much of my friends' house as the original bust does'.[48] Chantrey and Watt knew each other well, discussing together the copying machines, and as Chantrey portrayed Watt in life, so he also had the job of memorializing him in death. The two men exchanged final letters in May 1818, and the following year, on 19 August, Watt died at Heathfield, aged 83. Chantrey's bust was the basis for a full-size statue on his tomb at St Mary's Church, Handsworth, where Watt was interred as he wished, 'in the most private manner without show or parade'.[49] Other versions were placed in London, Glasgow and Edinburgh. It was acclaimed as the finest resemblance of a man eulogized on his monument in Westminster Abbey as one of 'the real Benefactors of the World'.

As well as the Chantrey and Turnerelli busts, Watt's workshop contains a mystery object that has only recently been identified. On the central workbench sat a highly complex plaster mould comprising 43 separate parts. In 2010 conservators painstakingly opened the mould and separated the individual pieces to reveal a man – but who? The parts were scanned with a laser to produce a digital image, and these were then combined electronically to reveal a previously unknown bust of Watt, which was rendered into a physical artefact using a three-dimensional printer that built up layers of nylon fused together by heat.[50] Establishing the author of the bust involved further detective work; among his sculpture collection was a small low-relief self-portrait of Watt that closely resembled the new bust. The small copy was signed on the back, in Watt's hand, 'Reduced from Gahagan's bust by scraping 1807' – giving a date for the original and a pointer to one of the Gahagan family of sculptors, although which of them remains unclear, being the artist commissioned to make the original.[51]

Watt was, then, generating images of himself in considerable quantities. Maria Edgeworth visited Heathfield in April 1820, and noted the array of portraits of Watt that greeted her: 'his picture, his bust, his image everywhere'.[52] His bust proved highly charismatic: when Edgeworth saw it she was struck 'almost breathless', and in 1841 a writer was inspired by it to write that 'As I came home, the booming rattle of the train seemed like the spirit of Watt still animating inert matter.'[53] By generating images of himself, Watt was carrying out on a small scale a process that was to be repeated much

Portrait bust of James Watt newly manufactured in 2010 from the original mould (1807), also shown in sections, by one of the Gahagan family of sculptors.

more widely after his death. Immortalized in marble, plaster or ivory, he became the human face of far wider changes transforming the face of industrial Britain.

Watt's copying machines represent a growing trend towards the mechanization of all sorts of manufactures. Their nearest industrial counterparts were the machines used by the Bank of England to make the dies for minting coins, which used a similar stylus and cutting tool arrangement to engrave the detail of an original produced by an artist onto a steel copy. The multiplication of the finished product fell to Matthew Boulton, who turned his attention to minting machinery driven by Watt's engine; a single set of eight coining presses could produce more than 460,000 halfpenny coins, each perfectly identical, in every twelve-hour working day.[54] Boulton's minting machines are suggestive of a broader trend towards mechanization; in cotton factories, an automatic spinning machine of 1825 could process 100 lb of cotton sixteen times faster than the equivalent machine in 1780, in only 125 hours as opposed to 2,000.[55] The changes in machine tools, machines for building other machines, were equally far-ranging, and their potentialities are demonstrated by the steam hammers built by James Nasmyth of Manchester, which replaced the team of sweating hammermen plying their sledges, or the water-powered helve wheel, with a giant steam-powered hammer head that could pound the heaviest forging or delicately crack the shell of an egg in a wine glass, as it was often called upon to do at public demonstrations. Faced with these new capabilities, Thomas Carlyle, in his essay 'Signs of the Times' of 1829, characterized the period as 'not an Heroical, Devotional, Philosophical, or Moral Age, but, above all others, the Mechanical Age. It is the Age of Machinery, in every outward and inward sense of that word.'[56] And these machines were increasingly 'self-acting', incorporating into their mechanisms the skills previously bred into the expert artisans who worked with them.

Watt's steam engine was the icon of Carlyle's age of machinery, instrumental in 'effecting the most remarkable revolution in all departments of industry that the world has ever seen'.[57] By 1850 Britain was using half as much steam power again as the whole of western Europe.[58] The historian Asa Briggs has written of a widely accepted 'gospel of steam' based, for example, on the creative power of invention that it represented, the universality of its expected capabilities and the rising living standards that it brought.[59] Although historians have realized since that the expectations of steam, and its status as a symbol of progress, ran somewhat in advance of its actual employment, and waterwheels actually provided more power generation than engines until the mid-nineteenth century, this did not reflect at that time on Watt himself.

The Romantic poet William Wordsworth believed Watt was, 'considering both the magnitude and the universality of his genius . . . perhaps the most extraordinary man that this country ever pro-duced'.[60] He became the first engineer to be commemorated in Westminster Abbey, with a memorial installed in 1834 following a decade of lobbying by many prominent figures representing Britain's new industrial interests. Watt became a new kind of industrial hero, compared to Isaac Newton in astronomy and William Shakespeare in literature. He was elevated into the traditional national pantheon of aristocrats and monarchs, military men and statesmen. And in this respect Watt blazed a trail for the community of engineers and inventors to attain heroic stature in the third quarter of the nine-teenth century. [61]

Images of Watt, in the shape of portraits and busts, statues and memorials, played a major role in his posthumous promotion; a whole genre of 'Watt art' sprang up. The story that, as a child, he had toyed with the steam issuing from a kettle to try to ascertain its nature acquired the status of a parable in Victorian Britain, and was depicted in a series of popular prints.[62] Another mezzotint by J. E. Lauder, dated 1860, shows Watt as a Romantic, philosophical figure, leaning over John Anderson's model of the engine, concentrating intently and solving its problems by the power of thought. And when portraits of Britain's 51 most distinguished men of science were put together into a single ensemble image of that name by William Walker in 1862, Watt sat prominently at the very centre, the focal point for the image and, by extension, the community of scientists and engineers standing around him.

The generation of so much iconography around Watt fed debates about the nature of his achievements throughout the nineteenth

James Scott after R. W. Buss, *Watt's First Experiment of Steam*, 1849.

century. First, these concerned his priority with the steam engine and how it measured up to that built by others. The earliest articles that surveyed the engine's development, in the *Encyclopaedia Britannica* of 1797, were written by Watt's friend John Robison with input from Watt.[63] An article in Olinthus Gregory's *Treatise on Mechanics* of 1807, accusing Watt of seeking to 'repress the energies of his contemporaries' and monopolize engine construction, was suppressed after pressure from Watt.[64] After Watt's death in 1819 his son remained avidly protective of his father's reputation; François Arago, who wrote the first biography of James Senior, wrote of 'the religious respect with which my friend the present Mr James Watt regards all that recalls the remembrance of his father'.[65]

This careful shaping of Watt's legacy reflects a second aspect of the debate about him: whether he was a philosopher or a craftsman. In his retirement Watt was keen to emphasize the 'philosophical' nature of his work on the steam engine. This was particularly manifested in manipulation of the story that, as a child, he was enthralled by the steam issuing from a kettle. Although the story as subsequently told concerned the potential industrial *power* of the steam, Watt and his son instead emphasized that it was about the steam's philosophical *properties* – in fact, Watt Junior himself modified the original account.[66] Watt's intention in emphasizing this was to explain his independence from Joseph Black in devising the theories of heat that underpinned the steam engine's performance. By comparison, subsequent biographers, most notably Samuel Smiles, gave Watt's workshop prominence in their accounts, identifying it as a place of handicraft rather than philosophy. Historian David Miller argues that in so doing, Smiles 'was effectively developing an image of Watt that projected the old craftsman of the Heathfield Hall workshop backwards, rather than the young philosopher of the kettle myth forwards, in time'.[67]

The controversy over Watt's legacy, and what he stood for, has raged up to the present day as engineering and science have been afforded differing degrees of priority.[68] Watt was at first perceived as a lone heroic engineer, but from the late 1820s, as the engineering profession transformed Britain with bold new railway and civil engineering projects, he was joined by others like Isambard Kingdom Brunel and George Stephenson. In the final quarter of the nineteenth century there was a move away from praising engineers and inventors to emphasizing the role of the scientist and 'basic scientific research', and replacing talk of inventions with 'applied science'.[69] By the centenary of Watt's death in 1919, however, he had been firmly reappropriated as a craftsman and engineer: it is telling that one of the largest groups of contributors to the commemorative appeal launched in 1919 'comprised workers in engineering and metalworking firms throughout the Birmingham region'.[70] Most recently the debate has come full circle, and Watt has been a case study in the interplay of ideas between science and industry, and the subject of detailed reconstructions of the philosophical world that he lived in. However, amid the books and two-dimensional material, the busts and other sculptural representations of Watt, his workshop itself has sometimes been mentioned but rarely considered in detail. Exploring what happened to the workshop after Watt's death in 1819 sheds new light on how to think about Watt, and all that he stood for.

As Watt was continuously reappraised and reappropriated by different groups, his workshop always remained as a presence in the background. Watt's wife Anne continued to live at Heathfield until her own death in 1832 but, in Watt's will, he carefully left all his 'books and prints . . . tools models book cases drugs and curiosities', the majority of which were in the workshop, to his son.[71] Watt Junior kept the workshop door firmly locked and the room remained entirely untouched until his own death in 1848. It was only opened for the first time for Watt's biographer J. P. Muirhead in 1853. Muirhead's description of the workshop indicates its tremendous imaginative power, for he wrote that

> The classical 'garret' and all its mysterious contents . . . have ever since been carefully preserved in the same order as when the hand and 'eye of the master' were last withdrawn from them . . . all things there seemed still to breathe of the spirit that once gave them life and energy; and only the presence of some reverend dust silently announced, that no profane hand, forgetful of the '*religio loci*' [place of sanctity], had been permitted to violate the sanctities of that magical retreat.[72]

For Muirhead the workshop was a place of religious significance, as it was for the biographer Samuel Smiles, who finished a detailed account of its contents by stating that in it the 'spirit' of Watt's work survived, as if embodied in the artefacts 'fast crumbling to decay'.[73] Here was the workshop as an industrial shrine. Even if it had remained untouched for so long, the mere fact of its existence cast a spell over those concerned with Watt and how he was presented. It particularly did so for Bennet Woodcroft, director of the Patent Office Museum.

Woodcroft (1803–1879) was chief among the nineteenth-century pursuers of Watt 'relics'. An engineer and inventor from Sheffield, he had worked in textile weaving and printing and in marine propulsion, where he patented a series of screw propellers. With growing expertise on the operation of Britain's patent system, in the 1850s he was charged with establishing the basic infrastructure to efficiently administer an expanding torrent of inventions seeking patent protection. As well as making information about patents more easily accessible, including the monumental task of publishing over 14,000 specifications in five years, Woodcroft also began the Patent Office library of technical literature, developed a portrait gallery of inventors and assembled a collection of artefacts that were housed in the Patent Office Museum in South Kensington, London.[74] Woodcroft was highly active, his patent work was strategically important to Britain as nineteenth-century industry expanded and, with the Patent Museum, he had the chance to indulge his antiquarian instincts. He was a forceful character, obstinate, determined and difficult to thwart in pursuit of historic artefacts for the collections, and high on his list of desirable acquisitions for the Patent Museum were artefacts associated with Watt.

Early among these was a 'tea kettle' said to be in the possession of Watt's descendants. James Gibson Watt, then head of the Watt family, wrote to the Patent Museum on 27 September 1863: 'I am satisfied it is not . . . the one which he originally observed the steam lifting the lid when boiling on the fire . . . The one I have was evidently made by his orders and used as an experimentalising steam kettle.'[75] Undaunted, the museum curator Francis Pettit Smith replied, 'As this one was actually constructed for and used by James Watt in his early investigations of the properties of steam it cannot fail to attract great notice and prove to be a very interesting & valuable acquisition to our present collection.'[76] The kettle was subsequently delivered to the Patent Museum by Mr Gibson Watt's solicitor and it remains on display today, close to two of Watt's oldest steam engines, also acquired for the museum in 1861: the 'Lap' engine of 1788, and fragments of 'Old Bess', dating from 1777.[77]

Alongside these items, however, Watt's workshop remained the ultimate prize. Bennet Woodcroft wrote to a Birmingham contact in May 1863, remarking on 'a rumour now current that the Trustees of the late Mr Watt contemplate opening the room at Heathfield Hall . . . which, by agreement with the tenant, has been hitherto kept closed'.[78] That came to nothing, but four months later, Francis Pettit Smith wrote rather unsubtly to James Gibson Watt, 'How often I have longed to take a peep into Heathfield . . . where I am informed a host of invaluable relics do still exist – which in honour to the illustrious man should once more see the daylight – and be preserved to the end of time in some public institute like this.'[79] By January 1864 no progress had been made, and Woodcroft, exasperated, wrote to Pettit Smith, 'I am ready to go with you any day to Birmingham whether Mr Gibson Watt gives his permission or not. If I can't go into the house I will stand outside.'[80] Woodcroft and Smith finally got into the workshop with Gibson Watt on Wednesday, 5 April 1864, having spent twenty minutes fighting with the door and then breaking the window frame in an attempt to open it. Woodcroft's subsequent letter to a colleague, Sir John Romilly, provided details of what he found within, from the initial 'stratum of dust', to the contents beneath, which were 'most systematically arranged'. Woodcroft continued,

> In drawers were found splendid works of art carved by [sculpture copying] machines & produced in a variety of substances from marble, mother of pearl, to common deal. At Christie and Mantons these works produced by James Watt's own hands with the aid of machinery made by himself would realize fabulous prices. Mechanical drawings, chemicals, optical instruments and almost every imaginable thing that room contains.

The visitors were so engrossed in what they saw that they spent seven hours exploring, and Woodcroft left his glasses behind; they

Watt's alleged 'experimentalising steam kettle', forming part of a self-contained 'bachelor's stove' with grate and cooking pan, *c.* 1760.

were later returned to him by Mary Pemberton, daughter of the tenant, accompanied by a 'kindly expressed' note.[81]

Woodcroft's fascination with the workshop reflected a very particular, mechanical view of the world and of Watt. This view was based on a realization that many of the industrial sites and machines of Britain's Industrial Revolution were, even in the 1860s, at risk of destruction. The Penydarren Ironworks in South Wales, one of the six largest in Britain, closed in 1859, and the buildings were ruined and abandoned before 1870.[82] Many other ironworks followed, unable to compete with cheaper steel production. In Birmingham the Soho establishments associated with Boulton and Watt were disappearing, too. The engineer J. C. Fischer revisited the Soho Foundry in July 1851, but reported that

this great plant had suffered a complete decline . . . The many workshops were quite empty, deserted, and decayed . . . I would never have believed so rapid a change possible had I not seen it with my own eyes. Here as in many another place the inscription 'sic transit gloria mundi' would indeed be appropriate.[83]

A short distance away, the Soho Manufactory was either empty or being sublet, and was demolished in early 1863.[84] The first items of correspondence between Woodcroft and Watt's descendants date from May 1863, suggesting that the loss of the Soho building may have piqued Woodcroft's initial interest in preserving Watt's workshop.[85]

Individual machines also faced an uncertain future. Just as Woodcroft was gearing up to acquire Watt's workshop, he was also pursuing the engine from Henry Bell's steamship *Comet*, which marked the beginning of steam navigation in Britain.[86] The engine had been built on the Clyde Estuary in 1812, not far from Watt's home town in Greenock. However, the vessel was wrecked on rocks at Craignish Point in the Sound of Jura. The engine was salvaged and put to work at two Glasgow factories before being moved to Glasgow Polytechnic which, in 1855, burned down: the engine was buried by the collapsing building. Unsurprisingly the engine was described as being 'in a very rusty dilapidated condition' by 1862.[87] This galvanized Woodcroft into action: he wrote to Francis Pettit Smith, 'Get the Comet engine as soon as possible in all its filth.'[88] Even with the main negotiations concluded, one further task remained: to obtain the engine's original cylinder. It was eventually obtained 'not by purchase but as a special gift from Mr Bell's widow, in whose home . . . it was doing duty as a chimney can!'[89] Given the viscitudes experienced by many historic machines before finding places of refuge, the survival of Watt's workshop is exceptional.

Even if an artefact did perchance find its way to a museum, its survival was still not guaranteed, because popular fascination with historic machines was manifested in a very tactile, hands-on way. Robert Southey had complained in 1807 that 'The English have a barbarous habit of seeing by the sight of touch . . . they can never look at any thing without having it in their hand, nor show it to another person without touching it with a stick.'[90] In 1782, upon visiting Stratford upon Avon to see William Shakespeare's chair, a popular attraction for visitors, Karl Phillip Moritz wrote that it 'was so cut to pieces that it hardly looked like a chair; for every one that travels through Stratford, cuts off a chip, as a remembrance which he carefully preserves, and deems a precious relique'.[91] In the 1860s visitors to the Patent Office Museum treated the historic machines in the same way. Francis Pettit Smith commented in 1864 that 'There is a very curious taste on the part of the English public to pull things about, and we are forced to put everything under glass cases, or else it would be taken to pieces.'[92] Later, in 1877, the then curator of the Patent Office Museum, Archibald Stuart Wortley, protested that the historic steam locomotive *Rocket* was 'suffering much from the public picking off scaling pieces of rust' and 'carrying them away as memorials'.[93] Just as inventors achieved heroic status after 1850, so did the objects they built. Flakes of rust replaced the remains of saints, and the splinters of Shakespeare's chair, as the holy relics of nineteenth-century industry.

As with so many other artefacts, the future of Watt's workshop was never entirely certain. Woodcroft forged ahead with the construction of a special room to accommodate it in his 'fire-proof, police guarded' offices at Southampton Row in London's Holborn district and, for good measure, had built for James Gibson Watt a

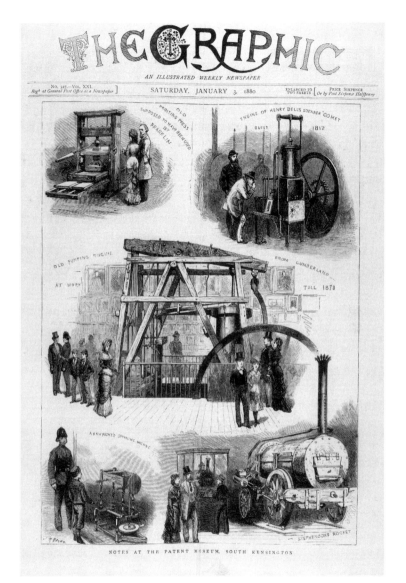

The Patent Museum on the front page of the *Graphic* newspaper (1878).
The heroic objects pictured include Richard Arkwright's spinning machine
at bottom left, the locomotive *Rocket* alongside it, and the 'Comet' marine
engine at top right.

facsimile of a small engine that had belonged to his illustrious predecessor, which was almost certainly intended as a gift to smooth the path of negotiation towards acquiring the workshop.[94] It was not for want of trying, then, that Woodcroft's work ultimately came to nothing. His masters at the Treasury complained at the cost of acquiring the workshop and the risk of a financial payout if, having been acquired, it was subsequently damaged or destroyed.[95] A competing group, the Birmingham-based Committee of the James Watt Memorial, was also attempting to preserve the workshop in April 1865. They were led by prominent local antiquarian Samuel Timmins, who had declared: 'It is most greatly to be desired that these great and priceless memorials of the genius of James Watt may . . . be preserved for ever for the veneration of the future pilgrims to the shrines of industrial heroes.'[96] Finding themselves caught between Timmins in Birmingham and Woodcroft in London, Watt's descendants adopted a policy of strict neutrality: Timmins tried to gain hold of the workshop again in 1876, getting as far as removing some of its contents before being ordered by telegram to put them back again.[97]

The workshop remained at Heathfield for the rest of the nineteenth century. The last word on the matter for Bennet Woodcroft came in April 1877, almost a year after he had officially retired. Reviewing his correspondence regarding the workshop, he wrote, 'I felt disappointed with my own productions. They fall far short of doing justice to the subject.'[98] This is uncharacteristic of a man who was usually so bullish, and it would have been a source of some regret to him that the sacred precincts of the workshop were being violated. After 1864 the Pemberton family, tenants of Heathfield, became guardians of the key for the workshop door. They had found all Watt's old furniture stored away in an outbuilding, and 'filled up corners and other odd spaces in play and bed-rooms with costly old cabinets and bureaux and within them displayed our treasures' – it remains a possibility that they found their way inside the workshop, too.[99] Worse was to come. In 1876 Heathfield was let to prominent Birmingham industrialist Sir George Tangye, and the events leading up to his moving in were only revealed after the workshop was acquired by the Science Museum. Major Gibson Watt, then head of the family, thinking Tangye would require the space in the workshop, wrote that his father

> had everything packed up . . . 20 cases were sent off . . . when Mr Tangye said he would be only too pleased to keep the attic as it was. Everything that had not been despatched was therefore unpacked & put back in its original position as near as possible. That is not generally known, & I have not mentioned it to anyone before.[100]

Far from being undisturbed, the workshop contents were subject to some considerable disruption.

Aside from unexpected removals, the workshop contents were in a parlous physical condition by the 1880s. Roasted in summer, frozen in winter, with woodworm attacking the framing of the sculpture machines, and even errant visitors moving or removing artefacts, the workshop entered a period of decline.[101] It may have been during this period that a lavatory pan dating from the 1850s found its way, upended, into one corner of the room. However, this deterioration also provided motivation to record its contents and, for the first time, a more detailed understanding was reached of what the workshop actually contained. Edward Collins, the man responsible for managing the Heathfield estate, made a detailed inventory that recorded 2,626 individual objects, or groups of items, and described what he thought they were.[102] What is clear from the inventory is the sheer diversity of the workshop's contents: although Bennet Woodcroft sought to acquire the workshop as a shrine to Watt the steam engineer, he was inadvertently preserving evidence of a very different Watt who worked on a wide range of other projects.

The multifaceted nature of the workshop had already been noted by Samuel Smiles when he visited it in 1864 or 1865, and his evocation of what he saw is valuable enough to be quoted in detail:

> Many objects lay about or in the drawers . . . busts, medallions, and figures, waiting to be copied by the sculpture machine, many medallion moulds, a store of plaster of Paris, and a box of plaster casts from London. Here are Watt's ladles for melting

lead, his foot-rule, his glue-pot, his hammer. Reflecting mirrors, an extemporized camera with the lenses mounted on pasteboard, and many camera-glasses laid about, indicate interrupted experiments in optics. There are quadrant glasses, compasses, scales, weights, and sundry boxes of mathematical instruments ... on the shelves are minerals and chemicals in pots and jars, on which the dust of nearly half a century has settled.[103]

Smiles wrongly identified a number of items in the workshop while describing them, including a model of the governor used by Watt to regulate the speed of the steam engine. But among all this, the number of objects connected with steam can be counted on the fingers of two hands. What in fact characterizes the workshop most of all is the close proximity of objects of 'craft' and 'philosophy': thermometers lie in drawers alongside tools for engraving scales, and sets of stamps for forming letters in metal. A surveyor's tripod rests against a shelf holding apparatus specially made for Watt's experiments on heat, and glass carboys for use in chemical experiments sit with an unfinished plaster mould of a male figure after the antique.

Only in 1924 did a plan for preserving this diverse range of items finally coalesce. The centenary of Watt's death in 1919 had passed amid growing interest from local people, the Institution of Mechanical Engineers and the American Society of Engineers in preserving Heathfield. However, their negotiations in pursuit of this end were ultimately unsuccessful, and the house was proposed for demolition so that the grounds could accommodate new houses for Birmingham's expanding population. In April 1924 Henry Lyons, director of the Science Museum in London, was in contact with Major Gibson Watt, and by November 1924 it was clear that the house would not be saved. Thereafter the Science Museum moved speedily: on 17 December a team arrived on site and began carefully to pack the workshop for transport to London. With the contents removed, the floorboards were lifted, and the door and frame, window skylight, even the fireplace, followed to their new home in London. The workshop contents were reassembled in an exact reconstruction of the workshop, and today they form the centrepiece of a major gallery.

Watt would most likely be embarrassed at the amount of attention the workshop receives.

To conclude, then, we return to the question of whether Watt was a philosopher or a craftsman. There are two things to consider: the historiography of Watt – what historians have argued and written about him – and the nature of the workshop itself. The former has been fluid, and evolved over time. In comparison, the workshop itself has remained a relative constant. A very small number of objects may have gone missing in the nineteenth century, but the gaps they left behind are hard to identify among the 8,434 items that remain, and which present us with one of the fullest physical pictures remaining anywhere of life in the workshop or laboratory in the late eighteenth century. All of them belonged to one man, and the sheer quantity of material, crossing the boundaries between philosophy and craft, makes it hard to categorize the contents against any one of the labels that have been applied to Watt over time: philosopher or craftsman primarily, but engineer and chemist, as well.

In the fields of science and technology conceptions of 'craft' were for a long time particularly mechanical in their outlook. That view was sustained right up to Henry Dickinson's acquisition of Watt's workshop for the Science Museum in 1924 and beyond. David Miller has referred to Dickinson's description of Watt as 'the young workman in his leathern apron', sitting with a model of the separate condenser resting on his lap, as representing Watt the craftsman.[104] We can bring the book to a close by amplifying another of Miller's points, that Watt the philosopher and Watt the practical chemist were one and the same person.[105] In a world where not only science and technology but art and consumption besides came hand in hand, a young workman in his apron might equally have been a chemist avoiding splashes of acid or watching the thermometers during a heat experiment, a sculptor pouring wet plaster into moulds, an instrument maker engraving the scale on a quadrant, or a foundryman fettling a cast Doric column-head for the framing of a beam engine. The mutual exclusivity of the labels applied to Watt – philosopher or craftsman, particularly – becomes hard to sustain: he lived in multiple worlds, and many of his associates would have done as well. All of those worlds were ultimately underpinned by one thing, however: without the ability to do and make as well as think, ideas will forever remain just ideas. To have a material effect on the world, they have to be given tangible form. The themes highlighted in this book – power, precision, consumption and the antique – informed how this could be done during Britain's Industrial Revolution.

JAMES WATT: A CHRONOLOGY

1736   Born in Greenock, Scotland

1753   Moves to Glasgow to act as his father's agent

1755–6   Trains as an instrument maker in London

1757   Appointed instrument maker to Glasgow College

1759   Enters partnership with John Craig and opens their shop

1763   Receives John Anderson's model engine to repair

1765   John Craig dies

1767   Enters partnership with John Roebuck to develop the engine

1768   First meets Matthew Boulton and acquires a share in the Delftfield Pottery

1769   First engine at Kinneil finished, and Watt patents the separate condenser

1773   Watt's first wife dies

1774   Boulton takes over Roebuck's share of the engine, and Watt moves to Birmingham

1776   Boulton & Watt's first engine at Bloomfield Colliery starts work, and Watt remarries

1781–2	Patents obtained on improvements to the rotative engine
1790	Builds his house, Heathfield, at Handsworth, Birmingham
1792–9	Legal actions against infringers of separate condenser patent
1795	Opening of Soho Foundry
1804	Begins work on his reducing sculpture-copying machine
1809	Starts building his equal-size copying machine, and Boulton dies
1819	Dies and is buried at St Mary's Church, Handsworth

REFERENCES

Introduction: Do We Want the Dust?

1 The foregoing description is based on Collins' photographs taken from the window. Science Museum technical file T/1924–792.

2 Science Museum technical file T/1924–792, E. Collins to H. W. Dickinson, 7 December 1924.

3 Science Museum technical file T/1924–792, E. Collins to H. W. Dickinson, 16 December 1924.

4 Science Museum technical file T/1924–792, E. Collins to H. W. Dickinson, 29 December 1924.

5 Science Museum technical file T/1924–792, E. Collins to H. Lyons, 23 February 1925.

6 T. Carlyle, 'Chartism', *Critical and Miscellaneous Essays*, v (1869), p. 399.

7 J. Mokyr, *The Enlightened Economy: Britain and the Industrial Revolution, 1700–1850* (London, 2009).

8 A. Turner, *Early Scientific Instruments: Europe, 1400–1800* (London, 1987), p. 226.

9 P. Jones, *Industrial Enlightenment: Science, Technology and Culture in Birmingham and the West Midlands, 1760–1820* (Manchester, 2008).

10 J. Mokyr, *The Enlightened Economy*, p. 61.

11 Jones, *Industrial Enlightenment*, pp. 126–7.

12 J. Moxon, *Mechanick Exercises or the Doctrine of Handy-works* (Mendham, 1994). Reprinted from the 1703 edition: p. 4 of preface.

13 Mokyr, *The Enlightened Economy*, p. 110.

14 C. Fox, *The Arts of Industry in the Age of Enlightenment* (New Haven, CT, 2009), p. 8.

15 Ibid., p. 6.

16 M. Berg, *The Age of Manufactures* (London, 1994), p. xiii.

17 M. Daumas, *Scientific Instruments of the Seventeenth and Eighteenth Centuries and their Makers* (London, 1972), p. 1.

18 H. W. Dickinson and R. Jenkins, *James Watt and the Steam Engine*,
    2nd edn (London, 1989), p. 261.

19 G. Miege, *The Present State of Great-Britain and Ireland in Three Parts*,
    4th edn (London, 1718), pp. 146–7.

20 R. Porter, *A Social History of England in the 18th Century* (London, 1982),
    p. 334.

21 A. P. Wadsworth and J.D.L. Mann, *The Cotton Trade and Industrial
    Lancashire, 1600–1780* (New York, 1968), p. 413.

22 J. B. Say, *A Treatise on Political Economy*, Book 1 (Philadelphia, PA, 1855),
    p. 16.

23 R. Samuel, 'Workshop of the World: Steam Power and Hand Technology
    in Mid-Victorian Britain', *History Workshop*, III (1977), pp. 6–72.

24 D. Landes, *The Unbound Prometheus* (Cambridge, 1969), p. 5.

25 M. Berg, *Luxury and Pleasure in Eighteenth-century Britain* (Oxford, 2005),
    p. 247.

26 M. Berg, 'From Imitation to Invention: Creating Commodities in
    Eighteenth-century Britain', *Economic History Review*, LV (2002), pp. 1–30:
    p. 1.

27 L.T.C. Rolt, *Tools for the Job: A Short History of Machine Tools* (London, 1965),
    p. 56; Dickinson and Jenkins, *James Watt and the Steam Engine*, p. 263.

28 N. Hewison, 'Ormolu Ornaments', in *Matthew Boulton: Selling What All
    the World Desires*, ed. S. Mason, exh. cat., Birmingham Museums and Art
    Gallery (New Haven, CT, and London, 2009), pp. 55–62: p. 55.

29 F. Arago, *Historical Eloge of James Watt*, trans. J. P. Muirhead (London,
    1839), p. 187.

30 Ibid., p. 192.

31 T. S. Ashton, *The Industrial Revolution, 1760–1830* (London, 1948), p. 58;
    Mokyr, *The Enlightened Economy*, p. 391.

32 D. P. Miller, *James Watt, Chemist* (London, 2009), p. 82.

33 H. Torrens, 'Some Thoughts on the History of Technology and Its Current
    Condition in Britain', *History of Technology*, 22 (2000), pp. 223–32: p. 226.

34 N. Scarfe, ed., *Innocent Espionage: The La Rochefoucauld Brothers' Tour of
    England in 1785* (Woodbridge, 1995), p. xix.

35 D. Cannadine, 'Engineering History, or the History of Engineering?
    Re-writing the Technological Past', *Transactions of the Newcomen Society*,
    LXXIV (2004), pp. 163–180: p. 167.

36 G. Head, *A Home Tour Through the Manufacturing Districts of England,
    in the Summer of 1835* (New York, 1836), p. 157.

37 R. W. Emerson, *English Traits* (Boston, 1866), pp. 88–9.

38 W. L. Webb, 'Patrick O'Brien' obituary, *The Guardian*, 8 January 2000,
    www.guardian.co.uk, accessed 24 September 2012.

39 K. Farrer, ed., *Letters of Josiah Wedgwood to 1770* (Manchester, 1903),
    pp. 325–6.

Chapter One: Sensible, Ingenious and Enterprising Men, 1736–56

1   D. Defoe, *A Tour through the Island of Great Britain* (London, 1748), vol. II, p. 91.

2   *Industrial Revolution: A Documentary History, Series Three* (Marlborough, 1999), Reel 15, JWP 6/36.34, J. Watt to J. Watt Senior, 19 June 1755.

3   J. Boswell, *The Life of Dr Johnson* (London, 1840), p. 539.

4   M. L. Mare and W. H. Quarrell, eds, *Lichtenberg's Visits to England, as Described in his Letters and Diaries* (Oxford, 1938), p. 45.

5   Defoe, *A Tour through the Island of Great Britain*, vol. II, p. 147.

6   Leather tanning often used immense vats of dog excrement, the enzymes in which softened the hides so they could be worked more easily. T. Covington, *Tanning Chemistry: The Science of Leather* (London, 2009), p. 166; B. Faujas de Saint Fond, *A Journey Through England and Scotland to the Hebrides in 1784*, ed. A. Geikle (Glasgow, 1907), vol. I, p. 114.

7   The boatmen who worked on the River Thames were renowned for their swearing. Peter Ackroyd even suggests that Handel's *Water Music* was composed to drown them out during George I's first formal trip on the river. Peter Ackroyd, *London: The Biography* (London, 2000), p. 553.

8   François de La Rochefoucauld, *A Frenchman in England*, ed. J. Marchand (Cambridge, 1933), p. 20.

9   G. Birkbeck, ed., *Boswell's The Life of Samuel Johnson, LLD, including a Journal of his Tour to the Hebrides* (London, 1839), p. 56.

10   *Travels of Carl Philipp Moritz in England, 1782: A Reprint of the English Translation of 1785* (London, 1924), pp. 30–31.

11   C. William, ed., *Sophie in London 1786; being the Diary of Sophie V. La Roche* (London, 1933), p. 43.

12   R. Porter, *A Social History of England in the 18th Century* (London, 1982), p. 23.

13   *Travels of Carl Philipp Moritz in England, 1782*, p. 18.

14   *The Letters of Horace Walpole, Earl of Orford*, vol. II: *1744–1753* (London, 1840), p. 419.

15   See his diary for 28 September 1665, for example.

16   W. Blackstone, *Commentaries on the Laws of England*, 15th edn (London, 1809), pp. 441–2.

17   J. Brewer, 'Commercialisation and Politics', in *The Birth of a Consumer Society*, ed. N. McKendrick, J. Brewer and J. H. Plumb (London, 1982), p. 211.

18   A. de Tocqueville, *Journeys in England and Ireland*, ed. Jacob Peter Mayer (London, 1979), pp. 106–7.

19 J. Mokyr, *The Enlightened Economy: Britain and the Industrial Revolution, 1700–1850* (London, 2009), p. 172; P. Deane and W. A. Cole, *British Economic Growth* (Cambridge, 1962), p. 75.

20 Mokyr, *The Enlightened Economy*, p. 178.

21 Peter Matthias, *The First Industrial Nation*, 2nd edn (London, 1983), p. 65.

22 Ibid., p. 166; Phyllis Deane, 'The British Industrial Revolution', in *The Industrial Revolution in National Context*, ed. Mikulas Teich and Roy Porter (Cambridge, 1996), pp. 13–35: p. 25.

23 Porter, *A Social History of England in the 18th Century*, p. 333.

24 Mokyr, *The Enlightened Economy*, pp. 306, 308.

25 Once arrived, he earned himself a job by wearing a wooden hat of oval cross-section, which he had ingeniously manufactured on a lathe.

26 C. Hibbert, ed., *An American in Regency England: The Journal of a Tour of 1810–11* (London, 1968), p. 15.

27 Robert Southey, *Letters from England* [1807], ed. J. Simmons (London, 1951), p. 202.

28 Science Museum inv. 1997–32/1, manuscript journal of Robert Hamilton, 1796–99.

29 R. L. Hills, *James Watt*, vol. 1: *His Time in Scotland, 1736–1774* (Ashbourne, 2002), p. 36.

30 J. P. Muirhead, *The Life of James Watt, with Selections from his Correspondence* (London, 1858), p. 13.

31 Ibid., p. 25.

32 A. E. Musson and E. Robinson, *Science and Technology in the Industrial Revolution* (Manchester, 1969), pp. 22–3.

33 Muirhead, *The Life of James Watt* , p. 487.

34 Ibid., p. 23.

35 Ibid., pp. 28–9.

36 Hills, *James Watt*, vol. 1: *His Time in Scotland*, p. 42.

37 H. Hamilton, *An Economic History of Scotland in the Eighteenth Century* (Oxford, 1963), p. 16.

38 Ibid., p. 237.

39 *Industrial Revolution: A Documentary History, Series Three* (Marlborough, 1999), Reel 1, JWP 4/11.160, J. Watt to J. Watt Senior, 11 June 1754.

40 *Industrial Revolution: A Documentary History, Series Three* (Marlborough, 1999), Reel 1, JWP 4/11.161, 'A List of James Watt Clothes Taken to Glasgow'.

41 *James Watt*, vol. 1: *His Time in Scotland*, p. 48.

42 Muirhead, *The Life of James Watt*, p. 23.

43 *Industrial Revolution: A Documentary History, Series Three* (Marlborough, 1999), Reel 1, 6/46.1, J. Watt to J. Watt Senior, 19 August 1756; R. Porter, *Enlightenment: Britain and the Creation of the Modern World* (London, 2000), pp. 35–36.

44 *Travels of Carl Philipp Moritz in England, 1782*, p. 87.

45 W. G. Hoskins, *The Making of the English Landscape* (London, 1955), p. 202.

46 P. Mantoux, *The Industrial Revolution in the Eighteenth Century*, 2nd edn (London, 1961), p. 114.

47 J. Langton and R. J. Morris, eds, *Atlas of Industrializing Britain, 1780–1914* (London, 1986), p. 80.

48 Mantoux, *The Industrial Revolution in the Eighteenth Century*, p. 115.

49 Langton and Morris, eds, *Atlas of Industrializing Britain*, p. 82, fig. 9.3.

50 Matthias, *The First Industrial Nation*, p. 104.

51 N. Scarfe, ed., *Innocent Espionage: The La Rochefoucauld Brothers' Tour of England in 1785* (Woodbridge, 1995), p. 158.

52 Langton and Morris, eds, *Atlas of Industrializing Britain*, p. 86.

53 Scarfe, ed., *Innocent Espionage*, p. 118.

54 P. Bagwell, *The Transport Revolution from 1770* (London, 1974), pp. 63–4.

55 Ibid., p. 22; *James Watt*, vol. 1: *His Time in Scotland*, p. 33.

56 M. Daunton, *Progress and Poverty* (Oxford, 1995), p. 287.

57 Matthias, *The First Industrial Nation*, p. 38; P. Hudson, *The Industrial Revolution* (London, 1992), pp. 52–3.

58 Porter, *A Social History of England in the 18th Century*, p. 91.

59 Jean Marchand, ed., *A Frenchman in England, 1784* (Cambridge, 1933), p. 197.

60 *Travels of Carl Philipp Moritz in England, 1782*, p. 66.

61 *Industrial Revolution: A Documentary History, Series Three* (Marlborough, 1999), Reel 1, JWP 4/11.117, J. Watt to J. Watt Senior.

62 E. Hobsbawm, *The Age of Revolution, 1789–1848* (London, 1995), p. 31.

63 *James Watt*, vol. 1: *His Time in Scotland*, p. 48.

64 Scarfe, ed., *Innocent Espionage*, p. 154.

65 Marchand, ed., *A Frenchman in England, 1784*, p. 29.

66 Mare and Quarrell, eds, *Lichtenberg's Visits to England*, p. xiv.

67 P. Langford, *A Polite and Commercial People: England, 1727–1783* (Oxford, 1999), p. 666.

68 Landes, *The Unbound Prometheus*, p. 62.

69 Mathias, *The First Industrial Nation*, p. 49.

70 K. Morgan, ed., *An American Quaker in Britain: The Travel Journals of Jabez Maud Fisher, 1775–1779* (Oxford, 1992), p. 235.

71 Landes, *The Unbound Prometheus*, p. 73.

72 Mantoux, *The Industrial Revolution in the Eighteenth Century*, p. 373.

73 Ibid., p. 395.

74 Porter, *A Social History of England in the 18th Century*, p. 336.

75 J. Tucker, *Instructions for Travellers* (Dublin, 1758), pp. 39–40

76 *Travels of Carl Philipp Moritz in England, 1782*, p. 122.

77 C. MacLeod, *Inventing the Industrial Revolution: The English Patent System, 1660–1800* (Cambridge, 1988).

78 Mokyr, *The Enlightened Economy*, p. 404.

79 D. Defoe, *The Complete English Tradesman* (London, 1727), vol. ii, p. 297.

80 Mokyr, *The Enlightened Economy*, pp. 384, 386.

81 *Travels of Carl Philipp Moritz in England, 1782*, p. 152.

82 *Industrial Revolution: A Documentary History, Series Three*, Reel 1, JWP 6/46.33, J. Marr to Watt Senior., 24 June 1755.

83 *Industrial Revolution: A Documentary History, Series Three*, Reel 1, JWP 6/46.

84 JWP 6/46.30, 21 July 1755.

85 JWP 6/46.31, 15 July 1755.

86 JWP 6/46.28, 6 August 1755.

87 JWP 6/46.31.

88 Scarfe, ed., *Innocent Espionage*, p. 55.

89 Morgan, ed., *An American Quaker in Britain*, pp. 285–6.

90 Jones, *Industrial Enlightenment*, p. 98.

91 *Travels of Carl Philipp Moritz in England, 1782*, p. 164.

92 JWP 6/46.7, 7 June 1756.

93 JWP 6/46.32, 1 July 1755.

94 JWP 6/46.26, 9 August 1755.

95 JWP 6/46.12, 18 March 1756.

96 JWP 6/46.8, 18 May 1756.

97 JWP 6/46.16, 27 December 1755; JWP 6/46.12, 18 March 1756.

98 JWP 6/46.17, 29 November 1755.

99 JWP 6/46.11, 18 March 1756.

100 JWP 6/46.29, 5 August 1755.

101 JWP 6/46.30, 21 July 1755; JWP 6/46.19, 25 October 1755.

102 A. McConnell, *Jesse Ramsden (1735–1800): London's Leading Scientific Instrument Maker* (Aldershot, 2007), p. 67.

103 T. S. Ashton, *Iron and Steel in the Industrial Revolution* (Manchester, 1924), p. 194.

104 JWP 6/46.28, London, 6 August 1755.

105 JWP 6/46.23, London, 2 September 1755.

106 JWP 6/46.11, London, 26 April 1756.

107 Morgan, ed., *An American Quaker in Britain*, p. 255.

Chapter Two: Artists of High Reputation, 1757–64

1 John Slezer, *Theatrum Scottiae* (1693), available at National Library of Scotland, http://digital.nls.uk, accessed 23 August 2012.

2 S. Smiles, *Lives of the Engineers: The Steam-engine. Boulton and Watt* (London, 1878), p. 29; J. A. Denholm, *The History of the City of Glasgow and Suburbs: Compiled from Authentic Records and Other Respectable Authorities* (Glasgow, 1798), p. 101.

3   E. Robinson and A. E. Musson, *James Watt and the Steam Revolution: A Documentary History* (London, 1969), pp. 24–5.

4   R. L. Hills, *James Watt*, vol. 1: *His Time in Scotland, 1736–1774* (Ashbourne, 2002), p. 71.

5   W. Smellie, *Literary and Characteristical Lives of John Gregory, Henry Home, Lord Kames, David Hume, and Adam Smith* (Edinburgh, 1800), p. 161. Smellie, from Lanarkshire in Scotland, founded the *Encyclopedia Britannica*.

6   J. Keir, *The First Part of a Dictionary of Chemistry &c.* (Birmingham, 1789), p. iii; P. Jones, *Industrial Enlightenment: Science, Technology and Culture in Birmingham and the West Midlands, 1760–1820* (Manchester, 2008), p. 1.

7   A. Turner, *Early Scientific Instruments: Europe, 1400–1800* (London, 1987), p. 183.

8   A. Morrison-Low, *Making Scientific Instruments during the Industrial Revolution* (Aldershot, 2007), p. 46.

9   Ibid., pp. 249–84.

10   M. L. Mare and W. H. Quarrell, eds, *Lichtenberg's Visits to England, as Described in his Letters and Diaries* (Oxford, 1938), p. 159.

11   B. Faujas de Saint Fond, *A Journey Through England and Scotland to the Hebrides in 1784*, ed. A. Geikle (Glasgow, 1907), vol. 1, p. 91.

12   A. McConnell, 'Jesse Ramsden, London's Leading Scientific Maker – Why?', *Bulletin of the Scientific Instrument Society*, 93 (2007), pp. 2–6: p. 4; Science Museum inv. 1952–73.

13   A. E. Musson and E. Robinson, *Science and Technology in the Industrial Revolution* (Manchester, 1969), p. 103.

14   Simon Schaffer, 'The Consuming Flame: Electrical Showmen and Tory Mystics in the World of Goods', in *Consumption and the World of Goods*, ed. J. Brewer and R. Porter (London, 1993), pp. 489–526: p. 492.

15   G. L'E. Turner, 'Eighteenth-century Scientific Instruments and their Makers', in *Cambridge History of Science*, ed. R. Porter (Cambridge, 2003), pp. 511–35: p. 516.

16   Peter Jones, *Industrial Enlightenment: Science, Technology and Culture in Birmingham and the West Midlands, 1760–1820* (Manchester, 2008), p. 75.

17   Larry Stewart, 'A Meaning for Machines: Modernity, Utility and the Eighteenth-century British Public', *Journal of Modern History*, LXX (1998), pp. 259–94: pp. 281, 282.

18   Larry Stewart, 'Science and the Eighteenth-century Public', in *The Enlightenment World*, ed. P. Jones, M. FitzPatrick, C. Knellwolf and I. McCalman (Abingdon, 2004), pp. 234–52: p. 240.

19   Morrison-Low, *Making Scientific Instruments during the Industrial Revolution*, p. 204.

20   Ibid., p. 282.

21 N.A.M. Rodger, *The Wooden World: An Anatomy of the Georgian Navy* (London, 1988), pp. 46, 48.

22 A. Chapman, 'Scientific Instruments and Industrial Innovation: The Achievement of Jesse Ramsden', in *Making Instruments Count: Essays in Honour of Gerard Turner*, ed. R.G.W. Anderson, J. A. Bennett and W. F. Ryan (Aldershot, 1993), pp. 418–30, pp. 419–20.

23 P. Wood, 'Anderson, John (1726–1796)', Oxford Dictonary of National Biography, www.oxforddnb.com, accessed 29 September 2011.

24 *Industrial Revolution: A Documentary History, Series One* (Marlborough, 1999), Part 8, Reel 114, Muirhead III 3/1, Waste Book 1757–1763, entries between 6 December 1757 and 19 August 1758.

25 J. P. Muirhead, *The Origin and Progress of the Mechanical Inventions of James Watt* (London, 1854), vol. I, pp. xxxv–xxxvi.

26 *Industrial Revolution: A Documentary History, Series Three* (Marlborough, 1999), Reel I, JWP 4/11.41, J. Watt to J. Watt Senior, 15 September 1758.

27 N.A.M. Rodger, *The Command of the Ocean* (London, 2004), pp. 382–3.

28 *Industrial Revolution: A Documentary History, Series One* (Marlborough, 1999), Part 8, Reel 114, Muirhead III 3/1, Waste Book 1757–1763, 3 January 1757. *Industrial Revolution: A Documentary History, Series Three* (Marlborough, 1999), Reel I, JWP 4/11.59 and 41, September 1758.

29 S. Bedini, *Thomas Jefferson and his Copying Machines* (Charlottesville, VA, 1984), p. 50.

30 Chapman, 'Scientific Instruments and Industrial Innovation', p. 420.

31 M. Daumas, 'Precision Mechanics', in *A History of Technology*, ed. C. Singer, E. J. Holmyard and A. R. Hall (Oxford, 1957), vol. IV, pp. 379–416: p. 400.

32 C. Holtzapffel, *Turning and Mechanical Manipulation* (London, 1846), vol. I, p. 438.

33 A. Turner, *Early Scientific Instruments: Europe, 1400–1800* (London, 1987), p. 209.

34 M. Daumas, *Scientific Instruments of the Seventeenth and Eighteenth Centuries and their Makers* (London, 1972), p. 115.

35 R. L. Hills, 'Richard Roberts', in *Henry Maudslay and the Pioneers of the Machine Age*, ed. J. Cantrell and G. Cookson (Stroud, 2002), pp. 54–73: p. 55.

36 M. Daumas, 'Precision Mechanics', p. 382.

37 Daumas, *Scientific Instruments of the Seventeenth and Eighteenth Centuries*, pp. 113–14.

38 McConnell, *Jesse Ramsden*, p. 36.

39 Ibid., p. 41.

40 Chapman, 'Scientific Instruments and Industrial Innovation', p. 423.

41 Turner, *Early Scientific Instruments*, p. 171.

42 D. Bryden, 'James Watt, Merchant: The Glasgow Years, 1754–1774', in

Perceptions of Great Engineers: Fact and Fantasy, ed. D. Smith (1994), pp. 9–22: p. 10.

43 Robert Campbell, *The London Tradesman* (London, 1747), p. 254.

44 Turner, *Early Scientific Instruments*, p. 211.

45 A. Morrison-Low, 'Making Scientific Instruments in the Industrial Revolution: "Location, Location, Location"', in *Bulletin of the Scientific Instrument Society*, 94 (2007), pp. 9–16: p. 14.

46 Morrison-Low, *Making Scientific Instruments during the Industrial Revolution*, p. 199.

47 Campbell, *The London Tradesman*, p. 254.

48 Hills, *James Watt*, vol. I: *His Time in Scotland*, p. 106.

49 Ibid., p. 107.

50 *Industrial Revolution: A Documentary History, Series One* (Marlborough, 1999), Part 7, Matthew Boulton Correspondence and Papers, Reel 104, box 343, letter 52, 13 December 1800.

51 C. Holtzapffel, *Turning and Mechanical Manipulation*, vol. I, p. 80.

52 Ibid., pp. 83–5.

53 Ibid., p. 101.

54 JWP 6/46.6, J. Watt to J. Watt Senior, 19 June 1756.

55 *Industrial Revolution: A Documentary History, Series Three* (Marlborough, 1999), Reel 33, JWP, CI/I, 'Accounts', 7 October 1759.

56 Later Wyke also made revolution counters for Watt's steam engine. See A. Smith, *A Catalogue of Tools for Watch and Clock Makers by John Wyke of Liverpool* (Charlottesville, VA, 1978), p. 7.

57 J. Moxon, *Mechanick Exercises or the Doctrine of Handy-Works* (Mendham, 1994).

58 G. L'E. Turner, 'The Auction Sale of Larcum Kendall's Workshop, 1790', *Antiquarian Horology*, VIII (1967), pp. 269–75.

59 H. W. Dickinson, *James Watt: Craftsman and Engineer* (Cambridge, 1935), pp. 57–8.

60 Moxon, *Mechanick Exercises*, p. 217.

61 Science Museum inv. 1924–792/1814.

62 Hills, *James Watt*, vol. I: *His Time in Scotland*, p. 133.

63 J. P. Muirhead, *The Origin and Progress of the Mechanical Inventions of James Watt* (London, 1854), vol. III, pp. 75–6.

64 Sotheby's, *The James Watt Sale: Art and Science* (London, 2003), lot nos 10, 12, 13.

65 JWP 4/11.9, 10 October 1757.

66 JWP 4/11.30, 15 May 1758.

67 JWP 4/11.40, 16 August 1758.

68 J. P. Muirhead, *The Life of James Watt, with Selections from his Correspondence* (London, 1858), p. 55.

69 Ibid., p. 56.

70 J. Rabone, 'Measuring Rules', in *The Resources, Products and Industrial History of Birmingham and the Midland Hardware District*, ed. S. Timmins (London, 1866), pp. 628–32: p. 631.

71 J. Rae, *Life of Adam Smith* (London, 1895), p. 74.

72 Muirhead, *The Life of James Watt*, p. 470.

73 A. Smith, *An Inquiry into the Nature and Causes of the Wealth of Nations* (London, 1778), vol. I, p. 7.

74 Muirhead, *The Life of James Watt*, p. 46. He wasn't alone. Robert Campbell, in his *London Tradesman*, complained that 'a refinement of our taste into a love of the soft Italian music, is debasing the martial genius of the nation, and may one day be a Means to fiddle us out of our Liberties', p. 92.

75 M. T. Wright, 'James Watt: Musical Instrument Maker', *Galpin Society Journal*, L (2002), pp. 104–29. This was the main source for the passage that follows.

76 Ibid., pp. 123–4.

77 Hills, *James Watt*, vol. I: *His Time in Scotland*, p. 113.

78 P. Holman, *Life after Death: The Viola Da Gamba in Britain from Purcell to Dolmetsch* (Woodbridge, 2010), p. 167.

79 Wright, 'James Watt: Musical Instrument Maker', p. 126.

80 Ibid., p. 127.

81 W. Johnson, ed., *Journals of Gilbert White* (Henley-on-Thames, 1982), pp. xxxv–xxxvi.

82 R. Blythe, ed., *The Diary of Thomas Turner, 1754–1765* (Oxford, 1984), p. 161, entry 19 August 1758.

83 Ibid., pp. 223–4, entry 28 April 1761. As Josiah Wedgwood wrote, 'Heavens once dreaded bolt is now called down to amuse your wives & daughters, – to decorate their tea boards & baubles!' K. Farrer, ed., *Letters of Josiah Wedgwood to 1770* (Manchester, 1903), p. 105.

84 D. J. Bryden, 'Evidence from Advertising for Mathematical Instrument Making in London, 1556–1714', *Annals of Science*, XLIX (1992), pp. 301–36: p. 332. See also entry for Sunday, 26 May, in *The Diary of Samuel Pepys*, ed. R. C. Latham and W. Matthews (London, 2000), vol. VIII.

85 Hills, *James Watt*, vol. I: *His Time in Scotland*, p. 104.

86 *Industrial Revolution: A Documentary History, Series One* (Marlborough, 1999), Part 2, Reel 19, M1/2/7, 'Cash Memorandum', *c.* 1769.

87 Hills, *James Watt*, vol. I: *His Time in Scotland*, p. 115.

88 Jean Bernoulli, *Lettres Astronomiques; ou l'on donne une idée de l'état actuel de l'astronomie pratique dans plusiers villes de l'Europe* (Berlin, 1771), p. 74.

89 Ibid., pp. 63–4.

90 Mare and Quarrell, eds, *Lichtenberg's Visits to England*, p. 77.

91 Turner, 'Eighteenth-century Scientific Instruments and their Makers', p. 527.

92 A. Morton and J. Wess, *Public and Private Science* (Oxford, 1993), p. 86. Cuff could take two weeks to make a single microscope.

93 Alison Morrison-Low, 'Feasting my Eyes with the View of Fine Instruments', in *Science and Medicine in the Scottish Enlightenment*, ed. C. Withers and P. Wood (East Linton, East Lothian, 2002), pp. 17–53: p. 39.

94 *Industrial Revolution: A Documentary History, Series Three* (Marlborough, 1999), Reel 33, JWP, CI/I, 'Accounts'.

95 D. J. Bryden, *Scottish Scientific Instrument-makers* (Edinburgh, 1972), pp. 50, 11.

96 Ibid., p. 19.

97 Hills, *James Watt*, vol. I: *His Time in Scotland*, p. 128.

98 JWP 4/II.137, 8 September 1766.

99 Musson and Robinson, *Science and Technology in the Industrial Revolution*, p. 24.

100 R. Law, *James Watt and the Separate Condenser* (London, 1969), p. 17.

101 Robinson and Musson, *James Watt and the Steam Revolution*, p. 27.

102 Hills, *Power from Steam*, p. 59.

103 A. Mills, 'The Manufacture of Precision Brass Tubing', *Bulletin of the Scientific Instrument Society*, XXVII (1990), pp. 10–15: p. 10.

104 T. Gill, *Gill's Technological and Microscopic Repository; or, Discoveries and Improvements in the Useful Arts* (London, 1830), vol. VI, p. 262.

105 D. Howse, 'Sisson, Jonathan (1690?–1747)', *Oxford Dictionary of National Biography* online, www.oxforddnb.com, accessed 30 October 2013.

106 Science Museum inv. 1951–691. J. Minns, *Model Railway Engines* (London, 1973), p. 6.

Chapter Three: Looking for a Living, 1764–74

1 J. Gibson, *The History of Glasgow, from the Earliest Accounts to the Present Time* (Glasgow, 1777), pp. 232–4.

2 Ibid., pp. 204–5. The records of the trade to and from Glasgow are immensely detailed because of the records kept for excise purposes, down to the export of 46 11/12 gross of ivory combs and 44 13/16 chalders of lime.

3 J. A. Denholm, *The History of the City of Glasgow and Suburbs: Compiled from Authentic Records and Other Respectable Authorities* (Glasgow, 1798), p. 213.

4 Daniel Defoe, *A Tour through the Island of Great Britain* (London, 1778), vol. IV, p. 117. Defoe's account of the city appears to be based on that in John Slezer's *Theatrum Scottiae* of 1693.

5 A. E Musson and E. Robinson, *Science and Technology in the Industrial Revolution* (Manchester, 1969), p. 178.

6   D. Daiches, 'The Scottish Enlightenment', in *A Hotbed of Genius: The Scottish Enlightenment, 1730–1790*, ed. D. Daiches, P. Jones and J. Jones (Edinburgh, 1986), pp. 1–42, p. 2.

7   Joel Mokyr, *The Enlightened Economy: Britain and the Industrial Revolution, 1700–1850* (London, 2009), p. 54; Musson and Robinson, *Science and Technology in the Industrial Revolution*, p. 179.

8   M. Berg, *The Age of Manufactures* (London, 1994), p. 45.

9   R. L. Emerson and P. Wood, 'Science and Enlightenment in Glasgow, 1690–1802', in *Science and Medicine in the Scottish Enlightenment*, ed. C. Withers and P. Wood (East Linton, East Lothian, 2002), pp. 79–142: p. 81.

10 A. L. Donovan, *Philosophical Chemistry in the Scottish Enlightenment: The Doctrines and Discoveries of William Cullen and Joseph Black* (Edinburgh, 1975), p. 60. Thanks to William Brock and John Christie for establishing the original source, University of Glasgow Special Collections, ref. Cullen MS1054.

11 M. Bartholomew and P. Morris, 'Science in the Scottish Enlightenment', in *The Rise of Scientific Europe, 1500–1800*, ed. D. Goodman and C. A. Russell (Sevenoaks, 1991), pp. 279–304: p. 298.

12 E. Robinson and D. McKie, *Partners in Science: Letters of James Watt and Joseph Black* (London, 1970), p. 87; R. Anderson, 'Joseph Black', in *A Hotbed of Genius*, ed. Daiches, Jones and Jones (Edinburgh, 1986), pp. 93–115: p. 93.

13 Bartholomew and Morris, 'Science in the Scottish Enlightenment', p. 300.

14 Anderson, 'Joseph Black', p. 107.

15 S. Smiles, *The Life of Thomas Telford* (London, 1867), p. 129.

16 I. J. Standing, 'Mushet, David (1772–1847)', *Oxford Dictionary of National Biography* online, www.oxforddnb.com, accessed 1 November 2012.

17 Anderson, 'Joseph Black', p. 99.

18 Musson and Robinson, *Science and Technology in the Industrial Revolution*, p. 134; Bartholomew and Morris, 'Science in the Scottish Enlightenment', p. 290.

19 R. L. Hills, *James Watt*, vol. III: *Triumph Through Adversity, 1785–1819* (Ashbourne, 2006), p. 137.

20 C. A. Whatley, *The Industrial Revolution in Scotland* (Cambridge, 1997), p. 29.

21 Daiches, 'The Scottish Enlightenment', p. 32.

22 L. Gittins, 'The Alkali Experiments of James Watt and James Keir, 1765–1780', *Transactions of the Newcomen Society*, LXVIII (1996), pp. 217–31: p. 222.

23 Musson and Robinson, *Science and Technology in the Industrial Revolution*, p. 231.

24 A. Clow and N. Clow, *The Chemical Revolution: A Contribution to Social Technology* (London, 1952), p. 130.

25 Gibson, *The History of Glasgow*, p. 114.

26 Ibid., pp. 115, 120.

27 Denholm, *The History of the City of Glasgow*, p. 224.

28 Clare William, ed., *Sophie in London, 1786; being the Diary of Sophie v. La Roche* (London, 1933), p. 40.

29 M. L. Mare and W. H. Quarrell, eds, *Lichtenberg's Visits to England, as Described in his Letters and Diaries* (Oxford, 1938), pp. 42–3.

30 M. Berg, *Luxury and Pleasure in Eighteenth Century Britain* (Oxford, 2005), p. 7.

31 J. P. Muirhead, *The Life of James Watt, with Selections from his Correspondence* (London, 1858), p. 50.

32 R. L. Hills, *James Watt*, vol. 1: *His Time in Scotland, 1736–1774* (Ashbourne, 2002), p. 126.

33 Sotheby's, *The James Watt Sale: Art and Science* (London, 2003), lot nos 15–20.

34 Muirhead, *The Life of James Watt*, p. 50.

35 H. W. Dickinson and R. Jenkins, *James Watt and the Steam Engine* (Oxford, 1927), pp. 29–33.

36 Muirhead, *The Life of James Watt*, p. 203.

37 Dickinson and Jenkins, *James Watt and the Steam Engine*, p. 106.

38 J. Insley, 'James Watt's Cookbook Chemistry', in *Notes and Records of the Royal Society*, LXV (2011), pp. 301–8: pp. 305–6.

39 Clow and Clow, *The Chemical Revolution*, p. 59.

40 D. P. Miller, *James Watt: Chemist* (London, 2009), p. 86.

41 Musson and Robinson, *Science and Technology in the Industrial Revolution*, p. 6.

42 Berg, *Luxury and Pleasure*, p. 130.

43 D. Friedley, 'English Eighteenth Century Pottery', *Metropolitan Museum of Art Bulletin*, VII/6 (1912), pp. 113–16: p. 116.

44 C. Hibbert, ed., *An American in Regency England: The Journal of a Tour of 1810–11* (London, 1968), pp. 163–4.

45 J. Aikin, *A Description of the Country from Thirty to Forty Miles Round Manchester* (Newton Abbot, 1968), p. 531.

46 Friedley, 'English Eighteenth Century Pottery', p. 115.

47 Berg, *Luxury and Pleasure*, p. 132; B. Faujas de Saint Fond, *A Journey Through England and Scotland to the Hebrides in 1784*, ed. A. Geikle (Glasgow, 1907), vol. 1, p. 96.

48 K. Farrer, ed., *Letters of Josiah Wedgwood to 1770* (Manchester, 1903), p. 127.

49 William, ed., *Sophie in London, 1786*, pp. 122–3.

50 P. Mantoux, *The Industrial Revolution in the Eighteenth Century* (London, 1961), pp. 385–6; Farrer, ed., *Letters of Josiah Wedgwood to 1770*, p. 127.

51 W. Mankowitz, *Wedgwood* (London, 1967), p. 43.

52 R. L. Hills, 'James Watt and the Delftfield Pottery, Glasgow', *Proceedings of the Society of Antiquaries of Scotland*, cxxxi (2001), pp. 375–420: p. 394.

53 Ibid., p. 398.

54 Insley, 'James Watt's Cookbook Chemistry', pp. 301–8: p. 305.

55 G. Quail, 'James Watt at Delftfield, the Work of James Watt as Potter at Delftfield, Glasgow, and the Development of Cream-coloured Earthenware', *Scottish Pottery Historical Review*, vi (1981), pp. 44–54: p. 52.

56 Hills, 'James Watt and the Delftfield Pottery, Glasgow', p. 400.

57 R. L. Hills, *James Watt*, vol. 1: *His Time in Scotland*, p. 175.

58 Ibid., p. 167.

59 Science Museum inv. 1924–792/1165.

60 Hills, 'James Watt and the Delftfield Pottery, Glasgow', p. 385. Science Museum inv. 1924–792/1246 and /1218.

61 Hills, *James Watt*, vol. 1: *His Time in Scotland*, p. 450.

62 Hills, 'James Watt and the Delftfield Pottery, Glasgow', pp. 387–8.

63 Science Museum inv. 1924–792/1045, /1048, /1049, /1051, /1056, for example. Hills, *James Watt*, vol. 1: *His Time in Scotland*, p. 170.

64 Hills, 'James Watt and the Delftfield Pottery, Glasgow', p. 390.

65 Miller, *James Watt: Chemist*, chap. 5, particularly pp. 122–3. A. Donovan, 'James Hutton, Joseph Black and the Chemical Theory of Heat', *Ambix*, xxv (1978), pp. 176–90.

66 D. P. Miller, 'Seeing the Chemical Steam through the Historical Fog: Watt's Steam Engine as Chemistry', *Annals of Science*, lxv (2008), pp. 47–72: p. 50.

67 Miller, *James Watt: Chemist*, p. 94.

68 Robinson and McKie, *Partners in Science*, p. 10.

69 Miller, *James Watt: Chemist*, p. 90.

70 Clow and Clow, *The Chemical Revolution*, p. 298.

71 S. Shaw, *History of the Staffordshire Potteries* (Newton Abbot, 1970), pp. 30, 62.

72 J. Black, *Lectures on the Elements of Chemistry* (London, 1803), vol. 1, p. 20.

73 Ibid., p. 330.

74 G. Smith, *The Laboratory; or, School of Arts* (London, 1810), vol. 1, p. 71. Author's italics.

75 E. Meteyard, *The Life of Josiah Wedgwood* (London, 1865), vol. 1, p. 168.

76 J. Wedgwood and J. Banks, 'An Attempt to Make a Thermometer for Measuring the Higher Degrees of Heat, from a Red Heat up to the Strongest that Vessels of Clay Can Support', *Philosophical Transactions of the Royal Society of London*, lxxii (1782), pp. 305–26: p. 306.

77 R. Reilly, *Josiah Wedgwood* (London, 1992), p. 156; B. Trinder, *The Making of the Industrial Landscape* (London, 1982), p. 84.

78 Farrer, ed., *Letters of Josiah Wedgwood to 1770*, pp. 225–6.

79 Wedgwood and Banks, 'An Attempt to Make a Thermometer', p. 306.

80 Robinson and McKie, *Partners in Science*, pp. 23, 39. Watt's workshop contains a considerable length of thermometer tube, indicating that Watt, when running his instrument making business in Glasgow, was producing these instruments in some quantity.

81 Wedgwood and Banks, 'An Attempt to Make a Thermometer', p. 310.

82 Ibid., p. 309.

83 J. Stock, *Development of the Chemical Balance* (London, 1969), p. 2.

84 Ibid., p. 11.

85 Aikin, *A Description of the Country from Thirty to Forty Miles Round Manchester*, p. 525.

86 Farrer, ed., *Letters of Josiah Wedgwood to 1770*, p. 106.

87 Donovan, *Philosophical Chemistry in the Scottish Enlightenment*, p. 107.

88 Clow and Clow, *The Chemical Revolution*, pp. 544–5. For a recent overview of Combrune's work, see J. Sumner, 'Michael Combrune, Peter Shaw and Commercial Chemistry: The Boerhaavian Chemical Origins of Brewing Thermometry', *Ambix*, LIV/1 (2007), pp. 5–29.

89 J. Golinsky, '"Fit Instruments": Thermometers in Eighteenth-century Chemistry', in *Instruments and Experimentation in the History of Chemistry*, ed. F. L. Holmes and T. H. Levere (Cambridge, 2000), pp. 185–210, pp. 187–8.

90 Smith, *The Laboratory*, vol. 1, p. 402.

91 Robinson and McKie, *Partners in Science*, p. 115.

92 W. White, *All Round the Wrekin* (London, 1860), p. 299.

93 Ibid., p. 304.

94 F. L. Holmes and T. H. Levere, 'Introduction: A Practical Science', *Instruments and Experimentation in the History of Chemistry* (Cambridge, 2000), pp. vii–xviii, p. ix; Black, *Lectures on the Elements of Chemistry*, vol. 1, p. 288.

95 L. Stewart, 'Assistants to Enlightenment: William Lewis, Alexander Chisholm and Invisible Technicians in the Industrial Revolution', *Notes and Records of the Royal Society*, LXII, pp. 17–29: p. 24.

96 Science Museum, *Josiah Wedgwood: 'The Arts and Sciences United'* (Barlaston, 1978), pp. 29, 31–3.

97 Black, *Lectures on the Elements of Chemistry*, vol. 1, p. 293.

98 Ibid., p. 333.

99 Hills, *James Watt*, vol. 1: *His Time in Scotland*, p. 331; R. Anderson, 'Joseph Black', p. 99.

100 Miller, *James Watt: Chemist*, p. 85.

101 Donovan, *Philosophical Chemistry in the Scottish Enlightenment*, p. 182.

102 Robinson and McKie, *Partners in Science*, p. 28.

103 Donovan, *Philosophical Chemistry in the Scottish Enlightenment*, p. 182.

104 Hills, *James Watt*, vol. 1: *His Time in Scotland*, p. 366.

105 Black, *Lectures on the Elements of Chemistry*, vol. 1, pp. 36–7.

106 Robinson and McKie, *Partners in Science*, p. 418.

107 Ibid., p. 77.

108 Miller, 'Seeing the Chemical Steam through the Historical Fog', p. 62.

109 R. L. Hills, *Power from Steam: A History of the Stationary Steam Engine* (Cambridge, 1989), p. 53. There is some disagreement over when Watt's walk on Glasgow Green took place; it may have been 1764. Thanks to Jim Andrew for pointing this out.

110 H. Hamilton, 'The Failure of the Ayr Bank, 1772', *Economic History Review*, VIII/3 (1956), pp. 405–17: p. 412.

111 Hills, *James Watt*, vol. 1: *His Time in Scotland*, p. 127.

Chapter Four: Gentlemen of Merit and Ingenuity, 1765–81

1 Henry Dickinson and Rhys Jenkins, *James Watt and the Steam Engine*, 2nd edn (London, 1989), pp. 113–14.

2 R. L. Hills, *James Watt*, vol. II: *The Years of Toil, 1775–1785* (Ashbourne, 2005), p. 59.

3 J. R. Harris, *Industrial Espionage and Technology Transfer: Britain and France in the Eighteenth Century* (Aldershot, 1998), p. 174.

4 J. Bisset, *A Poetic Survey Round Birmingham; with a Brief Description of the Different Curiosities and Manufactories of the Place. Intended as a Guide for Strangers* (Birmingham, 1800), p. 25.

5 S. Timmins, 'The Industrial History of Birmingham', in *The Resources, Products and Industrial History of Birmingham and the Midland Hardware District*, ed. S. Timmins (London, 1866), pp. 207–24: p. 221.

6 E. Hopkins, *The Rise of the Manufacturing Town: Birmingham and the Industrial Revolution* (Stroud, 1998), p. 21.

7 M. L. Mare and W. H. Quarrell, eds, *Lichtenberg's visits to England, as Described in his Letters and Diaries* (Oxford, 1938), pp. 98–9.

8 N. Scarfe, ed., *Innocent Espionage: The La Rochefoucauld Brothers' Tour of England in 1785* (Woodbridge, 1995), p. 114.

9 J. Simmons, ed., *Letters from England by Robert Southey* (London, 1951), p. 197.

10 P. Jones, *Industrial Enlightenment: Science, Technology and Culture in Birmingham and the West Midlands, 1760–1820* (Manchester, 2008), pp. 73–4.

11 R. B. Prosser, *Birmingham Inventors and Inventions* (Birmingham, 1881), p. 3.

12 W. Hutton, *An History of Birmingham* (Birmingham, 1795), p. 90.

13 K. Farrer, ed., *Letters of Josiah Wedgwood 1762 to 1770* (Manchester, 1903), p. 110.

14 Bisset, *A Poetic Survey Round Birmingham*, p. 12.

15 Rita McLean, 'Introduction: Matthew Boulton, 1728–1809', in *Matthew Boulton: Selling What All the World Desires*, ed. S. Mason, exh. cat.,

Birmingham Museums and Art Gallery (New Haven, CT, and London, 2009), pp. 1–6: p. 4.

16 K. Morgan, ed., *An American Quaker in Britain: The Travel Journals of Jabez Maud Fisher, 1775–1779* (Oxford, 1992), pp. 253–5.

17 H. W. Dickinson, *Matthew Boulton* (Cambridge, 1937), p. 73.

18 Peter Jones, '"I had Lords and Ladys to wait on yesterday . . .": Visitors to the Soho Manufactory', in *Matthew Boulton*, ed. Mason, pp. 71–9: p. 73.

19 J. Griffiths, *The Third Man: The Life and Times of William Murdoch, 1754–1839* (London, 1992), p. 71.

20 James Boswell, *The Life of Samuel Johnson* (London, 1799), p. 473.

21 Kenneth Quickenden, 'Matthew Boulton's Silver and Sheffield Plate', in *Matthew Boulton*, ed. Mason, pp. 41–6: p. 45.

22 Jenny Uglow, 'Matthew Boulton and the Lunar Society', in *Matthew Boulton*, ed. Mason (Birmingham, 2009), pp. 7–13: p. 10.

23 H. W. Dickinson, *James Watt: Craftsman and Engineer* (Cambridge, 1935), p. 54.

24 J. P. Muirhead, *The Life of James Watt, with Selections from his Correspondence* (London, 1858), p. 301.

25 W. Hutton, *An History of Birmingham to the End of the Year 1780* (Birmingham, 1781), p. 78.

26 Prosser, *Birmingham Inventors and Inventions*, p. 48.

27 J. Money, *Experience and Identity: Birmingham and the West Midlands, 1760–1800* (Manchester, 1977), p. 262.

28 British Museum inv. BM5454A.

29 British Museum object inv. BM5454B.

30 A. Rees, entry for 'Button', in *The Cyclopedia; or, Universal Dictionary of Arts, Science, and Literature* (London, 1819), vol. V; Morgan, ed., *An American Quaker in Britain*, pp. 253–5.

31 Dickinson, *Matthew Boulton*, p. 48.

32 Mare and Quarrell, eds, *Lichtenberg's Visits to England*, p. 113.

33 'Birmingham Toys: Manufacturing Techniques', *Revolutionary Players*, www.revolutionaryplayers.org.uk, accessed 30 October 2012.

34 Hopkins, *The Rise of the Manufacturing Town*, p. 8.

35 Raphael Samuel, 'Workshop of the World: Steam Power and Hand Technology in Mid-Victorian Britain', *History Workshop*, III (1977), pp. 6–72: p. 46.

36 Bisset, *A Poetic Survey Round Birmingham*, p. 155.

37 He was originally commissioned to make a set of wooden legs for Wedgwood when he had one of his amputated in 1768 – a resourceful man. Farrer, ed., *Letters of Josiah Wedgwood to 1770*, p. 203.

38 Hopkins, *The Rise of the Manufacturing Town*, p. 9.

39 E. G. Fitzmaurice, *Life of William, Earl of Shelburn* (London, 1912), vol. I, pp. 276–7.

40 John Turner, 'The Birmingham Button Trade', in *The Resources, Products and Industrial History of Birmingham*, ed. Timmins, pp. 432–51: p. 444.

41 J. S. Wright, 'The Jewellery and Gilt Toy Trades', in *The Resources, Products and Industrial History of Birmingham*, ed. Timmins, pp. 452–62: 456.

42 T. Gill, *Technological and Microscopic Repository; or, Discoveries and Improvements in the Useful Arts* (London, 1830), vol. VI, p. 279.

43 Ibid., vol. VI, p. 279.

44 Turner, 'The Birmingham Button Trade', pp. 432–451: p. 446.

45 Morgan, ed., *An American Quaker in Britain*, p. 253.

46 J. Tann, 'Boulton and Wat's Organisation of Steam Engine Production Before the Opening of Soho Foundry', *Transactions of the Newcomen Society*, LXIX (1977–8), pp. 41–56: pp. 44–5.

47 D. B. Barton, *The Cornish Engine* (Truro, 1969), p. 22.

48 Daniel Treadwell, 'On the Uses and Improvement of Cast-iron', in Gill, *Technological and Microscopic Repository*, vol. VI, pp. 222–7: p. 223.

49 Dickinson, *James Watt*, pp. 86–7.

50 S. Timmins, 'The Industrial History of Birmingham', in *The Resources, Products and Industrial History of Birmingham*, ed. Timmins, pp. 207–24: p. 221.

51 C. Edwards provides an introduction in *Tools and Techniques, 1600–1840*, available online at www.bafra.org.uk, accessed 24 October 2012.

52 C. Holtzapffel, *Turning and Mechanical Manipulation* (London, 1846), vol. I, pp. 327, 358.

53 Ibid., pp. 330–31.

54 Ibid., p. 350.

55 E. Roll, *An Early Experiment in Industrial Organisation: Being a History of the Firm of Boulton and Watt, 1775–1805* (London, 1968), p. 56.

56 Holtzapffel, *Turning and Mechanical Manipulation*, vol. I, p. 197.

57 Ibid., p. 206.

58 Ibid., pp. 196–7.

59 Dickinson and Jenkins, *James Watt and the Steam Engine*, p. 108.

60 Dickinson, *James Watt*, p. 110.

61 E. A. Forward, 'The Early History of the Cylinder Boring Machine', *Transactions of the Newcomen Society*, V (1924), pp. 24–38: p. 25.

62 M. Daumas, *Scientific Instruments of the Seventeenth and Eighteenth Centuries, and Their Makers* (London, 1972), p. 110.

63 Barton, *The Cornish Engine*, pp. 131–2.

64 Dickinson and Jenkins, *James Watt and the Steam Engine*, p. 258; Griffiths, *The Third Man*, p. 96.

65 Holtzapffel, *Turning and Mechanical Manipulation*, vol. II, p. 850.

66 Wielding the sledgehammer was usually a full-time job in a forge or engineering works, reserved for the younger, fitter men. In some

shipyards the sledges were referred to as 'Mondays', presumably because after that day their wielder was incapable of further exertions.

67 Holtzapffel, *Turning and Mechanical Manipulation*, vol. II, p. 850.
68 Hills, *James Watt*, vol. II: *The Years of Toil*, p. 111.
69 Holtzapffel, *Turning and Mechanical Manipulation*, vol. II, p. 558.
70 Griffiths, *The Third Man*, p. 44.
71 Dickinson, *James Watt*, p. 109.
72 Hills, *James Watt*, vol. I: *His Time in Scotland*, p. 218.
73 Hills, *James Watt*, vol. II: *The Years of Toil*, p. 79.
74 Roll, *An Early Experiment in Industrial Organisation*, p. 26.
75 Hills, *James Watt*, vol. II: *The Years of Toil*, p. 106; Roll, *An Early Experiment in Industrial Organisation*, p. 62; Dickinson and Jenkins, *James Watt and the Steam Engine*, p. 266.
76 S. Smiles, *Lives of the Engineers: The Steam-engine. Boulton and Watt* (London, 1878), p. 200.
77 Roll, *An Early Experiment in Industrial Organisation*, p. 61.
78 M. T. Wright, 'The Ingenious Mechanick', in *John Joseph Merlin: The Ingenious Mechanick* (London, 1985), pp. 47–84: pp. 48–9.
79 S. Timmins, 'The Industrial History of Birmingham', in *The Resources, Products and Industrial History of Birmingham and the Midland Hardware District*, ed. Timmins, pp. 207–24, p. 221.
80 Griffiths, *The Third Man*, p. 102.
81 Roll, *An Early Experiment in Industrial Organisation*, p. 151.
82 E. Robinson and D. McKie, *Partners in Science: James Watt and Joseph Black* (London, 1970), p. 96.
83 Science Museum inv. 1924–792/627.
84 Hills, *James Watt*, vol. II: *The Years of Toil*, p. 191.
85 Roll, *An Early Experiment in Industrial Organisation*, p. 85.
86 Dickinson and Jenkins, *James Watt and the Steam Engine*, p. 264.
87 J. Andrew, J. Stein, J. Tann and C. MacLeod, 'The Transition from Timber to Cast Iron Working Beams for Steam Engines: A Technological Innovation', *Transactions of the Newcomen Society*, LXX (1998–9), pp. 197–220: p. 204.
88 Science Museum inv. 1876–1370.
89 Roll, *An Early Experiment in Industrial Organisation*, p. 43.
90 Ibid., p. 29.
91 Hills, *James Watt*, vol. II: *The Years of Toil*, p. 101.
92 Holtzapffel, *Turning and Mechanical Manipulation*, vol. I, p. 245.
93 Ibid., p. 370.
94 Ibid., p. 202.
95 Ibid., p. 209.
96 Harris, *Industrial Espionage and Technology Transfer*, p. 206.
97 W. Pole, *The Life of Sir William Fairbairn* (London, 1877), pp. 46–7.

98 Hills, *James Watt*, vol. 11: *The Years of Toil*, p. 98.

99 Barton, *The Cornish Engine*, p. 27.

Chapter Five: Steam Mill Mad? 1781–95

1   N. Scarfe, ed., *Innocent Espionage: The La Rochefoucauld Brothers' Tour of England in 1785* (Woodbridge, 1995), pp. 60, 61.

2   J. Simmons, ed., *Letters from England by Robert Southey* (London, 1951), p. 213.

3   W. H. Chaloner, 'Manchester in the Latter Half of the Eighteenth Century', *Bulletin of the John Rylands Library*, XLII/1 (1959), pp. 40–60: pp. 41–2.

4   C. Bruyn Andrews, ed., *The Torrington Diaries* (New York, 1938), vol. 11, p. 195.

5   M. W. Thompson, ed., *The Journeys of Sir Richard Colt Hoare* (Gloucester, 1983), p. 155.

6   K. Morgan, ed., *An American Quaker in Britain: The Travel Journals of Jabez Maud Fisher, 1775–1779* (Oxford, 1992), pp. 235–6.

7   W. Hardy, *The Origins of the Idea of the Industrial Revolution* (Oxford, 2006), p. 11.

8   A. Rees, entry for 'Cotton', *Cyclopaedia of the Useful Arts* (London, 1819), vol. x.

9   W. Bowden, *Industrial Society in England Towards the End of the 18th Century* (London, 1965), p. 122.

10 M. B. Rose, *The Lancashire Cotton Industry: A History since 1700* (Preston, 1996), p. 7.

11 R. Kennedy, *Mr Jefferson's Lost Cause: Land, Farmers, Slavery and the Louisiana Purchase* (New York, 2003), p. 100.

12 S. Levitt, 'Clothing', in *The Lancashire Cotton Industry*, ed. Rose, pp. 154–86: pp. 154–5.

13 H. J. Voth, *Time and Work in England, 1750 to 1830* (Oxford, 2000), pp. 196–7; M. Edwards, *The Growth of the British Cotton Trade, 1780–1815* (Manchester, 1967), pp. 32–3; P. Deane, *The First Industrial Revolution* (Cambridge, 1979), p. 87.

14 T. Carlyle, *Chartism* (London, 1840), pp. 84–5.

15 R. S. Fitton, *The Arkwrights: Spinners of Fortune* (Manchester, 1989), p. 210.

16 Arkwright's prototype machine, capable of spinning four threads simultaneously, survives in the Science Museum collection. Science Museum inv. 1860–4.

17 Rees, 'Cotton'.

18 S. D. Chapman, 'The Arkwright Mills: Colquhoun's Census of 1788 and Archaeological Evidence', *Industrial Archaeology Review*, VI/1, pp. 5–26: pp. 5, 8.

19 Bruyn Andrews, ed., *The Torrington Diaries*, pp. 195–6.

20 Morgan, ed., *An American Quaker in Britain*, pp. 235, 250.

21 A. E. Musson, 'Industrial Motive Power in the United Kingdom, 1800–70', *Economic History Review*, XXIX/3 (1976), pp. 415–39: p. 429.

22 D. B. Barton, *The Cornish Beam Engine* (Truro, 1969), p. 23.

23 R. L. Hills, *James Watt*, vol. III: *Triumph Through Adversity, 1785–1819* (Ashbourne, 2006), p. 19.

24 Matthew Boulton purchased 250 kg for one of the trials on the wheel. R. L. Hills, *James Watt*, vol. I: *His Time in Scotland, 1736–1774* (Ashbourne, 2002), p. 432.

25 J. P. Muirhead, *The Origin and Progress of the Mechanical Inventions of James Watt* (London, 1854), vol. II, p. 102.

26 S. Smiles, *The Lives of Boulton and Watt* (London, 1878), p. 252.

27 Patent No. 1213, 1779. *Specification of Matthew Wasborough: Steam Engines, Propelling Vessels, &c.*, p. 2.

28 Smiles, *The Lives of Boulton and Watt*, pp. 228–9.

29 R. L. Hills, *Power from Steam: A History of the Stationary Steam Engine* (Cambridge, 1989), p. 64.

30 H. W. Dickinson, *James Watt: Craftsman and Engineer* (Cambridge, 1935), p. 156.

31 H. Hazelton, *The Boulton and Watt Engine Book* (Birmingham, 1855)

32 J. Kanefsky and J. Robey, 'Steam Engines in 18th Century Britain: A Quantitative Assessment', *Technology and Culture*, XXI (1980), pp. 161–86: p. 176.

33 V.A.C. Gatrell, 'Labour, Power, and the Size of Firms in Lancashire Cotton in the Second Quarter of the Nineteenth Century', *Economic History Review*, XXX (1977), pp. 95–139: p. 125.

34 Gatrell's claim of manufacturers that 'some giants were as labour-intensive as some pygmies, some pygmies as power-intensive as some giants' is telling in this respect. See ibid., p. 113.

35 Chapman, 'The Arkwright Mills', p. 10.

36 By comparison the author's car, with a 1 litre engine, is three times more powerful. A. E. Musson, 'Industrial Motive Power in the United Kingdom, 1800–70', *Economic History Review*, XXIX (1976), pp. 415–39: p. 420.

37 E. Roll, *An Early Experiment in Industrial Organisation: Being a History of the Firm of Boulton and Watt, 1775–1805* (London, 1968), p. 62.

38 J. Farey, *A Treatise on the Steam Engine: Historical, Practical and Descriptive* (London, 1828), vol. I, p. 422.

39 J. Aikin, *A Description of the Country from Thirty to Forty Miles Round Manchester* (Newton Abbot, 1968), p. 175.

40 Farey, *A Treatise on the Steam Engine*, p. 275.

41 Musson, 'Industrial Motive Power in the United Kingdom', p. 419.

42 He was slightly underestimating. Morgan, ed., *An American Quaker in Britain*, p. 235.

43 R. L. Hills, *Power in the Industrial Revolution* (Manchester, 1970), p. 113.

44 Musson, 'Industrial Motive Power in the United Kingdom', p. 419.

45 Chapman, 'The Arkwright Mills', p. 10.

46 W. Pole, *The Life of Sir William Fairbairn* (London, 1877), p. 116. Boulton & Watt retaliated by purchasing land next to Murray's works to prevent him from expanding onto it.

47 Aikin, *A Description of the Country from Thirty to Forty Miles Round Manchester*, p. 177.

48 A. E. Musson and E. Robinson, *Science and Technology in the Industrial Revolution* (Manchester, 1969), p. 424.

49 Farey, *A Treatise on the Steam Engine*, p. 422.

50 Aikin, *A Description of the Country from Thirty to Forty Miles Round Manchester*, p. 176.

51 H. W. Dickinson, *Matthew Boulton* (Cambridge, 1937), p. 115.

52 Kanefsky and Robey, 'Steam Engines in 18th Century Britain', pp. 171, 174.

53 R. Gard, ed., *The Observant Traveller* (London, 1989), p. 73.

54 A. E. Musson and E. Robinson, 'The Early Growth of Steam Power', *Economic History Review*, XI/3 (1959) pp. 418–39: p. 419; E. T. Svedenstierna, *Svedenstierna's Tour of Great Britain, 1802–3* (Newton Abbot, 1973), pp. 173–4.

55 W. Cooke Taylor, *Notes of a Tour of the Manufacturing Districts of Lancashire* (London, 1842), p. 2.

56 J. P. Mayer, ed., *Journeys to England and Ireland* (New Haven, CT, 1979), p. 107.

57 J. Bischoff, *A Comprehensive History of the Woollen and Worsted Manufactures* (London, 1842), vol. I, p. 233.

58 M. Edwards, *The Growth of the British Cotton Trade, 1780–1815* (Manchester, 1967), p. 51.

59 E. Baines, *History of the Cotton Manufacture in Great Britain* (London, 1835), p. 6.

60 Pole, *The Life of Sir William Fairbairn*, p. 26.

61 W. Fairbairn, *Treatise on Mills and Millwork*, Part I: *On the Principles of Mechanism* (London, 1871), p. ix.

62 Pole, *The Life of Sir William Fairbairn*, p. 72.

63 Fairbairn, *Treatise on Mills and Millwork*, Part I, p. xii.

64 G. White, 'A Digest of the First Part of the Minutes of Evidence Taken before the Committee on Artizans and Machinery', *Hume Tracts* (London, 1824), p. 278.

65 It is interesting in this regard that Fairbairn described his one-time boss, John Rennie, as being highly regarded 'both as an engineer and a millwright'. Pole, *The Life of Sir William Fairbairn*, p. 88; Fairbairn, *Treatise on Mills and Millwork*, Part I, p. xi.

66 R. Buchanan, *Practical Essays on Millwork and other Machinery*, 3rd edn (London, 1841), vol. I, p. 176.

67 Buchanan, *Practical Essays on Millwork*, vol. II, p. 545.

68 Pole, *The Life of Sir William Fairbairn*, p. 117.

69 Ibid., pp. 113–14.

70 Buchanan, *Practical Essays on Millwork*, vol. I, p. xix.

71 M. Berg, *Luxury and Pleasure in Eighteenth-century Britain* (Oxford, 2005), p. 227.

72 Robert Campbell, *The London Tradesman* (London, 1747), p. 252.

73 J. P. Muirhead, *The Life of James Watt, with Selections from his Correspondence* (London, 1858), p. 223.

74 R. L. Hills, *James Watt*, vol. I: *His Time in Scotland, 1736–1774* (Ashbourne, 2002), p. 75; see Watt's workshop, Science Museum inv. 1924–792/30, for an example.

75 A. Rees, entry for 'Clock-maker', *Cyclopaedia of the Useful Arts* (London, 1819), vol. VIII.

76 Robert Campbell, *The London Tradesman* (London, 1747), p. 252.

77 W.T.R. Pryce and T. A. Davies, *Samuel Roberts, Clock Maker* (Cardiff, 1985), p. 61.

78 B. Loomes, *Complete British Clocks* (Newton Abbot, 1978), p. 84.

79 R. Barclay, *The Art of the Trumpet Maker* (Oxford, 1992), p. 78.

80 T. Crom, *Horological Shop Tools, 1700 to 1900* (Melrose, 1980), p. 41.

81 Loomes, *Complete British Clocks*, p. 89.

82 P. Mantoux, *The Industrial Revolution in the Eighteenth Century*, 2nd edn (London, 1961), p. 296.

83 R. Willis, 'Machines and Tools for Working Metal, Wood, and Other Materials', *Lectures on the Results of the Great Exhibition Delivered before the Society of Arts, Manufactures and Commerce* (London, 1852), pp. 230, 231.

84 Roberts's advert was on the front page of the first edition of the *Manchester Guardian* on 5 May 1821. As *The Guardian*, it is still going strong today.

85 Aikin, *A Description of the Country from Thirty to Forty Miles Round Manchester*, p. 172.

86 A. E. Musson and E. Robinson, 'The Origins of Engineering in Lancashire', in *The Industrial Revolutions: The Metal Fabrication and Engineering Industries*, ed. R. A. Church and E. A. Wrigley (Oxford, 1994), vol. IX, pp. 233–65: p. 262.

87 A. Rees, entry on 'Manufacture of Cotton', *Cyclopaedia of the Useful Arts*, vol. XXII.

88 R. S. Fitton, *The Arkwrights: Spinners of Fortune* (Manchester, 1989), p. 15.

89 Rees, 'Manufacture of Cotton'.

90 J. Andrew, J. Stein, J. Tann and C. MacLeod, 'The Transition from Timber to Cast Iron Working Beams for Steam Engines: A Technological Innovation', *Transactions of the Newcomen Society*, LXX (1998–9), pp. 197–220: p. 212.

91 C. Hibbert, ed., *An American in Regency England: The Journal of a Tour of 1810–11* (London, 1968), pp. 132–3.

92 Hibbert, ed., *An American in Regency England*, pp. 118–19.

93 R. L. Hills, *James Watt*, vol. III: *Triumph Through Adversity, 1785–1819* (Ashbourne, 2006), p. 96.

94 Buchanan, *Practical Essays on Millwork*, vol. I, p. xx. This didn't stop it being destroyed in a fire in 1791, caused by a fire started by a 'large corn machine . . . wanting grease'. See Dickinson and Jenkins, *James Watt and the Steam Engine*, p. 167.

95 Mantoux, *The Industrial Revolution in the Eighteenth Century*, p. 331.

96 Hills, *James Watt*, vol. III: *Triumph Through Adversity*, pp. 191–224.

97 J. Tann, 'Mr Hornblower and His Crew: Watt Engine Pirates at the End of the 18th Century', *Transactions of the Newcomen Society*, LI (1979–80), pp. 95–109: p. 99.

98 Hills, *James Watt*, vol. III: *Triumph Through Adversity*, p. 216.

99 Kanefsky and Robey, 'Steam Engines in 18th Century Britain', p. 174.

100 Farey, *A Treatise on the Steam Engine*, p. 677.

101 T. S. Ashton, *An Economic History of England: The 18th Century* (London, 1964), p. 107.

102 Musson, 'Industrial Motive Power in the United Kingdom', p. 424.

103 Pole, *The Life of Sir William Fairbairn*, p. 112.

104 G. Head, *A Home Tour Through the Manufacturing Districts of England, in the Summer of 1835* (New York, 1836), p. 120.

Chapter Six: Inventive, Creative Genius, 1795–1819

1 G. Yates, *An Historical and Descriptive Sketch of Birmingham; With Some Account of Its Environs, and Forty-Four View of the Principal Public Buildings* (Birmingham, 1830), pp. 225, 242.

2 Ibid., pp. 225–6.

3 W. O. Henderson, *J. C. Fischer and his Diary of Industrial England, 1814–51* (London, 1966), p. 131.

4 Ibid., p. 132.

5 Ibid., pp. 133–4.

6 D.S.L. Cardwell, *Steam Power in the Eighteenth Century; A Case Study in the Application of Science* (London, 1963), p. 75.

7 Roll, *An Early Experiment in Industrial Organisation*, pp. 312, 270.

8 Ibid., pp. xv, 291–304.

9 L. Ince, 'The Soho Engine Works, 1796–1895', *Stationary Power: The Journal of the International Stationary Steam Engine Society*, XVI (2000), pp. 1–132: p. 58.

10 E. C. Smith, *A Short History of Naval and Marine Engineering* (Cambridge, 1937), pp. 52, 105–10.

11 *Industrial Revolution: A Documentary History; Series One; The Boulton and Watt Archive Part 11* (Marlborough, 2003), p. 7.

12 J. Tann, 'Marketing Methods in the International Steam Engine Market: The Case of Boulton and Watt', *Journal of Economic History*, XXXVIII/2 (1978), pp. 363–91: pp. 363–4, 387.

13 Ince, 'The Soho Engine Works', p. 28. The original engine yard at the Soho Manufactory only finally closed down, with its work transferred to the Soho Foundry, in 1850.

14 Ibid., p. 19.

15 H. W. Dickinson, *James Watt: Craftsman and Engineer* (Cambridge, 1935), p. 168.

16 E. Robinson, 'Training Captains of Industry: The Education of Matthew Robinson Boulton and the Younger James Watt', *Annals of Science*, X (1954), pp. 301–13: p. 303.

17 J. Griffiths, *The Third Man: The Life and Times of William Murdoch, 1754–1839* (London, 1992), p. 284.

18 Robinson, 'Training Captains of Industry', p. 312.

19 P. Jones, 'Living the Enlightenment and the French Revolution: James Watt, Matthew Boultonm and Their Sons', *Historical Journal*, XLII/1 (1999), pp. 157–82: p. 178.

20 L. Hunt and M. Jacob, 'The Affective Revolution in 1790s Britain', *Eighteenth-century Studies*, XXXIV (2001), pp. 491–521: p. 496.

21 Ibid., p. 495.

22 Ibid., p. 506.

23 J. Hall, 'Joshua Field's Diary of a Tour in 1821 Through the Midlands', *Transactions of the Newcomen Society*, VI (1925–6), pp. 1–42: p. 20.

24 V. Coltman, *Fabricating the Antique: Neoclassicism in Britain, 1760–1800* (Chicago, IL, 2006), p. 12.

25 This fascination with the antique is often referred to as Neoclassicism – but that word was actually a pejorative coined by the Victorians.

26 I. Ware, *A Complete Body of Architecture* (London, 1756), p. 4.

27 N. Goodison, 'The Context of Neo-Classicism', in *Matthew Boulton: Selling What All the World Desires*, ed. S. Mason (Birmingham, 2009), pp. 31–40: p. 33.

28 R. Reilly, *Josiah Wedgwood* (London, 1992), p. 80.

29 J. Tann, *The Development of the Factory* (London, 1970), p. 153.

30 A. W. Skempton, 'Samuel Wyatt and the Albion Mill', *Architectural History*, XIV (1971), pp. 53–73.

31 K. Farrer, ed., *Letters of Josiah Wedgwood to 1770* (Manchester, 1903), p. 250.

32 R. L. Hills, *James Watt*, vol. I: *His Time in Scotland, 1736–1774* (Ashbourne, 2002), p. 91. Author's italics.

33 Archives of Soho, Birmingham Central Library, MS 3029/2, 'Notes and drawings by William Creighton of Soho'.

34 As well as this amazing work, some items show Creighton's wicked sense of humour. The very last is is titled 'A Rat in a Trap', and shows a rat with a male head (presumably one of his colleagues), declaring: 'Oh I'm caught, my genius has deserted me I suffer and cannot save my bacon ah!'

35 G. Battista Piranesi, *Diverse maniere* (Rome, 1769), p. 33.

36 N. Goodison, 'The Context of Neo-Classicism', in *Matthew Boulton: Selling What All the World Desires*, ed. S. Mason, exh. cat., Birmingham Museums and Art Gallery (New Haven, CT, and London, 2009), pp. 31–40: p. 32.

37 Mason, ed., *Matthew Boulton*, cat. nos 140–142.

38 Ibid., cat. nos 149–51.

39 Presumably he means 'taken from James Stuart's *Antiquities of Athens*'.

40 K. Farrer, ed., *Letters of Josiah Wedgwood to 1770* (Manchester, 1903), pp. 387–8.

41 Sotheby's, *The James Watt Sale: Art and Science* (London, 2003), lot nos 21–7.

42 V. Coltman, *Fabricating the Antique: Neoclassicism in Britain, 1760–1800* (Chicago, IL, 2006), p. 77.

43 Francis Chantrey's bust of Watt of 1816, and his one of John Rennie of 1818, copies of both of which are in Watt's workshop, comprise fine examples of this trend.

44 See the portrait medallion by Peter Rouw of Matthew Robinson in the Victoria & Albert Museum, London, inv. A.51–1970, for example.

45 W. Chambers, *A Treatise on the Decorative Part of Civil Architecture* (London, 1825), pp. 4–5.

46 J. Farey, *A Treatise on the Steam Engine: Historical, Practical and Descriptive* (London, 1828), vol. I, p. 574.

47 Ibid., pp. vii, 596, 468.

48 T. Tredgold, *The Steam Engine* (London, 1827), p. vi.

49 A. P. Woolrich, 'John Farey and His *Treatise on the Steam Engine* of 1827', *History of Technology*, XXII (2000), pp. 62–106: p. 71.

50 Ibid., p. 70.

51 Tredgold, *The Steam Engine*, p. 211.

52 A. Gray, *The Experienced Millwright* (Edinburgh, 1806), p. 20. O. Gregory, entry for 'Architecture', *Pantologia* (London, 1813), vol. I.

53 *Industrial Revolution: A Documentary History; Series One; The Boulton and*

Watt Archive, Part II: *Engineering Drawings* (Marlborough, 2003), Reel 175, portfolio 387.

54 *Industrial Revolution: A Documentary History; Series One; Part II: Engineering Drawings* (Marlborough, 2003), Reel 175, portfolio 377.

55 J. Bourne, *Treatise on the Steam Engine* (London, 1868), p. 163.

56 Tann, *The Development of the Factory*, p. 161.

57 R. Buchanan, *Practical Essays on Millwork and Other Machinery*, 3rd edn (London, 1841), vol. I, p. 394.

58 H. Schaefer, *Nineteenth Century Modern: The Functional Tradition in Victorian Design* (New York, 1970), p. 28. For more on this theme, see A. P. McMahon, 'Would Plato Find Artistic Beauty in Machines?', *Parnassus*, VII (1935), pp. 6–8: p. 8.

59 Farey, *A Treatise on the Steam Engine*, vol. I, pp. 473, 575.

60 Tredgold, *The Steam Engine*, p. 44.

61 Bourne, *Treatise on the Steam Engine*, pp. 176–7.

62 Tredgold, *The Steam Engine*, p. 170.

63 Archives of Soho, Birmingham Central Library, MS 3147/3/248/70, W. Creighton, 29 April 1803.

64 Farey, *A Treatise on the Steam Engine*, vol. I, p. 575.

65 Ibid., p. 473.

66 Ibid.; Schaefer, *Nineteenth Century Modern*, p. 25.

67 Tredgold, *The Steam Engine*, p. 212.

68 L. Mumford, *Technics and Civilization* (Chicago, IL, 2010), p. 209.

69 J. Tann, 'Marketing Methods in the International Steam Engine Market: The Case of Boulton and Watt', *Journal of Economic History*, XXXVIII/2 (1978), pp. 363–91: p. 382.

70 E. Vale, *The Harveys of Hayle, Engine Builders, Shipwrights and Merchants of Cornwall* (Truro, 1966), pp. 106–7.

71 G. Bathe, *An Engineer's Miscellany* (Philadelphia, PA, 1938), p. 27.

72 Bourne, *Treatise on the Steam Engine*, p. 166.

73 Farey, *A Treatise on the Steam Engine*, vol. I, p. 612; Bourne, *A Treatise on the Steam Engine*, p. 165.

74 C. Holtzapffel, *Turning and Mechanical Manipulation* (London, 1846), vol. I, p. 328.

75 T. Tredgold, *Practical Essay on the Strength of Cast Iron* (London, 1824), pp. 10–11.

76 S. Clegg Junior, *Architecture of Machinery: An Essay on Propriety of Form and Proportion* (London, 1842), pp. 2–3.

77 Bathe, *An Engineer's Miscellany*, p. 25.

78 J. Wosk, *Breaking Frame: Technology and the Visual Arts in the Nineteenth Century* (New Brunswick, NJ, 1992), p. 179.

79 See Science Museum inv. 1915–128, for example, a six-column engine by an unknown maker, *c.* 1840.

80 Thomas Tredgold, *The Principles, Practice and Explanation of the Machinery Used in Steam Navigation* (London, 1851), vol. ii, Part 2, plates for the engines of the *Wilberforce* and *Ruby* steam vessels.

81 Bonhams, *The Jonathan Minns Collection of Industrial Archaeological Artefacts* (London, 2006), lot no. 9, for a fine example of the type. This design also found favour with the 'compound' engines having more than one steam cylinder, built by Thomas Horn of Westminster, of which several examples survive.

82 Farey, *A Treatise on the Steam Engine*, vol. i, plate xviii; Bonhams, *The Jonathan Minns Collection*, lot nos 4–6.

83 Henderson, *J. C. Fischer and his Diary of Industrial England*, p. 131.

84 L. Ince, 'Maudslay, Sons & Field, 1831–1904', in *Henry Maudslay and the Pioneers of the Machine Age*, ed. G. Cookson and J. Cantrell (Stroud, 2002), pp. 166–84, p. 166. For an example of Maudslay's Gothic engines from 1832, see Tredgold, *The Principles, Practice and Explanation of the Machinery Used in Steam Navigation*, Plate 6.

85 Science Museum inv. 1933–30.

86 Science Museum inv. 1966–230. See also the *Illustrated London News*, 6 September 1851, p. 298; N. Pevsner, *High Victorian Design: A Study of the Exhibits of 1851* (London, 1951), p. 23.

87 The Henry Ford, inv. 30.489.1. See also Bathe, *An Engineer's Miscellany*, p. 32.

88 J. S. Fletcher, *The Story of the English Town: Leeds* (London, 1919), pp. 78, 80.

89 The mill survives on Marshall Street in Leeds today and is listed as Grade i by English Heritage.

90 The builder's model of this engine, displayed at the Great Exhibition of 1851 and weighing an impressive 276 kg, remains in the Science Museum, inv. 1935–513/1.

91 See Cantrell and Cookson, eds, *Henry Maudslay and The Pioneers of the Machine Age* for a detailed survey.

92 S. Smiles, ed., *James Nasmyth, Engineer: An Autobiography* (London, 1885), p. 127; J. Hamilton, *London Lights: The Minds that Moved the City that Shook the World* (London, 2007), p. 141.

93 A. Rees, entry on 'Machinery', *The Cyclopedia; or, Universal Dictionary of Arts, Science, and Literature* (London, 1819), vol. xxii.

94 A series of articles describing them in *Engineering* of 18 January and 1 February 1901 includes excellent photography.

95 S. Clegg, *Architecture of Machinery: An Essay on Form and Proportion* (London, 1842), pp. 3–4.

96 One of the finest examples was the side-lever engine built by Maudslay for the Paddle Ship *Dee* in 1832, with gothic framing. See Science Museum inv. 1900–41.

97 Schaefer, *Nineteenth Century Modern*, p. 25.

98 D. Scott, *The Engineer and Machinist's Assistant* (Edinburgh, 1847): description of the Plates, 42.

99 M. Wright, 'Henry Maudslay's Contribution to Machine Design', *Henry Maudslay* seminar, Kew Bridge Steam Museum, 2001.

100 Tredgold, *The Steam Engine*, p. 354. The 'table' engine was so called because it did away with the rocking beam, and sat the piston on a table of cast iron, from which it turned the crank and flywheel beneath.

101 A. Turner, *Early Scientific Instruments: Europe, 1400–1800* (London, 1987), p. 201.

102 A. McConnell, *Instrument Makers to the World: A History of Cooke, Troughton and Sims* (York, 1992), pp. 21–2.

103 Bonhams, *The Jonathan Minns Collection of Industrial Archaeological Artefacts* (London, 2006), lot no. 3.

104 Christie's, *Exceptional Scientific and Engineering Works of Art, Instruments and Models* (London, 9 April 1997), lot no. 16.

105 Christie's, *Exceptional Scientific and Engineering Works of Art* (London, 15 April 1999), lot no. 80; Christie's, *Exceptional Scientific and Engineering Works of Art* (London, 8 April 1998), lot nos 12–13.

106 Christie's, *Exceptional Scientific and Engineering Works of Art* (15 April 1999), lot no. 81; Christie's, *Exceptional Scientific and Engineering Works of Art* (8 April 1998), lot nos 14–15.

107 Clegg, *Architecture of Machinery*, p. 1.

108 G. C. Boase and T. I. Williams, 'Clegg, Samuel (1781–1861)', *Oxford Dictionary of National Biography* online, www.oxforddnb.com, accessed 8 June 2012.

109 H. Louw, *Greeks, Romans and Goths in an Age of Iron* (1999), www.arct.cam.ac.uk, accessed 8 June 2012.

110 Tredgold, *The Steam Engine*, vol. 1, p. 344.

111 Ibid., p. 207.

112 H. C. Escher, 'Escher's Letters from England in 1814', in *Industrial Britain under the Regency, 1814–18*, ed. W. O. Henderson (New York, 1968), pp. 34–5.

113 G. Head, *A Home Tour Throught the Manufacturing Districts of England, in the Summer of 1835* (New York, 1836), p. 119.

114 Ibid., p. 154.

115 M. Berg, 'From Imitation to Invention: Creating Commodities in Eighteenth-century Britain', *Economic History Review*, LV/1 (2002), pp. 1–30: p. 3.

116 E. H. Robinson, 'Watt, James (1736–1819)', *Oxford Dictionary of National Biography* online, www.oxforddnb.com, accessed 17 August 2012; Jones, 'Living the Enlightenment and the French Revolution', p. 182.

Chapter Seven: Life after Death, 1800–1924

1 This account is based on the surviving structural elements and contents of the workshop, Science Museum inv. 1924–792, and the plan of Heathfield held by Handsworth Historical Society, ref. 7/3397.

2 W. O. Henderson, *J. C. Fischer and his Diary of Industrial England, 1814–51* (London, 1966), p. 131.

3 C. Hankin, ed., *Life of Mary Anne Schimmelpennick*, 3rd edn (London, 1859), pp. 285–6. Science Museum 'Z' Archive, z24/D, letter 980, B. Woodcroft to Sir J. Romilly, 10 May 1864.

4 M. Arago, *Life of James Watt* (Edinburgh, 1839), p. 85.

5 The items sent from Glasgow possibly include a 38-drawer cabinet that remains in the workshop, containing many of the tools and materials from Watt's earlier career. R. L. Hills, *James Watt*, vol. III: *Triumph Through Adversity, 1785–1819* (Ashbourne, 2006), p. 237.

6 The workshop is part of a tradition of men's hiding places away from their wives. Josiah Wedgwood wrote of a friend getting married, whose 'Study is hoisted up into the Garret, & the Parlour newly cleared of its learned lumber is fitted up in the most modern & Elegant fashion': *Letters of Josiah Wedgwood to 1770*, ed. K. Farrer (Manchester, 1903), p. 170.

7 H. W. Dickinson research file 'James Watt', Science Museum, transcript of Watt's will, provided by E. C. Smith to H. W. Dickinson, 22 January 1920.

8 T. E. Pemberton, *James Watt of Soho and Heathfield: Annals of Industry and Genius* (Birmingham, 1905), p. 52.

9 J. P. Muirhead, *The Life of James Watt, with Selections from his Correspondence* (London, 1858), pp. 468–9.

10 The first definite mention of this machine in Watt's correspondence dates from March 1811. H. W. Dickinson, *The Garret Workshop of James Watt* (London, 1970), p. 14.

11 Ibid., p. 16.

12 J. P. Muirhead, *The Origin and Progress of the Mechanical Inventions of James Watt* (London, 1854), vol. II, pp. cccxlvi–cccxlvii.

13 John Limbird, ed., *Arcana of Science and Art* (London, 1831), p. 94.

14 Muirhead, *The Origin and Progress of the Mechanical Inventions of James Watt*, vol. I, p. ccxlviii.

15 *Register of Aliens, 1803–1825*, Edinburgh City Archives (Ref: SL115/2/2), www.edinburgh.gov.uk, accessed 18 July 2012.

16 London's National Portrait Gallery has been compiling details of some of those who worked in Britain, 'British Bronze Founders and Plaster Figure Makers, 1800–1980', www.npg.org.uk, accessed 19 July 2012. Pierotti is not among those listed.

17 Science Museum inv. 1924–792/2164.

18 Science Museum inv. 1924–792/2163.

19   Science Museum inv. 1926–1075/301.

20   Science Museum invs 1926–1075/326, 1924–792/1753.

21   Science Museum inv. 1924–792/2162. Jane Insley made the connection between the numbers and those on the jars in the course of exhibition research, for which many thanks.

22   G. Stuart, ed., *Peacham's Compleat Gentleman, 1634* (London, 1906), pp. 107–8.

23   A. Yarrington and C. Sicca, eds, *The Lustrous Trade: Material Culture and the History of Sculpture in England and Italy c. 1700–c. 1860* (Leicester, 2000), pp. 13–14.

24   V. Coltman, *Fabricating the Antique: Neoclassicism in Britain, 1760–1800* (Chicago, IL, 2006), p. 163.

25   J. Northall, *Travels through Italy, Containing New and Curious Observations on that Country* (London, 1766), p. 362.

26   F. Haskell and N. Penny, *Taste and the Antique: The Lure of Classical Sculpture 1500–1900*, 4th edn (New Haven, CT, 1994), p. 85.

27   It is still possible to visit Selborne and see the statue.

28   M. Craske, 'Contacts and Contracts: Sir Henry Cheere and the Formation of a New Commercial World of Sculpture in Mid-eighteenth Century London', in *The Lustrous Trade*, ed. Sicca and Yarrington, pp. 94–113, p. 104.

29   Ibid., pp. 104–5.

30   M. Droth, 'Small Sculpture *c.* 1900: The "New Statuette" in English Sculptural Aesthetics', in *Sculpture and the Pursuit of a Modern Ideal in Britain, c. 1880–1930*, ed. David Getsy (Aldershot, 2004), pp. 141–66: p. 145.

31   T. Clifford, 'The Plaster Shops of the Rococo and Neo-classical Era in Britain', *Journal of the History of Collections*, IV/1 (1992), pp. 39–65: p. 39.

32   Coltman, *Fabricating the Antique*, p. 129.

33   Haskell and Penny, *Taste and the Antique*, p. 122.

34   J. Insley, 'Sculpture for the Masses: James Watt and the Reproduction of Art', ICOHTEC 'Consumer Choice and Technology' conference, Glasgow, 6 August 2011. Review, J. T. Smith, ed., 'Nollekens and His Times', *Gentleman's Magazine, and Historical Chronicle. From July to December 1828*, XCVIII/2 (London, 1828), pp. 536–40: p. 538.

35   Droth, 'Small Sculpture, *c.* 1900', p. 142.

36   'Obituary, John Isaac Hawins, 1772–1855', *Minutes of the Proceedings of the Institution of Civil Engineers*, XXV (1866), pp. 512–14: p. 512.

37   S. Bedini, *Thomas Jefferson and his Copying Machines* (Charlottesville, VA, 1984), p. 172.

38   D. Brewer, 'Review of J. P. Muirhead's *The Origin and Progress of the Mechanical Inventions of James Watt*', *North British Review*, XXIII (May and August 1855), pp. 103–24: p. 119.

39 Cheverton never patented the machine. *Report of the Select Committee on Arts and their Connexion with Manufactures: With the Minutes of Evidence, Appendix and Index*, 16 August 1836, paragraph 618.

40 British Association for the Advancement of Science, 'Minutes of Evening Meeting, 11 September 1837', *Mechanics Magazine*, XXVII (1837), pp. 449–56: p. 453.

41 M. Shedd, 'A Mania for Statuettes: Achille Collas and other Pioneers in the Mechanical Reproduction of Sculpture', *Gazette des Beaux-Arts*, CXX (July–August 1992), pp. 36–48: p. 40.

42 British Association, 'Minutes of Evening Meeting', p. 453.

43 J. P. Muirhead, *The Origin and Progress of the Mechanical Inventions of James Watt* (London, 1854), vol. I, p. ccl.

44 Coltman, *Fabricating the Antique*, p. 155.

45 Shedd, 'A Mania for Statuettes', p. 44.

46 M. Whinney, *Sculpture in Britain, 1530 to 1830* (London, 1964), p. 226.

47 Science Museum inv. 1926–1075.

48 F. Arago, *Historical Eloge of James Watt* (London, 1839), pp. 181–2; Dickinson, *The Garret Workshop of James Watt*, p. 21.

49 H. W. Dickinson research file 'James Watt', Science Museum, transcript of Watt's will, provided by E. C. Smith to H. W. Dickinson, 22 January 1920.

50 M. Hess and S.Robson, 'Re-engineering Watt: A Case Study and Best Practice Recommendations for 3D Colour Laser Scans and 3D Printing in Museum Artefact Documentation', *Lasers in the Conservation of Artworks*, IX (London, 2013), pp. 154–62.

51 J. Insley, 'Sculpture for the Masses: James Watt and the Reproduction of Art', icohtec 'Consumer Choice and Technology' conference, Glasgow, 6 August 2011. For more on the Gahagans, see I. Roscoe, *A Biographical Dictionary of Sculptors in Britain, 1660–1851* (London, 2009), pp. 489–97.

52 A.J.C. Hare, ed., *The Life and Letters of Maria Edgeworth* (London, 1894), vol. I, p. 153.

53 Ibid., p. 154; Whinney, *Sculpture in Britain*, p. 226.

54 H. B. Hancock and N. B. Wilkinson, 'Joshua Gilpin: An American Manufacturer in England and Wales, 1795–1801 – Part II', *Transactions of the Newcomen Society*, XXXIII (1960–61), pp. 57–66: p. 57.

55 R. Porter, A *Social History of England in the 18th Century* (London, 1982), p. 331.

56 D. Eastwood, 'The Age of Uncertainty: Britain in the Early Nineteenth Century', *Tranactions of the Royal Historical Society*, VIII (1998), pp. 91–115: p. 104.

57 S. Smiles, *Lives of the Engineers: The Steam-engine. Boulton and Watt* (London, 1878), p. 408.

58 F. Crouzet, *The Victorian Economy* (London, 1982), p. 7.

59   A. Briggs, *The Power of Steam: An Illustrated History of the World's Steam Age* (London, 1982), pp. 70–103.

60   Smiles, *Lives of the Engineers: Boulton and Watt*, p. 405.

61   C. MacLeod, *Heroes of Invention* (Cambridge, 2007), chaps 4 and 5; C. MacLeod, 'The Nineteenth-Century Engineer as Cultural Hero', in *Brunel: In Love with the Impossible*, ed. A. and M. Kelly (Bristol, 2006).

62   Science Museum inv. 1992–163, *Watt's First Experiment of Steam*, engraving by James Scott after the painting by R. W. Buss, 1849; inv. 1995–746, *Watt's First Experiment*, engraving by Herbert Bourne after the painting by Marcus Stone, 1879.

63   D. P. Miller, '"Puffing Jamie": The Commercial and Ideological Importance of being a "Philosopher" in the Case of the Reputation of James Watt (1736–1819)', *History of Science*, xxxviii (2000), pp. 1–24: p. 4.

64   H. Torrens, 'Jonathan Hornblower (1753–1815) and the Steam Engine: A Historiographic Analysis', in *Perceptions of Great Engineers: Fact and Fantasy*, ed. D. Smith (London, 1994), pp. 23–34: p. 26.

65   Arago, *Historical Eloge of James Watt*, pp. 128–9.

66   D. P. Miller, 'True Myths: James Watt's Kettle, his Condenser, and his Chemistry', *History of Science*, xlii (2004), pp. 333–60: p. 343.

67   Miller, 'True Myths', p. 345.

68   MacLeod, *Heroes of Invention*, chaps 4, 7 and 8; D. P. Miller, *James Watt: Chemist* (London, 2009).

69   C. MacLeod and J. Tann, 'From Engineer to Scientist: Reinventing Invention in the Watt and Faraday Centenaries, 1919–31', *British Journal for the History of Science*, xl (September 2007), pp. 389–411: pp. 411, 409.

70   David Miller, 'True Myths', p. 345; 'Craftsman and Engineer' was the subtitle to H. W. Dickinson's 1936 biography of Watt. MacLeod and Tann, 'From Engineer to Scientist', p. 397.

71   H. W. Dickinson research file 'James Watt', Science Museum, transcript of Watt's will, provided by E. C. Smith to H. W. Dickinson, 22 January 1920.

72   J. P. Muirhead, *The Origin and Progress of the Mechanical Inventions of James Watt* (London, 1854), vol. I, p. cclv.

73   Smiles, *Lives of the Engineers: Boulton and Watt*, p. 409.

74   A. McConnell, 'Woodcroft, Bennet (1803–1879)', *Oxford Dictionary of National Biography* online, www.oxforddnb.com, accessed 20 June 2012. See also J. Hewish, *The Indefatigable Mr Woodcroft* (London, 1979), and *Rooms Near Chancery Lane: The Patent Office Under the Commissioners, 1852–1883* (London, 2000).

75   Science Museum technical file T/1924–792, J. W. Gibson Watt to B. Woodcroft, 27 September 1863.

76   Science Museum technical file T/1924–792, F. P. Smith to J. W. Gibson Watt, 28 September 1863.

77 Science Museum technical file T/1924-792, J. W. Gibson Watt to
    F. P. Smith, 30 September 1863. Science Museum inv. 1863–15.

78 Science Museum 'Z' Archive, fol. Z24/D, B. Woodcroft to E. Price,
    11 May 1883.

79 Science Museum technical file T/1924–792, B. Woodcroft to J. W.
    Gibson Watt, 28 September 1863.

80 Science Museum technical file T/1924–792, B. Woodcroft to F. P. Smith,
    13 January 1864.

81 Science Museum technical file T/1924–792, M. Pemberton to F. P. Smith,
    6 May 1864, and B. Woodcroft to J. Romilly, 7 May 1864.

82 P. Wakelin, *Blaenavon Ironworks and World Heritage Landscape* (Cardiff,
    2006), p. 14; B. Trinder, *The Making of the Industrial Landscape* (London,
    1982), p. 109.

83 W. O. Henderson, *J. C. Fischer and his Diary of Industrial England, 1814–51*
    (London, 1966), p. 134.

84 H. W. Dickinson and R. Jenkins, *James Watt and the Steam Engine*
    (Oxford, 1927), p. 270.

85 P. Jones, 'Matthew Boulton: Enlightenment Man', keynote lecture, 'Where
    Genius and the Arts Reside: Matthew Boulton and the Soho Manufactory
    1809–2009' conference, Birmingham, 3 July 2009.

86 E. C. Smith, *A Short History of Naval and Marine Engineering* (Cambridge,
    1937), p. 14.

87 Science Museum technical file T/1862–53, G. Allan & Sons to J. S. Russell,
    16 July 1862.

88 Science Museum technical file T/1862–53, B. Woodcroft to F. P. Smith,
    21 July 1862.

89 Science Museum technical file T/1862–53, A. B. McGeorge to F. P. Smith,
    21 December 1862.

90 J. Simmons, ed., *Letters from England by Robert Southey* (London, 1951),
    p. 132.

91 *Travels of Carl Philipp Moritz in England, 1782; A reprint of the English
    translation of 1785* (London, 1924), p. 162. Moritz shamefacedly noted
    that 'I also cut myself a piece of it; but, reverencing Shakespeare as
    I do, I am almost ashamed to own to you, it was so small that I have
    lost it.'

92 *Report from the Select Committee on the Patent Office Library and Museum;
    Together with the proceedings of the committee, minutes of evidence, appendix
    and index, 19 July 1864* (London, 1864), p. 93. Readers will forgive the
    author for noting that nothing has changed.

93 MacLeod, *Heroes of Invention*, p. 261.

94 Science Museum 'Z' archive, Z24/E, fols 1097 and 1148, B. Woodcroft to
    J. W. Gibson Watt, 12 April 1865 and 7 November 1866. The model
    survives today, Science Museum inv. 1866–57.

95 Science Museum 'Z' archive, z24/D, Patent Office Museum outgoing letter book, fol. 987, Lord Chancellor's private secretary to J. Romilly, 28 May 1864.

96 H. W. Dickinson, *The Garret Workshop of James Watt*, p. 9.

97 Pemberton, *James Watt of Soho and Heathfield*, p. 66.

98 Science Museum 'Z' archive, z24/I, letter 1842, B. Woodcroft to H. R. Lack, 25 April 1877.

99 Pemberton, *James Watt of Soho and Heathfield*, pp. 61, 64.

100 Science Museum nominal file 1814, J. M. Gibson Watt to H. Lyons, 12 February 1926.

101 Science Museum technical file T/1924–792, H. Stuart Wortley to Mr Lack, 21 July 1883.

102 The inventory, dated 1885, remains in Science Museum technical file T/1924–792.

103 Smiles, *Lives of the Engineers: Boulton and Watt*, pp. 408–9.

104 D. P. Miller, *James Watt: Chemist* (London, 2009), p. 28.

105 Ibid., p. 86.

SELECT BIBLIOGRAPHY

Berg, Maxine, *The Age of Manufactures* (London, 1994)
——, *Luxury and Pleasure in Eighteenth-century Britain* (Oxford, 2005)
Clow, Archibald, and Nan L., *The Chemical Revolution: A Contribution to Social Technology* (London, 1952)
Dickinson, Henry W., *Matthew Boulton* (Cambridge, 1937)
——, and Rhys Jenkins, *James Watt and the Steam Engine*, 2nd edn (London, 1989)
Fox, Celina, *The Arts of Industry in the Age of Enlightenment* (New Haven, CT, 2009)
Hills, Richard L., *James Watt*, vol. I: *His Time in Scotland, 1736–1774* (Ashbourne, 2002)
——, *James Watt*, vol. II: *The Years of Toil, 1775–1785* (Ashbourne, 2005)
——, *James Watt*, vol. III: *Triumph through Adversity, 1785–1819* (Ashbourne, 2006)
Jones, Peter, *Industrial Enlightenment: Science, Technology and Culture in Birmingham and the West Midlands, 1760–1820* (Manchester, 2008)
Langford, Paul, *A Polite and Commercial People: England, 1727–1783* (Oxford, 1999)
MacLeod, Christine, *Heroes of Invention* (Cambridge, 2007)
Mantoux, Paul, *The Industrial Revolution in the Eighteenth Century*, 2nd edn (London, 1961)
Mason, Shena, ed., *Matthew Boulton: Selling What All the World Desires*, exh. cat., Birmingham Museums and Art Gallery (New Haven, CT, and London, 2009)
Miller, David P., *James Watt: Chemist* (London, 2009)
Mokyr, Joel, *The Enlightened Economy: Britain and the Industrial Revolution, 1700–1850* (London, 2009)
Morrison-Low, Alison, *Making Scientific Instruments during the Industrial Revolution* (Aldershot, 2007)
Musson, A. E., and Eric Robinson, *Science and Technology in the Industrial Revolution* (Manchester, 1969)

Sotheby's, *The James Watt Sale: Art and Science* (London, 2003)

Uglow, Jenny, *The Lunar Men: The Friends who Made the Future, 1730–1810* (London, 2002)

ACKNOWLEDGEMENTS

I have been very lucky in writing this book to have drawn upon a big pool of expertise and interest. The Science Museum Library staff have patiently dealt with a constant stream of requests and questions. Curatorial colleagues past and present, in the Science Museum and elsewhere, have chipped in with all manner of advice and encouragement. Peter Morris has provided invaluable editorial support, and the team who worked on the redisplay of Watt's workshop in 2011 at the Science Museum, Jane Insley, Andrew Nahum, Helen Peavitt, Adrian Whicher and Sarah Stallard, thrashed out many of the broad themes and turned them into a physical exhibition. Jane also read the manuscript and removed some of the 'Ben-isms'. Jim Andrew gave valuable advice, as has an anonymous referee, and Merel van der Vaart provided reassurance that the whole thing might be of some interest beyond the history of technology community. Any blunders remaining are, of course, entirely down to the author.

All images are courtesy of the Science Museum / Science & Society Picture Library, except the images on pages 25 and 35, which are courtesy UIG History / Science & Society Picture Library.

INDEX